Becoming a Digital Designer

A Guide to Careers in Web, Video, Broadcast, Game, + Animation Design

Steven Heller + David Womack

John Wiley & Sons, Inc.

Published by John Wiley & Sons, Inc., Hoboken, New Jersey
Published simultaneously in Canada

For general information about our other products and services, please contact our Customer Care Department within the United States at (800) 762-2974, outside the United States at (317) 572-3993 or fax (317) 572-4002.

Wiley also publishes its books in a variety of electronic formats. Some content that appears in print may not be available in electronic books. For more information about Wiley products, visit our Web site at www.wiley.com.
Wiley Bicentennial Logo: Richard J. Pacifico

Library of Congress Cataloging-in-Publication Data:

Heller, Steven.

Becoming a digital designer : a guide to careers in Web,
video, broadcast, game and animation design/
Steven Heller, David Womack.
p. cm.

Includes bibliographical references and index.

ISBN 978-0-470-04844-3 (pbk.)

1. Technology—Vocational guidance. 2. Digital media—Vocational guidance. 3. Digital electronics—Vocational guidance.
I. Womack, David, 1971 II. Title.

T65.3H45 2007

006.7—dc22
2007011323

Printed in the United States of America

10 9 8 7 6 5 4 3 2 1

Other Books in this Series

Becoming a Graphic Designer, Third Edition
by Steven Heller and Teresa Fernandes

Becoming a Product Designer
by Bruce Hannah

Becoming an Interior Designer
by Christine Piotrowski, ASID, IIDA

Becoming an Architect
by Lee W. Waldrep, Ph.D.

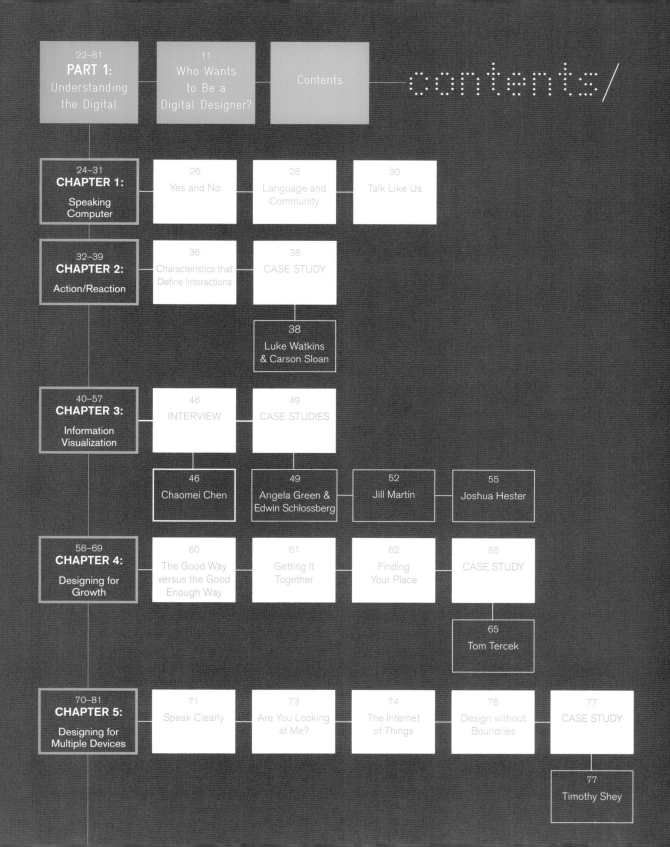

contents/

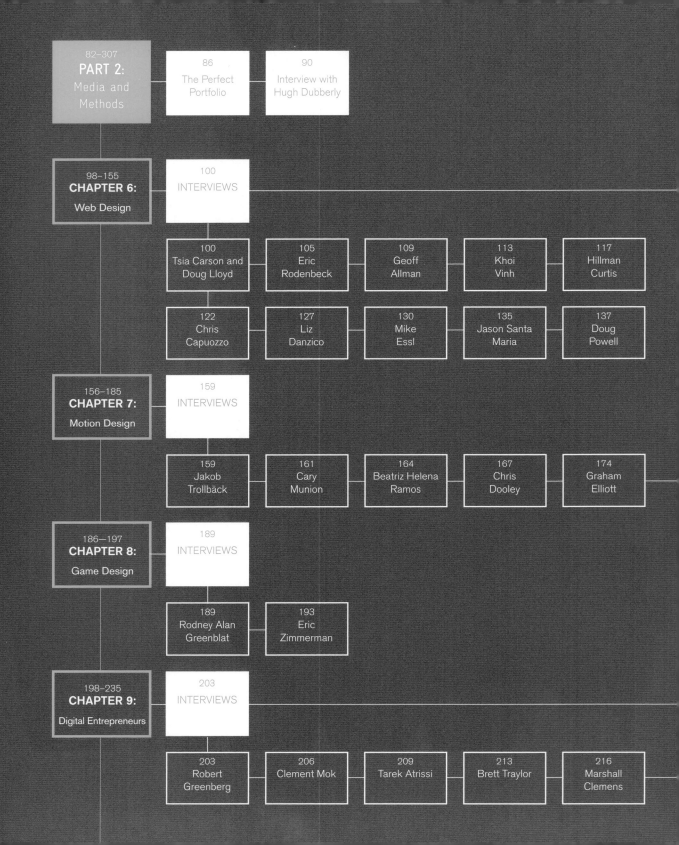

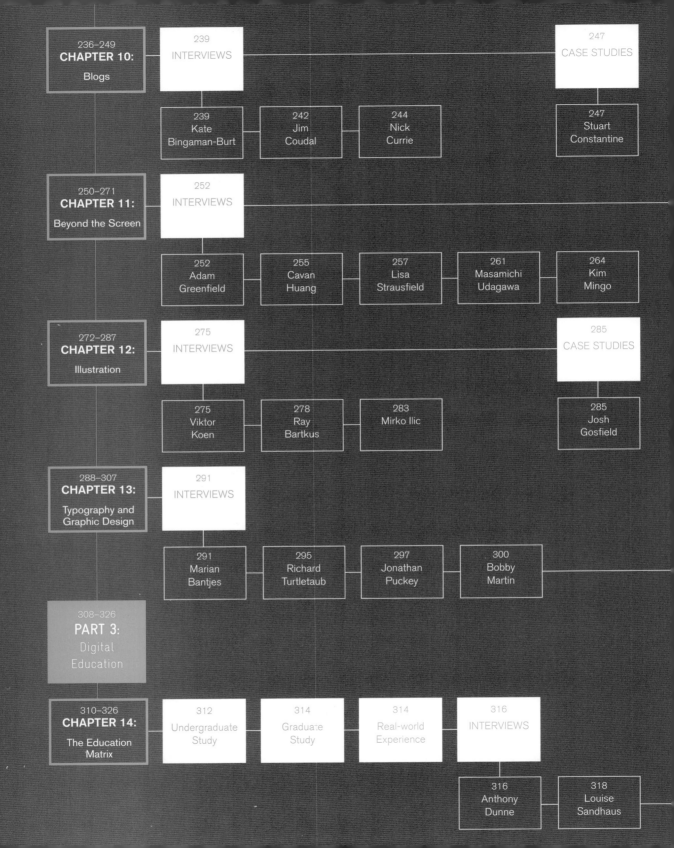

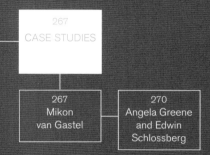

Acknowledgments

We are indebted to our editor, Margaret Cummins,
for the care and oversight on this project, and for the
delectable lunches, and to our designer, Rick Landers,
for his scrumptious design. And Mike Olivo who has
offered up a diet of nutritious production suggestions.
In keeping with our culinary theme, our gratitude as well
goes to our chefs de digital, all the interviewees, case
studies, and others who have helped us put together
this delicious mix of insight and inspiration.

But enough food talk: We are also grateful to the
following for the extra attention to our project and the
additional content they provided: Ed Schlossberg, Hugh
Dubberly, Khoi Vinh, Debbie Millman, Chris Capuozzo,
Fred Seibert, Melina Rodrigo, and Randy J. Hunt.

– SH & DW

Who Wants to Be a Digital Designer?

In the late 1980s I was given a Macintosh and told to throw out my glue pots, rulers, and Xactos, because digits were the future. So I dutifully learned Quark, Illustrator, and Photoshop on my new beige box and bid adieu to obsolete methods. Unlike some other old-schoolers, I was not nostalgic for acetone fumes and paper cuts; the magic of wysiwyg (what you see is what you get) and high-rez repro made the days of paste-up and mechanicals seem positively antediluvian.

The computer certainly liberated this designer from drudgery. But setting type, composing pages, and cropping and retouching photos in a digital environment was nonetheless ostensibly the same basic process I had previously done, only with different, more efficient tools. What I was creating on the Mac was not really digital design per se. Therefore, I was not really a digital designer—though I had certainly become more of a souped-up traditional one.

The real digital design revolution, as some pundits are fond of calling it, did not occur until a few years later, when sound and motion—and some amazing CGI visual aids—were added to the designer's desktop tool kit. But one person's revolution is another's devolution. Visionaries foresaw the multifaceted potential of desktop computing, while semi-Luddites, like me, failed to grasp how multisensory and interactive the field of graphic design was to become. We feared how it would change the fundamental definition of graphic design. In fact, we longed to maintain the simplicity of our craft, even though it was never as simple as one remembers.

Yet now, barely twenty years into the digital revolution, most of the methodologies, much of the media, and many of the standards have inexorably changed. Arguably, the digital revolution created an upheaval as significant to the big round world—no less the smaller, flat design world—as Gutenberg's printing press was for centuries after it was invented.

The digital ethos has become so much a part of our daily lives (from iTunes to cable, from iChat to satellite phones) that we take most every technological advance for granted. Technology has so thoroughly altered the way designers now practice that it is as necessary to be a technologist as it is to be an artist—and many young designers are more involved with the latter than the former, only later fusing technology and art into design.

A designer cannot be print-centric any longer, although many of the best in the world still produce their wares on paper—not coincidentally, the very material on which this book is printed. Yet a well-rounded "graphic designer" (the term is in quotes because it is seriously being reevaluated as this introduction is being written; see sidebar on page 30) must be versed, if not practiced, in video, audio, and all manner of programs to be functionally fluent in contemporary methods.

Just as decades ago I had to learn how to make the most out of limited technologies, the new breed of designer must embrace scads of tools such as html and Flash to achieve contemporary outcomes. And just as I was more or less a one-person band when it came to designing editorial pages or posters, today's designers must collaborate with bands of creative people—directors, producers, programmers, and engineers, as well as artists, photographers, and typographers—to produce their desired results on such a broad media stage.

Being a digital designer now demands striding various media platforms, but this does not mean you have to be a day-tripping generalist, either. Many digital designers are consumed with decidedly singular obsessions; some are expert in all things Web, others with video and Internet games. Still others are helping pioneer miniature graphics and video displays on handheld multiple devices, such as PDAs and cell phones.

Still, *going digital* (not the same as *going postal*) emphatically means that designers must be open to learning new tricks (the thing that old dogs can't seem to do, although some old designers are trying). In the digital world, it is necessary for designers to be abreast of the new and what tool or effect can be harnessed for which ends.

It used to be that a novel development would surface every few years. Today's basic software and operating systems, as well as media theories and philosophies, change like the tides. And so do the definitions of design.

While designers (graphic and otherwise) continue working in most of the traditional areas—advertising, editorial, environmental, entertainment—they are also finding ways to augment their respective communications techniques through novel methods. Consider advertising, for example. Decades ago it shifted its focus from print to television commercials, and now the Web is becoming a primary venue on which to expand the boundaries of sight, sound, and interactivity. Magazines and newspapers are increasingly supplemented by videos and motion graphics on the Web and digital tablets. Environmental designers (who produce signage and wayfinding systems indoors and out) have tapped into all manner of digital displays—kiosks, marquees, illuminated and kinetic "spectaculars" (of the kind on Times Square or the Ginza)—to carry messages and direct traffic. Moreover, digital designers are producing a manner of entertainments from personal games to massive scenic displays, from handy gimmicks to major motion pictures.

A designer does not have to be born into the digital world to create within it. Young designers take to the computer technologies like the proverbial fish to water, but many older ones are just as adventuresome; they clearly envision the potentials of making, say, typography dance and sing, and have incorporated new tools and methods into their venerable practices. Although the digital age seemed to have sneaked up on us (remember when compact discs were introduced, and then took over the world, and now they are virtually obsolete?) it is endemic to everything that designers now do. And designers now do more things on their desktops than was conceivable only a few short decades earlier. For this reason, and so as not to turn into a *designosaur*, I want to become a digital designer. This book is one way, even for me, to understand the terrain.

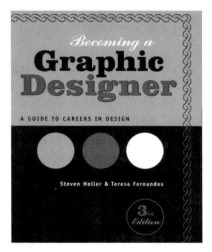

Heller, Fernandes. *Becoming a Graphic Designer*. Wiley, 2005.

Becoming a Digital Designer is aimed at those who want to assume creative roles in digital design, whatever the format, medium, or platform. It is further intended as a guide for those who are passionate about *traditional design* yet want to expand the options of *graphic* communications, and those who are not bound to any one method. This book serves as a complement to the popular *Becoming a Graphic Designer* (BaGD), by Steven Heller and Teresa Fernandes, which continues to offer useful advice and inspiration to wannabe print designers and typographers. Moreover, it is the next generation in the Wiley "Becoming" series, building on sections in BaGD devoted to interactive design but taking this material in completely new directions.

Toward this end, David Womack and I have not duplicated, or even overlapped, the contents of BaGD. All the interviews and case studies are new, most with designers, design managers, and producers who were not known to me at the time BaGD was being written. Moreover, the organization of this new BaDD is not based on conventional job descriptions, per se. The chapters provide glimpses and insights into the various trajectories that design is taking in the digital age.

This book uses an analogy to the big bang theory to express the explosion in digital technology in the media universe. We provide some basic information on the clusters of energy and information (which are quickly becoming galaxies themselves) and how a designer might survive (and even thrive) in these volatile new environments. This book does not address questions as to how to design in a particular medium, however; it is not a how-to book. Rather, we invite the readers to imagine a home for themselves in the new universe, a home they will no doubt have to build (and rebuild).

Still, within each chapter, through custom interviews and sidebars, insights and information are provided into how designers now work in traditional (i.e., type and illustration) and nontraditional (i.e., streaming TV for the Web) jobs. Also examined are how design standards have changed (or not) owing to the advent of new tools, new strictures, and new paradigms. And since new technologies have produced new aesthetics, these concerns are addressed as well.

For some readers, however, becoming a digital designer may suggest working more with software than imagination. Nothing is farther from the truth. In fact, the adjective *digital* is merely a means of distinguishing (until a viable new term is coined) those who, fluent in the current tech, have branched out beyond the confines that so rigidly defined design B.C. (before computer). *Digital designer* is probably not the title one will use on business cards, but rather a category of expertise that underscores all manner of design skills, disciplines, and activities. It is the next stage of design and designer, but not the final one. It is the present and, for some time to come—though we don't know how long—the future of practice.

It's been a fairly long time since I traded in those crusty old glue pots and blood stained Xactos for keyboards and mice, but a relatively short, albeit frantic, time since the design field has opened up to new frontiers. It seems like almost anything is possible as technology pervades design and designers revel in the digital. David Womack and I provide an overview (and more) of the options available to those looking to join the interconnected and interactive communications revolutions that have digitized the world (if not the universe).

Role-playing: What Are the Jobs for Digital Designers?

The roles within digital design can be confusing. Often different titles define the same thing. Other times, the same title means something altogether different. For example, a graphic designer can be a digital designer, but a digital designer can be more than a graphic designer. An art director or design director can be a digital designer, but not all *digital designers* are art directors or design directors. In short, *digital designer* is a catchphrase for anyone who designs using digital tools.

It is not necessarily a term that will show up in a job posting or even a résumé. More likely a posting will demand "art director with digital fluency" and a resume will say "art director" with a list of digital competencies as a point of information. Usually role descriptions change somewhat, depending on the needs of the company or firm, so it is important to carefully read the job description and listing of necessary skills before deciding on a role. What's more, many titles define unique roles that have only of late become viable jobs. If all this is confusing, here is a list of selected roles that are found in the design world today.

Design Director

This is a cross-disciplinary title, from print to Web. It often requires different skills and experience, depending on the platform. A design director is usually responsible for all design-related issues, from the actual look of a designed entity to the management of art directors, designers, and others.

Creative Director

This is often a design director, but usually encompasses more than just design. In advertising or branding agencies, it involves concept development. A creative director might even manage the design director, as well as writers and other creative and production personnel.

Executive Art Director

In the art director genus are many strata and substrata. In some firms the design or creative director is the top echelon. In others, the art director rules the roost. In companies or firms where there are lots of layers, the art director title may be made hierarchical. An executive art director will be higher on the totem pole than a mere art director in some places, while the art director in others may not be mere at all.

Art Director

Usually an art director is one who oversees design and "art" (illustration, photography, and other graphic or visual material). An art director is not necessarily a designer, but must know how to manage, hire, and otherwise oversee designers and other creative and production support personnel. In large firms there may be many art directors, each responsible for specific projects, under the auspices of an executive or managing art director.

Senior Designer

In some companies the designer is directly answerable to the creative or art director without any middle levels. The senior designer is usually the hands-on designer—whether in print or virtual space—who has the most experience, and therefore does the lion's share of the creative work. A senior designer can be an art director, but is usually more involved with only the design, not the management of a project.

Junior Designer

An experiential level down from senior designer is the junior designer or design assistant. This is an entry-level position that requires design skills, may work on independent projects, but usually reports to or is overseen by a senior.

Studio Manager

A studio manager handles resources including staffing, resource allocation, and employee benefits. Studio managers work in visual design, technology, animation, games, and production.

Production Manager

Not all design jobs involve designing things. With the advent of desktop computers and the increasing number of sophisticated tools, designers are taking on a larger production load. A production manager is also responsible for the efficient time management of resources on a companywide level, ensuring that all resource needs for internal and external projects are met.

Information Architect

An information architect (IA) creates user experiences by organizing content and developing intuitive interfaces. IA personnel usually work with producers, designers, and tech teams to develop the overall conceptual framework, navigation, and user interface for both medium- to large-scale projects.

Design Strategist

This can be a design or art director turned manager, or a nondesigner who understands the nexus between design and business. The role is usually to determine how design will best suit a client's needs and develop a plan to incorporate design into an overall strategy.

Human Factors Designer

Particularly in industrial design, but also in Web and other digital areas, the human factors designer (HFD) is responsible for developing design elements that are in sync with the users' behavior and habits.

Interface Designer

The interface designer is also known in some companies as an interaction designer. This involves creating graphic elements while employing a user-centered design approach.

Producer

The producer is often in the multimedia area and is primarily responsible for the client relationship, overseeing the development of projects for a particular client. Business is often key. The producer is involved in exploring project feasibility, creating proposed project plans, estimating budgets, creating top-level schedules, and assessing the availability of internal resources. Once the project is under way, the producer is responsible for all aspects of project management, including client relations, project specification, budgets, resource allocation, and defining and maintaining large project schedules and work plans.

Director

In multimedia companies the director establishes the fundamental creative ideal for animation, live-action, and so on. Also necessary is expertise in creating the standard and setting the tone for all work, as well as training others. A director often works with an assistant director, too.

Site Developer

Site developer is a quasi-design title, and deals with writing the code that makes Web sites work well. This person ostensibly works with designers, interpreting their files into functioning XHTML documents.

Flash Designer

As long as Flash is a principal animation program on the Web, a Flash designer will be a key player in Web design. This person is the architect, designer, and maintainer of Flash files, often under the direction of a creative director. Flash designers collaborate with the design, animation, games, and production departments in multimedia companies.

Game Designer

One multimedia company describes the game designer as "the creative lead on a project [who] collaborates with the client and the creative director to brainstorm innovative concepts." Game designers are responsible for articulating ideas in the form of treatments. Game designers work with producers to plan the execution of the game (including but not limited to the creation of storyboards, game play flow documents, and scripts) and to oversee and mentor the production team of programmers, graphic designers, and production assistants through completion of the project.

Illustrator

An Illustrator, particularly on multimedia, is able to draw in a wide variety of styles, emphasizing expressive poses and character development. Illustrators work in animation or static forms.

Intern

Depending on the focus of a company or firm, the intern—usually an unpaid (though not always) temporary employee—is often the gofer. Yet internships are extremely valuable for learning tricks and other tools of the trade, as well as networking for full-time jobs later on.

Authors' Dialogue:

Steven Heller and David Womack Talk about the Digital Revolution

WOMACK: Taking a cue from a quote in Orwell's *1984*: "Within twenty years at the most, the huge and simple question, 'Was life better before the Revolution than it is now?' would have ceased once and for all to be answerable." [Orwell, George. *1984*. Middlesex: Penguin Books, 1961. (77)] What, in your view, has been lost in either design process or product because of the digital revolution?

HELLER: Technology always costs something—jobs, quality, even knowledge. In terms of graphic design, technology—and specifically the digital revolution (which I believe has been as big a revolution as Gutenberg's storied invention of the printing press)—it has cost graphic design its tradition. To say this is pretty obvious.

The new invariably entombs the old. The handcraft tradition, so integral to graphic design, has been replaced by pixels. The traditional definitions of graphic design have also been, more or less, tossed aside. And traditional standards of design "beauty" have been usurped by what I'd call the digital aesthetic. With new technologies come new ways of judging excellence. When the digital emerged, we tried to find

corollaries to the nondigital. But in the same way that photo typesetting altered the look of the page compared to hot-metal typesetting, digital tools and filters have introduced new veneers and patinas. Those who were weaned on tradition find it difficult to get used to the new aesthetics. Those who were born into the digital simply accept and perpetuate them. Still, for some of us it seems that the cost of progress is high.

WOMACK: What has been gained?

HELLER: Perhaps the greatest gain of the revolution: We're exposed to multiple media and numerous platforms—from motion and sound to film and the Web. The digital designer (as opposed to the more limited graphic designer) has a world of options at her fingertips. Of course, this is not exactly new to graphic design—some of our number specialized in film and TV title sequences, animation, and other multimedia displays—but where once it was the province of technical experts, today the options are much more accessible. In fact, to be a graphic designer today demands being a digital designer, too.

WOMACK: You run a Masters of Fine Arts program at the School

of Visual Arts called "Designer as Author." Do you think that there are more opportunities for designers to take creative control of their work now than there used to be?

HELLER: Yes, yes, yes. With so much software power on the desktop, one cannot help but control the work like never before. One can also author or initiate creative work owing to direct access to tools that once belonged only to the expert-experts. Yet at the same time, it means others can control the work, too. Technically, anyone with the same skill set can intervene in another's work and make alterations. At this relatively early stage of digital production and digital creativity, a do-it-yourself quality prevails. So if you, the digital designer, can do it herself, then so can the so-called nondesigner. In fact, these days I wonder what makes someone a bona fide designer rather than a dabbler (an erstwhile amateur) playing with all these wonderful new tools (i.e., Garage Band or iMovie)? You are not a designer—though you work with many—what determines who wears this mantel?

WOMACK: In order to understand how the term *designer* is changing, it may be helpful to look at the term *writer.* Back in the old days, a writer, or scribe, was a person who could make marks on a piece of papyrus that others could read. As the skill of writing became more widespread, the meaning of the term changed. A writer became someone who takes the skill and tries to use it to say something interesting and new. Like writing, the skill of design—of creating form—is becoming more accessible. But in the same way that not everyone who can spell c-a-t should now call themselves a writer, not everyone who can make a form should call themselves a designer. I mean, you can call yourself anything you want—designer, artist, writer, musician, or lingerie model.

HELLER: You work with many designers. So, how do you define a designer?

WOMACK: The designers I bring in for projects are willing to do the really hard work of creating interesting and useful forms. Not everyone wants to do this—I don't. But I want to work with people who do. The computer may have made some design processes easier, but creating something interesting—something that delivers on the intentions of the project and uses the materials in a new and exciting way—is still extremely difficult. I don't think that part has become any easier. It's still the same old problem of turning sows' ears into silk purses.

I have a huge amount of respect for the sheer tenacity of the designers I work with, as well as for their wit and insight.

HELLER: What makes a good designer?

WOMACK: I don't know. I think that designers can be good in very different ways. Some designers I bring on because of their ability to create beautiful forms. Some because of their ability to think through complicated structures. Rarely do I find that one person is equally good at both. Part of the fun I have in putting design teams together is trying to find people with compatible skills who will balance one another.

HELLER: Is there a single creative or technical trait that is common to all digital designers?

WOMACK: You mean as opposed to other creative people? Well, I think that design is in a period of tremendous flux at the moment, and new types of people are entering the field. Design in the digital age has become much more systems focused, which makes it relevant to all sorts of issues—from structuring a business to understanding climate change. Hopefully designers also develop an appreciation for how systems influence their own work. In particular, software influences the final product. But I think that all creative work shares the most important characteristic. In the end, I think any creative work requires

perseverance and a willingness to suffer to make it good.

HELLER: Suffering, huh? I'm not sure I'm ready to work with you as my boss.

WOMACK: A person who is willing to suffer for their work and persevere doesn't need a boss. Bosses are for people who need to be told what to do.

HELLER: I'll change the subject: Much of what is stated in this book is based on our respective views of the digital design world—me from the traditional design world, and you from a loftier perch above the vortex of progress (if I may be so bold). So tell me, what do you think a digital designer must know and understand, that the traditional typographer and graphic communicator did not apply to their art and craft? And how much of this is totally new or just a modification?

WOMACK: Digital design lends itself to creating interactions with your audience—rather than presenting a finished form. This is why it's sometimes called *interaction design*. I think designers have always created interactions, but they generally involved less back-and-forth. The designer put something out there, and the viewer responded . . . and that was it.

Now the designer puts something out there, and the viewer responds, and the designer (or their system) makes a modification based on that response, and so on.

To be really successful, digital design should get better the more often it is used. The audience should add something to the system. I think that's fairly new.

HELLER: In a traditional context—whether in print or on-screen—the designer alone controls the experience. I find the user more involved is downright scary. It's like saying, "I'll give you my best work; now you play with it any way you like." Its kind of like the days of paint-by-numbers, where the artist gives you a basic concept, but the user can screw it up (or make it better, I guess) in any way they like.

WOMACK: Well, most successful interactions require very rigid rules for how the audience can interact with the Web site or installation. The job of the digital designer is not pushing pixels—it's pushing people. It's getting people to interact with the system in a way that is constructive. That's the trick. If you think of yourself as a fine artist who delivers a perfect, finished vision to the world, then you're probably going to be upset. But if you see yourself as more of a scientist who creates experiments and observes behavior and makes adjustments—you can learn some very interesting things about how people work. But I'm interested in finding out more about your perspective as a print designer and also as a celebrated design writer. What about digital design inspires you?

HELLER: I can honestly say—and this may be heresy in terms of this book—but the most exceptional work is indistinguishable. I know that certain things could have been accomplished only in a digital environment (like all those fantastic Pixar films, and certainly all Web sites, etc.), yet genius is genius regardless of media. That said, there are geniuses in different media—Picasso might not have been a good Web designer, in the same way that Khoi Vhin, a guru of the digital world, may not be the best traditional typographer.

Yet to answer the basic question of what "inspires" me: I'd say the

Plus ça Change

The more things change, the more they stay the same. This old chestnut may be trite, but it is often true. In the design world, the past ten years have brought considerable change, even upheaval, in the communication fields. But the basic job structures—with the exception of those unique to digital technology—remain the same, only different.

Therefore, it is useful for readers of this book—particularly those who are interested in pursuing print design—to refer to *Becoming a Graphic Designer: A Guide to Careers in Design* by Steven Heller and Teresa Fernandes for a complete understanding of the contemporary visual design scene. Almost all of the design disciplines represented in this book are still current—editorial, corporate, book, information, advertising, branding, environmental, and type (music in the form of CD packaging is, however, being phased out). The book further covers some of the crossover categories in this volume—interactivity, motion, and Web. It also addresses ways of establishing a personal business—as freelancer, small studio, partnership, or larger firm. BaGD also touches on authorship and entrepreneurship, which have since become more pronounced in the digital world.

The digital revolution (a term that will doubtless fade as digital becomes increasingly endemic to current practice) may have launched new options and served to integrate various media under unique rubrics, but it is simply a set of new tools. Like many that came before and passed, these tools have replaced old ones, yet have not always fundamentally altered the ways designers practice. So if you are passionate about magazines, books, and logos, the jobs are there if you have the skills.

Designers Beware: The Pen Is Still Mightier than the Pixel

Being a digital designer is not entirely about being tied to the box (or whatever other shape the computer comes in). Being a designer means creating form, conceiving ideas, and developing objects—both physical and virtual. But never for a minute think that this can be done only on the computer.

Don't feel you must shut down when the power goes off. Design is thought. Design is a process of translating thought to surface. Draw, sketch, sculpt—your fingers are still the most venerable and versatile digital tool. Beware of false prophets claiming that drawing is dead and the mouse or joystick is ascendant. Do not forsake the primary design machine, the brain, and its support mechanism, the hand.

ability to expand on every possible mode of graphic expression. If nothing else, the digital revolution has heightened the ability of creative people to translate theory into reality. Would you agree?

WOMACK: That's an interesting way of putting things. To me, the designers who were best able to translate theory into reality were Charles and Ray Eames. And they were working in the 1950s. If it has become easier to translate theory into reality, it's because of pioneers like the Eameses who made it look easy—and therefore inspired others to try—rather than a particular technology.

That said, I do think that digital technology has made design tools more available and also created opportunities for engaging your audience in new ways. So, there are more designers and they have

more to work with. I think that what inspires me most about digital design right now is just the spirit of independence I see. Designers are giving the finger to "the man" and setting up their own practices to work on their own projects. This really didn't used to be possible—for one thing, the equipment was too expensive. But now, you no longer need to rely on some jerk in a suit to give the thumbs-up to your project. You can just do it and put it out there and let your audience decide if it is beautiful and true. What bliss!

I'm not sure how much longer this situation will last. Some of the technology I see coming around the corner may make it expensive and/or more difficult for one designer and one computer to make their way in the world. But let's enjoy it while it does . . .

HELLER: Fertile periods exist between the introduction of new technologies and that moment when the suits take over. It's hard to believe that Steve Jobs and Bill Gates and his crew were hippies and now they're suits in jeans. Some people say that the designer of the future will continue to have more power. As American industry becomes more about "concepts" than hardware, designers will play a more inventive role in the process, and embracing the digital tools will allow these inventors to push the edges. Do you think that there is a rosy future for the digitally savvy, or will they simply be operators of new machines?

WOMACK: I think that it's important not to get too attached to a particular technology. When people talk about the digital revolution it sometimes seems as if they believe we are going through some period of particular upheaval and that, sooner or later, things will settle down again. I think the pace of change will continue to accelerate and that it may well happen that, thirty years from now, people will talk about digital technology the way we now talk about fax machines. I think it's more important for students to understand trends, their causes and effects, rather than to focus on mastering a particular technology. It may well be that they'll need to specialize later on, but there are risks in just doing one thing well.

HELLER: Agreed. Yet nonetheless, new machines and software have definitely changed how contemporary designers practice. But rather than debate the issue further, herein we'll learn from others in the trenches how the traditional and the digital designer intersect and diverge, given the new paradigms that technology has produced. ■

Word Up: A Glossary

Digital design has a language all its own, and the jargon can be confusing. Here's a guide to a few select terms: what they mean, and what they really mean.

Word + Definition	Meaning	Last Heard
Conceptual Model: A metaphor that explains an unknown product or system, often by comparing it to something familiar.	We're flying blind here, people, but we need to tell the client something.	Last heard from an information architect.
Guru: A master or spiritual leader.	A guy who has outlived his usefulness but can't be fired because he founded the company.	Last heard in an all-company meeting.
Innovation: A new and exciting idea or product that has the power to create change.	I don't know what this means and it scares me—but I can't let them know that.	Last seen in *BusinessWeek*.
Phase Two: The second phase of a project following the initial launch.	It will never, ever happen.	Last heard from a creative director during a client brainstorming session.
ROI: Return on investment. The value gained through an innovation.	I don't know what these designers are talking about, but now they're all looking at me. I'd better say something.	Last heard in a project pitch meeting.
Synergy: The energy created when like minds collaborate.	I don't like you, and you don't like me. But we have to work together, so suck it up.	Last heard shortly before a merger.
Viral Marketing: A process for publicizing an event or product through informal connections such as e-mail and word of mouth.	I don't like this. Do you like this? Will anybody like this?	Last heard at an ad agency that is dabbling in digital.

USING THEM IN A SENTENCE:
That viral campaign is a real innovation, but I'm not sure I see the ROI. We may have to save it for phase two, unless we can find a conceptual model that creates some synergy. But why am I rambling on when we have a guru in the room?

Understanding the Digital

To understand digital design, it is important to look beneath the surface. Digital designs can take a million different forms, but they all share common traits based on a common language. If you understand the principles that are driving change, you will be able position yourself to anticipate and create future opportunities. This section looks at the primary issues that feed the key disciplines of digital design, from understanding interaction, to visualizing information, to designing for multiple devices.

So, before you move on to Part Two, where we survey the jobs and career options that are available today, take some time to understand the digital principles that will shape the future. Chances are the best job will be the one you invent for yourself.

IN THIS SECTION:

Speaking Computer

Sometimes how you design is as important as what you design.

I received a letter from a human-rights group the other day and, even before opening the envelope, I knew a friend of mine had designed the stationery. There were very few clues to go on—actually, just the return address—but something about the choice of fonts and colors and the way the words related to one another tipped me off. I recognized the unique impression her style and personality had made upon her work.

This isn't uncommon. If you've ever been in a class where the teacher held up an example of a design or artwork and you knew, before he told you, which of your classmates had made it, then you know what I mean. Who we are shapes what we make.

Dutch social anthropologist Dr. Geerte Hofstede has studied this phenomenon on a cultural, as well as a personal, level. "The influence of culture is so powerful that one can almost always, when reading a book for instance, recognize the nationality of the author, even if it has not been mentioned," Hofstede writes. "This applies to our work too—we are from Holland, and even when we write in English, the Dutch software of our minds will remain evident to the careful reader."[1]

Hofstede has developed a system for understanding how the *software of our minds* affects and even determines what we make. His theory attempts to explain why, for instance, Italians design beautiful cars and shoes and Americans were the first to put a rocket on the moon.

It's no coinctidence that Hofstede compares our mental processes to software. Just like our personalities, the software we use leaves its mark on our design. Whether we choose to hand-code a Web site in HTML or use Dreamweaver will make a difference in the final result. Hand-coding, for example, allows us to focus on the details and make every page unique, while *wysiwyg* (what you see is what you get) programs such as Dreamweaver encourage templating. How you make something determines what you make.

But we're not just talking about Web sites here. Tools also leave their mark on print projects, motion graphics, and product design. One of the reasons that these traces are sometimes difficult to detect is that, at the moment, almost every designer in the world is using the same software made by the same companies. There just aren't very many cultures to compare. This may be changing, as more and more designers begin to create and modify their own software.

[1] Hofstede, *Geert. Cultures and Organizations, Software of the Mind.* McGraw-Hill, 1996.

But regardless of what software you use or whether you make Web sites, running shoes, or movies, there is a language that we all have in common, and that is the language of the computer.

The good news is that to speak computer you have to learn only two words. But those two words make all the difference.

Yes and No

At its core, the binary language of the computer is very simple. In fact, it has only two words: yes and no, which are represented as one or zero. It's just like being in court. Please answer the question: Did you commit the crime? Yes or no? The prosecutor does not want to hear about who said what to whom first or whether you skipped breakfast. In the same way the language of the courtroom affects the final verdict, the language of the computer affects what is produced and how.

The binary language of computers has led to some amazing efficiencies, perhaps the most basic being that almost no one has to actually input ones and zeros. The digits have been clumped together into words (which are a collection of six or eight numbers or bits), and the words have been structured into languages. The languages generate visual interfaces that allow you to draw instead of type. So, rather than playing twenty questions every time you want to make a shape—say a circle—you can simply draw the circle and the computer will translate the shape into ones and zeros for you. And, because the computer is using an algorithm to describe the shape, the form is perfectly precise. The computer can also replicate forms perfectly. If you want to make a hundred or a thousand or a million circles of the same size or of all different sizes, all you have to do is ask.

"Computer programming is just like speaking a language," digital designer Jonathan Puckey told me. "As long as I can describe in words what I want to accomplish, I can put those ideas into code."

The ability of the computer to create precise forms and to replicate forms exactly has had an enormous impact on the way things that surround us look and behave. The revolution brought about by computers can be seen as a continuation of the revolution that began with the assembly line. Each of the Model T cars coming off the assembly line used the same parts, and each car looked identical (or very close to identical).

What Ford did to production, digital technology has done to design. By automating the design process, we can work much more rapidly, and with greater precision. Of course, as in the case of the Model T, we might eventually get tired of everything looking more or less similar.

And this is where things start to get interesting. You can ask the computer to draw a perfect circle, but you can also ask it to draw an imperfect circle, or a thousand circles, each of which is imperfect in a different way. Video game designers do this all the time—it's the reason why, as you plow through the bushes in Grand Theft Auto, each leaf on each bush looks realistic: By *realistic* we mean that they are all slightly different though more or less the same.

But the imperfections don't need to be slight. I often hear digital designers say that one of the things they really love about computers is that computers allow them to screw things up fast. One small change in the code—a one here, a zero there—and things can get really weird. Digital designers, even those who really know their code, often can't guess what the results of their experiments will be. But that's the fun of it. And, once in a while, something unexpected will catch their eye and cause them to see a shape or line in a different way and they will play around a little more. That is how new tools and new ideas in design are born.

But, lest you think that all experiments are successful, the language of ones and zeros can also cause trouble, as you will already know if you've ever had your computer crash. There are lots of different reasons for computer crashes, but here's one way to make software failure almost inevitable.

Let's say you are working on a project and the deadline is approaching. You are writing code, and suddenly you remember that your partner did a project kind of like this a few months back. So you pick up the section of code that approximates the effect or function you are looking for. You make a few modifications. Although you know it's not the best way to solve the problem, you really only care about one question: Does it work? Yes or no. You get a yes, and you move on. A few weeks later, your partner is working on another project, and this time she picks up the code you just wrote and makes more modifications.

Does it still work? Well, the real answer is barely, but in code, as in the courtroom, there is no room for nuance. So the answer goes down as yes. Over time, all of these yes answers pile up as the code gets passed around, and each time it gets uglier and less efficient. Finally, you ask, "Does it work?" and the answer is a resounding *no*. Because so many replications and modifications have been made to the program in the interest of saving time, trying to figure out exactly what went wrong is like untangling a really awful knot. In fact, sometimes it's easier to scrap the whole thing and start over.

LeWitticisms

In the late 1960s, the artist Sol LeWitt decided that the thinking behind a piece of art is just as interesting as the final result. So, he put down his paintbrush and started issuing instructions. Here are his instructions for Wall Drawing #46: "Vertical lines, not straight, not touching, covering the wall evenly."

That's it. Then it was up to the galleries to follow his instructions and create the actual piece, usually by drawing with pencils directly on the gallery wall. By allowing for the separation of insight and execution, LeWitt anticipated the digital age.

Like LeWitt, digital designers are often in a position of issuing instructions, which are then interpreted by computers and the people who use them. The fact that no two galleries executed his instructions in exactly the same way did not bother LeWitt—in fact, the variation is part of what makes the artwork interesting.

Computers don't always interpret instructions in exactly the same way, either. The instructions, or lines of code, will yield different results when they are interpreted by NASA's supercomputers and a cell phone. Likewise, many of the most successful online experiments rely on millions of individual users to interpret instructions. For example, eBay, with its plaster figurines and paintings of ponies, isn't going to win any beauty contests, but what makes it so effective is the simplicity of the instructions. In effect, eBay says, "Post your treasures online and let people bid on them." When you are evaluating digital design, it's important to understand not only what something looks like, but also the instructions that led to its creation.

Free Software
(Your Design Will Follow)

Although commercial software dominates digital design, there are enough free tools available to complete a project if you are willing to be creative. The advantages of using free software—other than that it's free—are that it forces you to take a detour from the mainstream. By using different tools, you are likely to get different results. You are also likely to learn more about your tools because you will be part of the process of developing them.

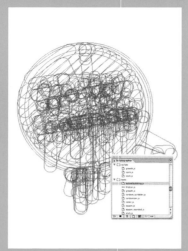

▲ **Scriptographer** ©2000 - 2007, Jürg Lehni

Libre Graphics is an international organization devoted to developing and using free graphics software. The organization supports the development of tools such as Gimp, an image-manipulation program; Inkscape, a vector-drawing package similar to Adobe Illustrator; and Scribus, a page-layout program.

Recently, the idea of free tools has been getting some major mainstream support. Google has been adding free tools to its repertoire. In addition to photo, document, and spreadsheet software, it also has a free 3-D software tool called Sketch Up that allows you to create elaborate models of anything from cities to software systems. Meanwhile, over at MIT Media Lab, John Maeda is working on a project called OpenStudio, which currently includes free drawing tools but may be expanded and developed to allow collaboration in multiple media.

If you're not ready to "go open" all at once, there are groups of designers creating free plug-ins that extend the functionality of commercial software. One of my favorites is Scriptographer.com, which creates new tools that run on top of Adobe Illustrator.

Language and Community

In the early 1900s, hundreds of Native American children were sent off to boarding schools run by missionaries so that they could receive a Christian education. One of the rules the children had to follow was that they must not speak their tribal language. Even after they were fluent in English, the children, now old, recall sneaking out to have whispered conversations in their native tongues.

From one perspective, this seems pretty odd—after all, isn't what they were saying more important than the language it was said in? But the children recognized that their languages provided a connection to their heritage and home, a way to identify one another and distinguish themselves from white society. When speaking their own languages, they once again felt part of the tribe.

In the frontier landscape of digital technology, language also gives people something to rally around and can serve as a means of protest. What is now called the *open-source movement* was an attempt to establish a programming language that was not dominated by a single corporation. The *source* in open source refers to source code. The idea is that anyone should have access to the code that drives a piece of software. And not only should you be able to see the code, you should also be able to use, adapt or refine, and distribute the code—or use it to create new tools of your own.

Initially started by a small group of maverick programmers, open source has become a revolution that has changed the way software—and many other things—is made. The pioneers of open source discovered that not only was their software *free-er*, it was often better too. It turned out that the informal, unpaid community of program-mers sharing tips and tools and working for the good of the community was producing software as good as or better than the large corporation's.

Open source has worked so well, in fact, that I just saw a headline on ZDNET that asked if open-source software was beginning to challenge the mother of all technology companies: "Are Mircrosoft's Problems Due to Opensource?"[1]

The Open Source Initiative's Web site (www.opensource.org) describes the advantages of opening up: "People improve it, people adapt it, people fix bugs. And this can happen at a speed that, if one is used to the slow pace of conventional software development, seems astonishing. We in the open source community have learned that this rapid evolutionary process produces better software than the traditional closed model, in which only a very few programmers can see the source and everybody else must blindly use an opaque block of bits."[2]

The success of open-source platforms such as Gnu and Linux has inspired some businesses to get on board. Hang on, you say, how does a business that gives away its code stay in business? Here are two possibilities: Companies give away the software but charge for maintenance or support. Or, they hope that the software will encourage people to purchase a related project. For instance, the gaming software itself may be open source, but you still need to purchase the processor and controls to run it. Plus, open source saves businesses money because they no longer need to employ an army of programmers—they get help from the people who use it.

Open does not always mean free. Sometimes software or products that are developed on an open-source platform are moved behind closed doors. Or part of their code is open source and the rest is proprietary. Google may be the world's largest open-source company—it is built using Linux. Although Google keeps many secrets to itself, it also actively encourages users to adapt and modify the public facing code. In fact, Google sponsors a competition for the biggest innovations in open source: $25,000, and the competition is open to anyone. Google recognizes that what is good for the open-source community is also good for Google.

The founders of the open-source movement believe that we (meaning them, you, and I) will take over the world. Wikipedia is a great example of an open-source product being used to pro-mote the open-source philosophy. Wikipedia has set out to create an open-source encyclopedia of all human knowledge—anyone can view an entry, edit, or create an entry. Because most facts link to other pages, you can always trace a piece of information to find out more or see who added what piece of information when. And, if you want to make a Wiki of your own, you can go to the "view source" section and copy the code. Wikipedia now has more than 1,500,000 entries in many different languages.

But what does this have to do with design? The design of systems that allow and encourage people to work together has been the defining challenge of the last few years. Although it may not look like it, Wikipedia is a brilliant example of digital design. It is easy to navigate, easy to add

[1] Dana Blankenhorn, ZDNet.com, April 28, 2006.   [2] www.opensource.com

to, easy to access, and, most important, actually useful (you might be surprised at how often this last point is overlooked). Other projects that fit in this category include Flickr, MySpace, and, of course, about 50 million blogs and counting. With this kind of competition, it is not always easy to gain what the pros call *mind share*—people need to find your site, remember it, and want to come back.

The success of these projects has inspired other open-source projects in different disciplines. There are a number of open-source projects related to science—these encourage scientists to share data and methods, not just results. There are some movements that advocate an open-source government.

Linus Torvalds, the founder of one the most successful open-source platforms, Linux, says, "The future is *open-source everything*." With rumors circulating that the Chinese government is switching to an open-source platform for all its computers, he may just be right.

Talk Like Us

One of the main ideas behind open source is that having more people contributing to a project is better. Of course, one of the largest barriers to getting more people involved in programming has been programming languages, which, like any language, can be difficult to pick up.

That may not be a bad thing. The reason languages are difficult, in addition to some rote memorization, is that they force you to think differently. Languages affect more than just what you can get done or how quickly you can do it. Designer and programmer Jurg Lehni told me, "When working with different programming languages, it is quite interesting to see how the different paradigms affect both my way of thinking and the outcome."

Still, programming languages are pretty unforgiving—put a comma instead of a semicolon and you may be left with a blank screen. This is beginning to change, says Lehni. "Recently, there have been a lot of exciting things going on around Ruby, a programming language from Japan. Ruby is very flexible, elegant, and sometimes astonishingly close to human language." A dialect of Ruby called *Ruby On Rails* has been used to create groundbreaking networking applications. Looking ahead, it seems very likely that programming languages—or at least some of them—will continue to evolve to resemble "natural" or human language. As a result, more people will be able to participate in creating and sharing digital tools.

A Designer by Any Other Name . . .

 Define digital designer. Given the growing intersection of graphic design with Web, time-based media, information design, and associated disciplines, including writing and producing (as well as the blurring between fine art and design), who and what we are is becoming more complicated to define and, therefore, to name.

Yet it wasn't always this confounding. Before W. A. Dwiggins famously coined the term *graphic design* in a 1922 Boston newspaper article as a means to describe the wide range of jobs he personally tackled, *commercial artist* was the accepted label for the interrelated acts of drawing and laying out. Dwiggins, however, was a true jack-of-many-graphic-trades, including, but not exclusively, illustrating books; composing pages; designing typefaces; producing calligraphic hand lettering, stencil ornament, book covers, and jackets; creating book interiors and title pages, advertising, and journal formats, along with handbills, stationery, labels, and signs; and writing his own critical essays, fiction stories, and marionette plays.

Dwig (as he was called) wanted to distinguish his prodigious activities from less prolific commercial artists, so he coined a term that was uniquely his own. Graphic design, originally derived from, but much broader than, graphic arts (signifying drawing and printmaking), defined such an esoterically personal pursuit that he could not have predicted that decades later it would become the standard professional nomenclature. Although he never actually called himself a graphic designer, this coinage was cast like bread upon the sea and eventually washed up on professional shores.

When asked if they called themselves commercial artists, not one member of a recent graduating class of design students raised a hand, but surprisingly, only two-thirds of the students embraced the term *graphic designer*. Over a decade ago, when design schools and design firms started affixing highfalutin monikers to academic degrees and business cards, the most common newbie was *communications design*, which, along with *graphic communications* and *visual communications* (or *Viz-Com*) seemed to address the transition from old to new digital media.

In 1975, when computers first began to be an integral part of design—and well before most people thought of setting PCs in the middle of their desks—Richard Saul Wurman gave the field his quixotic appellation information architects.[1] In the mid- to late 1990s, when the Web became a dominant presence in design practice, this tag became much more commonly applied. Other terms now include *user interface designers*, *human-centered interface designers*, and *experiential interface designers*.

Currently there is a schism between *digital designers* and a newly coined, curiously pejorative affixation, *conventional designers*, which indicates solely print orientation. The term *conventional design* was originally uttered by a guru in the Web standards movement, who was making a huge distinction between Web designers and print designers, who, by implication, were designosaurs (try that on your business card—or Web site). If graphic design is synonymous with print, and print is conventional, then a priori anything in the nonprint realm is unconventional.

Indeed, the Web and other digital platforms are the proverbial new frontier. With the evolutionary onslaught of new tech already upon us, the day may come when designers will be called ologists, as in designologists, typologists, or interfaceologists.

In a few years it might not be farfetched that the design academies and profession will sweep out all the dysfunctional nomenclature for new terminologies that alter outside and inside perceptions of what we do and who we are. Which, after all, makes sense in this radically integrated new digital media world.

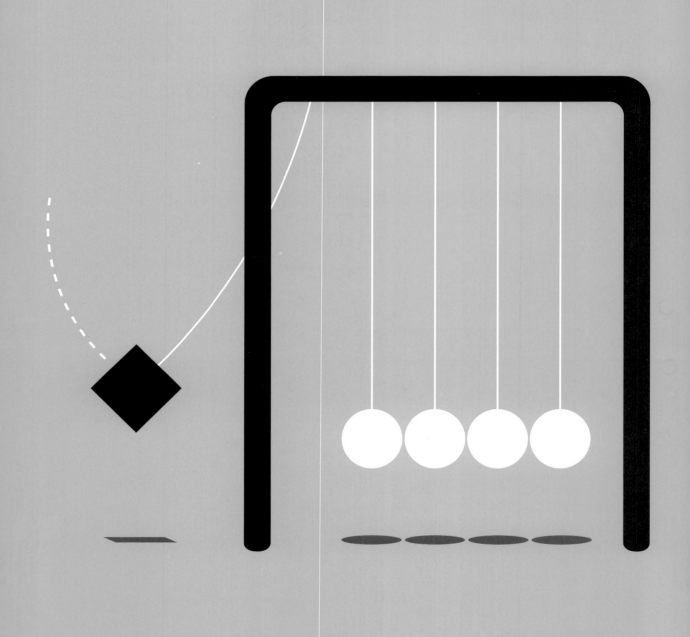

Action/Reaction

What do we mean by interactive? This chapter takes a look at some of the most basic concepts underlying the way we use technology.

On a summer's evening in New York City, people passing the Bloomingdale's department store on 3rd Avenue at 59th Street may have noticed something unusual. Five-foot-tall blue neon flowers suddenly lit up as they strolled past and then slowly faded out. A couple walking hand in hand stopped, took a few steps backward, then stepped forward again. Again the flower illuminated. After a few seconds of discussion, they walked on, more slowly than before, and watched the flowers light up beside them as they went.

Seeing what was happening, a child raced up and down beside the windows with his arms outstretched. The flowers trailed him. After a few minutes the couple and the child continued on their way and the windows went dark again. Most of the people passed too far from the windows to cause the flowers to illuminate. Others were too caught up in their own thoughts or conversations to notice anything at all.

One old woman leaning on a cane looked slightly annoyed to find herself suddenly bathed in a blue glow. But she passed too slowly to connect the flowers to her own progress, failed to recognize the pattern, and so was annoyed anew each time one lit.

How many Power Flowers does it take to establish a pattern? It might take two flowers before you realize something strange is going on, and three more flowers before you realize that you are causing it. In fact, there were thirty-six. How quickly should the flowers light up, and how soon should they fade? The passersby trip the motion sensors just slightly before they reach the flowers. If they fade too quickly or snap off, we might lose the fluid feeling created by the lingering trails of light. If the light stays on too long and there are many people passing, it looks like the display is malfunctioning, with the flowers turning on and off at random.

How close to the window should someone have to pass to trip the motion sensor? On a busy street like 3rd Avenue, flowers must compete with headlights and streetlights reflecting off the window glass; the flower-light is easily lost in the cacophony of lights and colors. But if you set the sensors so that one has to pass too close to the glass, you reduce the likelihood that someone will set a flower off by accident—and so you would deprive your audience of an unexpected delight: the point of the project in the first place.

PowerFlower. 2001

Sponsored by: Häagen-Dazs and Bloomingdales

Design: Masamichi Udagawa and Sigi Moeslinger

Photo: Ryuzo Masunaga

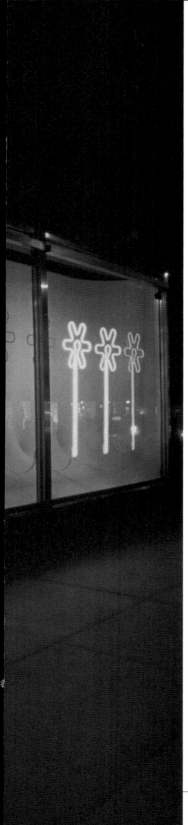

Interactive technology has far outpaced our understanding of interaction. It would be hard to imagine a large-scale public system that is much simpler, at least in its components, than Power Flowers. And yet one could spend a very long time studying the questions that the project raises.

In the meantime, Masamichi Udagawa and Sigi Moeslinger of Antenna have gone on to design subway cars, vending machines, and complex data displays for financial companies. They are currently working on a new interface for McDonald's. "The most important thing in designing interactive systems is not to rely on your assumptions," Mafundiqua told me. "If you go into a project thinking you know how things are, then you might not be able to see how they really are. You have to start with a hypothesis, but then you have to test it. Even simple interactions can be complex, and understanding these hidden complexities can mean the difference between success and failure. If you start with an incorrect hypothesis, then no matter how good the execution is, the project will not work."

A hypothesis is essentially a guess. Your ability to make accurate and practical guesses will evolve over time as you become more familiar with technology as well as the social and business landscapes in which your projects live. Your ability to make interesting guesses—to dream up a hypothesis that will reveal some aspect of an interaction that has gone unnoticed or unexplored—will probably not improve. Chances are that this is as good as it gets.

Young designers and students often have insights into problems that a more experienced designer would either discard or overlook. There is a reason that so many ground-breaking projects were started by people barely, or not even, out of school. Your chances of coming up with a breakthrough idea that will change the way the world works will only diminish as you become more familiar with the way the world works already. So cherish, covet, and write down your hypotheses. But, most important, test them.

Figuring out the hypothesis for a project can be difficult. Antenna's hypothesis, for example, was that their flowers would produce "unexpected delight." Qualities such as unexpected delight are difficult to quantify and difficult to test. This is one of the reasons why projects that set out to be beautiful or meaningful or moving so often fail. The designer starts with the best intentions but doesn't do the really hard work necessary to make sure his or her project will actually produce the desired effect.

In the case of the Power Flowers it would be almost impossible to test in advance whether the project would produce the desired result when it was actually on the street. Based on their years of insight and experience, Sigi and Masamichi made a guess. Because they couldn't test the big idea, it was particularly important that every other aspect of the project was honed to perfection.

Characteristics that Define Interactions

Whether you are talking about books or Web sites or giant glowing flowers, there are some common characteristics that define a successful interaction.

Casuality

This is the relationship between what you do and how the object or system responds. In the case of the Power Flowers, it took a while for people to realize that they were causing an effect, and that element of surprise is part of what made the project work.

Affordance

Is it obvious how the system works? Antenna chose to hide the sensors so that the flowers would turn on as if by magic. However, when they designed a new ticket machine for the New York subway, they wanted riders to know intuitively what to expect: You put your money in the top and the ticket comes out the bottom. When you think about it, there is no reason that a ticket machine has to work this way. The ticket could just as easily spit out the side. But, because we have become used to vending machines where the Coke or candy bar drops down, Antenna decided to build on the user's past experience rather than asking their audience to learn something new.

Mapping

How close to the window do you have to stand to make the flower light up? Do the flowers get brighter if you put your nose against the glass? Mapping occurs after causality is established: You know you are causing an effect, and now you want to find out if you can vary that effect by doing something a little different.

Telling Stories: All Abuzz

The new buzzword in design is storytelling. It is not an altogether inaccurate designation, but it has become something of a fashion to say, "My design has a story to tell." Well, the fact is, designers are storytellers—visual mostly, but typographic, too. And in the digital world, designers have the potential to express their stories. Of course, this notion flies in the face of conventions that uphold designers as packagers, organizers, and decorators. And while designers are all of these, in the digital world designers also author messages that are construed as stories.

The Web site is a case in point. It is a series of panels forming a narrative. It may not be the traditional linear narrative because any page or panel can be accessed at any time, randomly or systematically, yet who decreed that stories must follow such a rigid format?

Digital tools have changed the standards of design—some for the better, but not all—so why not accept that it's changed the definition of designer? The designer as a storyteller, extending the idea of the designer as author, is one of the great attributes of the new media revolution.

Learnability

Now that you've mastered the principles of the Power Flower, can you apply that same logic to street lamps? Sadly, no, but you can get pretty fast at buying a subway ticket using one of Antenna's vending machines, especially with that weirdo standing behind you muttering about how the flowers are following him.

Scalability

This was a big one for the Power Flower project—how many people can interact with the project at the same time? Antenna controlled the scale by setting the sensors at a depth of about one person. Two people, walking in different directions, couldn't activate the same flower at the same time without bumping into each other.

In this sense, projects that exist in physical space are different from Web sites. With Web sites, it is very difficult to control the number of people accessing the site at once. I once worked on a Web site that was the subject of a national radio program. Just after we popped the cork to celebrate our new found fame, we realized that the entire site had gone down. So many people had tried to log in at the same time that the servers had simply given up—and not only was our site down, the traffic had taken down other sites hosted on the same network. It took us three days to add enough servers to cope with the increase in traffic.

Repeatability

If you learn how to do something once, you should be able to do it the same way again. This may seem obvious, but have you ever noticed how different software programs use the same key commands for different functions? As we engage more and more frequently with different digital tools, repeatability is going to become a big problem. (The solution to problems of repeatability is often standardization.) ■

Gameboy Homeboy by Wyld File

Retro Tech

It's not enough to be up on the new technology. You have to be up on the old technology, as well. Some of the most interesting artists and animators are hacking into old video games in order to reclaim the graphic landscape. Corey Arcangel has hacked into an old Nintendo Super Mario Brothers cartridge, and now, instead of ducking fireballs, Mario sits alone on a cloud reflecting on his life and shedding tiny, pixelated tears.

Similarly, many designers and artists are finding creative freedom in using old, familiar software in new ways. The design duo Wyld File made a lo-fi video for Beck's song "Gameboy Homeboy" using Flash—a program that was never intended to create broadcast graphics.

These experiments are important because they give us a different perspective on technology. These artists and designers prove that you don't need the latest version of the latest software in order to do interesting work. Using an old tool in new ways can be more interesting than using a new tool in predictable ways. So before you invest in the latest upgrade, take your dad's old Atari for spin.

◀ TRAN.sit Studio Tour

Date: November 22, 2006

Client: Design Students

Designers: Luke Watkins and
Carson Sloan

Additional Credits: Everyone who
supported us, put us up for the night,
and let us stop by their studio.

Software: Adobe Illustsrator, GoLive,
Photoshop, Final Cut

CASE STUDY:

Two for the Road

Luke Watkins + Carson Sloan, TRAN.sit Studio Tour

What inspired you to take a studio road trip
across America to so many design studios—
and then post your adventures on the Web?

SLOAN: When we graduated we felt confident in our
understanding of the technical and conceptual skills
needed to begin our personal careers, but we realized
that one of the major things that we were lacking was
a firm grasp on the current state of design and what
the "real world" had to offer before we could make any
decisions about our personal futures. We agreed that
even a great school can only teach you so much, and
if we were struggling with this information, then other
students were in a similar situation. This journey was
our chance to see what was happening in the design
community and meet the creative minds behind the
work.

WATKINS: The Web provided us with the opportunity to
receive direct feedback from our audience. By posting
our experiences, we wanted to expose some of the real
world to other young designers, and we agreed that
the Web was the most accessible, expandable, and effective way to reach as many people as possible.

Experts always advise students to make their marks
by leaving a memorable promotion card or designing
a "killer" site. This is brilliant. But what kind of work
do you hope to get from this adventure?

SLOAN: We don't think this tour is about getting work, but
we do hope to leave our mark on the design community
through it. Instead, we see the benefit of this trip and the
Web site in terms of the experience and networking possibilities. Considering neither of us have any real Web or
motion training, creating this resource proves to employers that we're not only conceptually smart, but we're also
passionate, dedicated, and willing to learn.

Would you agree that this "scheme" would never be
possible without digital media?

WATKINS: We would agree this venture wouldn't be nearly
as successful if it were not for digital media. Were it not for
the emergence of communication methods like blogging
and podcasting, the idea to attempt this feat might never
have happened. Even in our travels the Internet has been
an amazing resource in terms of making contacts and
providing some credibility to our cause. In the beginning,

we had thought about printing promotional mailers, but working within our budget the site became our primary promotional piece. In order to reach as many people as we hoped, the Web was definitely the best way.

What about the medium is giving you the most satisfaction—and the least?

SLOAN: We enjoy that our site can act as a starting point for numerous tangents of exploration. Since it's not about us directly, we aren't particularly concerned with keeping the viewer within our site. Unlike a book, the Internet offers the speed and versatility to link information, creating a portal to exploring other resources.

WATKINS: The least satisfying aspect of the Web is the intangibility. Although we know that the site is being viewed, we cannot be sure if the information we're providing is reaching the right audience, or whether it is actually becoming beneficial. We hope that a more direct interaction with students will come about once we return from the tour and can focus more on the resource aspect.

What about the adventure has opened your eyes the most—and the least?

SLOAN: When we began the interview process we thought that after a handful of interviews we would start to experience repeat answers and overlapping opinions on design, but the more we experience the more we realize that no two studios are the same. We've come to realize there is no wrong way to go about working, and everyone we've met genuinely has a unique outlook on design philosophy. Also, it's astonishing to find out how many great designers are out there that you never hear about. On occasion, our personal ideals might disagree with those of the interviewee, but we agree there is no least aspect aside from that there is no absolute truth to design.

Do you want to do Web- or motion-related work when this is all over? And do you have a Web- or motion-related project in the wings?

WATKINS: Through this experience we have both developed a greater appreciation for Web and motion graphics. Although we both hope to continue expanding the TRAN.sit site, we still feel we have a long way to go before either of us would be fluent enough to pursue digital media as a career.

SLOAN: Currently, we have no plans for any additional Web—or motion-related work following this venture. However, there is no telling what form our next hare-brained scheme might take. We have discussed the possibility of a follow-up tour in the future.

Apart from meeting all these people and visiting all these studios, what have you learned that is unique to this unique experience?

WATKINS: Taking on this adventure has taken away much of the fear I first perceived around the idea of entering into the real world. This has become more than an educational experience; it's helped me in terms of finding out who I am personally and has allowed me to move in a new direction in the way I work and my way of thinking.

SLOAN: This trip has provided me with more stories to tell and a better understanding of what I want out of life. As a recovering student-workaholic, this trip has shown me that there is so much more to life than design, and that I can't control everything. I am exploring what that means, and I'll let you know when I have all the answers.

What's next?

WATKINS: We're not really sure; a job would be nice. We've considered writing a book as a follow-up to the trip and to expand the Web site in order to create a community online where professionals and students can interact and share opinions on topics of life and design.

SLOAN: Sit down and have a beer with Steven Heller.

WATKINS: I don't know . . . I'd kind of like a beer and a sandwich. ∎

Information Visualization

One of the most basic goals of design is to help people understand the world through the visual interpretation of complex information. As digital technology has made more information available, these visualizations are becoming increasingly important.

In the book *The Hitchhiker's Guide to the Galaxy* by Douglas Adams, the "Ultimate Answer to Life, the Universe, and Everything" is sought using the supercomputer Deep Thought. After several million years of processing, the computer finally comes up with the ultimate answer to the ultimate question, which turns out to be 42.

Back in 1978 when the *Guide* was written, computers were seen as machines that could provide simple numeric answers to complicated questions. You stuff data in and push a few buttons. Lights would flash and the machine would beep and whir until it spit out the "Ultimate Answer to Life, the Universe, and Everything" (42).

We've come a long way since then. Now, instead of looking for simple answers to complicated questions, we are increasingly looking for complicated answers to complicated questions. When addressing issues such as "How is pollution affecting global temperatures?" the result is not a number. It is an image, or a series of images. Images are able to convey a large amount of detailed information without sacrificing the big picture. In a single glance, we can take in millions of numbers.

Laying things out and arranging them visually can turn unstructured data into information we can use. To-do lists and calendars are examples of nondigital information visualizations that help us to map our activities over time. Not only do calendars serve as external memory devices, helping us remember dates and details, they also create a visual impression of how busy we are by representing the density of activities. If our calendars are packed with tiny scribbles, underlines, and exclamation points, we are in a condition conventionally known as screwed. We don't need to read every single item over to ascertain our overall situation—a quick glance tells us what we need to know.

Information visualization takes data and organizes it—often by arranging it along one or more axes. All charts and graphs are information visualizations. You can think of an ordered list, for instance, as a graph with only one axis. This axis might be awesomeness—as in the top ten hair-rock albums of the eighties. In the case of a to-do list, the axis is usually time. You can arrange things simply in the order in which they have to be completed or you can also indicate how much time each task is likely to take. However, what if instead of just writing out the tasks you add another axis: fun-ness. For tasks that are fun, you draw a line going up; for tasks that suck, you draw a line going down. And the more fun it is, the farther up line extends. The more it sucks, the farther down. Now you have a much more interesting picture of the week ahead, and it might even change the way you've planned it. You might want to alternate between fun and sucky tasks, or you might get all of the tasks that suck out of the way at once.

Information visualizations are so powerful because they allow us to ignore some aspects of our data in order to focus our attention on others. By taking a complex piece of data (a task) and ignoring everything but time and level of enjoyment, you can get a clear perspective on those aspects of the data. But if you replaced enjoyment with, say, the amount of money you'd earn by completing the task, you might get a very different graph and, based on that graph, might make very different decisions as to how to organize your schedule. For example, the tasks you dislike might yield more money, which you do like—so the enjoyment axis is more complicated than it first appeared. Information visualizations make the complex clear by ignoring some aspects of the data and highlighting other aspects, and which aspects you choose to highlight or ignore determines the meaning of the graph.

One of the famous examples cited by information visualization guru Edward Tufte in his book *The Visual Display of Quantitative Information* was a map of a cholera epidemic made by Dr. John Snow in 1854. The map shows a neighborhood in London overlaid with two types of data: the location of the homes of the cholera victims and the location of the pumps for getting water. By examining the map, we can easily see that most of the deaths occurred close to a particular pump. Observing this, Dr. Snow ordered that the handle of that pump be removed, thus stopping an epidemic that had killed more than 500 people.

But, before Dr. Snow could come up with the right answer—removing the pump handle—he had to ask the right question—what do all the sick people have in common? Answering this question required that Snow look at the problem from a different angle—he made a map and plotted the data. Following Snow's example, information visualization is increasingly being used by scientists in order to develop and test hypotheses.

Chris Henze is the technical lead of the visualization group in the Advanced Supercomputing Division at NASA's Ames Research Center. He works with scientists and engineers to turn what in some cases represents many years' worth of data collected by hundreds or thousands of instruments positioned all over the world into an image or sequence of images that can be viewed in a matter of minutes.

When dealing with complex trends such as climate change, the ability to compress space and time as well as highlight certain types of data is crucial. Henze told me "Visualizations allow us to zoom around at will, run forwards or backwards in time at any rate, and transform and filter the data."

For example, the Finite Volume Circulation Modeling Group is using visualizations to predict the landfall of hurricanes. These scientists study how hurricanes form and how they move. Then, combining the information on an approaching storm with what they know about how storms usually develop, they "fast-forward" into the future. Currently, using these simulations, NASA can see about three days into the future when predicting where a storm will hit.

The amount of data necessary to predict a hurricane is huge—for some projects, 70 terabytes is necessary in order to generate a visualization. That's about equal to the amount of data that could be contained in a stack of books 400 miles tall. Air temperature, wind speed, and ocean temperature are just a few examples of variables that influence how a hurricane will develop. Even

High-tech Graffiti

When you think of computer programmers, you may think of kids with thick glasses sitting in their parents basement. But a new breed of programmer is taking technology to the street. One of my favorite examples of the new generation of digital artists is Hektor, a robot made by Jurg Lehni and his brother Urs. Dangling from a string that can be stretched between two windows, Hektor is able to paint any image that appears on a computer screen onto the side of a building.

But Hektor is not the only new kid on the block. A graffiti gun shoots paintballs with incredible precision, printing out pictures and spelling words using the paintball spots. Another graffiti machine leaves a more subtle message by writing with water. It releases droplets of water at precisely timed intervals so that, as they fall, the drops spell out words. It's like reading a waterfall. One of the great things about digital design is that for every person who is using a piece of technology in the way it was intended, someone else is figuring out how to use it to make his own unique mark.

Hyperwall
NASA. May 2004

with this amount of data, however, it is still difficult to make predictions with 100 percent accuracy. NASA uses a tool called the hyperwall to run different scenarios simultaneously in order to compare the results. The hyperwall is a seven-by-seven cluster of flat-panel screens, each driven by its own dual-processor computer with a high-end graphics card. Each screen displays a slightly different interpretation of the data, allowing scientists to dissect the various factors—simultaneously watching how temperature and pressure are affected even as the clouds begin to swirl.

Predicting the path of hurricanes is comparatively simple compared to dealing with the really big issues, such as global climate change. The most famous, and perhaps most powerful, tool for understanding climate change is a relatively simple graph that shows the rate of change of average temperature over the last thousand years. This graph has been nicknamed the hockey stick graph, because it is long and flat and then suddenly turns upward at the end—and because it is frequently used in fights.

If you don't think design can be controversial, consider this: The scientists who created this graph have been hauled in front of Congress and accused of accepting bribes. The reason that the graph has created so much controversy is because it takes a complicated issue and paints a rela-

tively simple picture. Just like a calendar covered in exclamation points, you don't need to read each individual item in order to come away with a distinct impression that the Earth is getting warmer.

Designers are sometimes mistaken for stylists. But, while there's nothing wrong with being able to clearly articulate why a black belt should or should not be worn with brown shoes, designers are also being asked to explain how rising temperatures might affect the circulation of ocean currents and how a shift in those currents would impact the rate at which ocean levels rise. Designers are responsible for making images that clearly communicate these important issues to voters, politicians, scientists, and decision makers who might actually be able to solve some problems—if only they understood them. But that's just the beginning. Increasingly, designers are at the cutting edge of scientific inquiry, working with scientists to conduct primary research. Not only are designers helping to understand the results; they are also helping to come up with the questions.

So the next time some aging hippie pats your hand and says, "That's nice, dear . . ." when you tell them you're studying design, just let them know that the answer to Life, the Universe, and Everything is not likely to be 42. If they ask why, then draw them a picture. ■

Visualizing Patterns and
Trends in Scientific Literature

Designer: Chaomei Chen

Software: CiteSpace

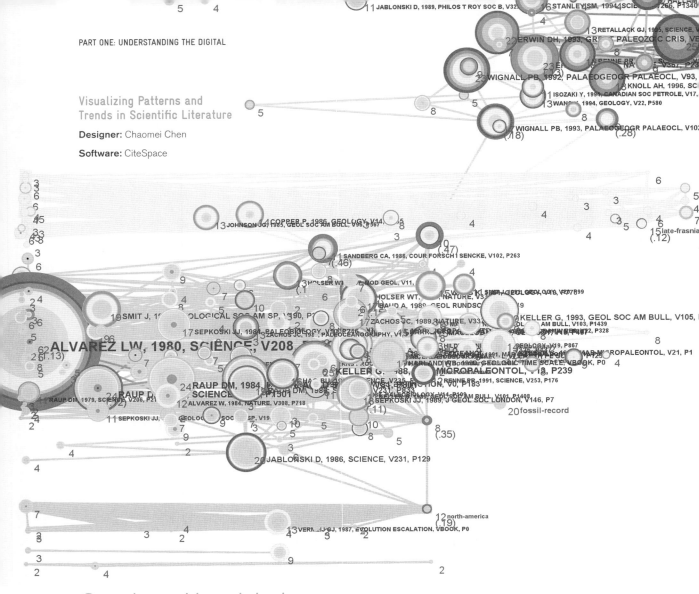

Seeing the Links

An interview with Chaomei Chen, professor at Drexel University and editor of
the journal, *Information Visualization*

How did you start making these maps?

My earlier interest was in visualizing large-scale hypertext structures—an example is a Web site
with lots of interrelated links. Naturally, people want a map that allows them to navigate these links.
So that's how I started thinking about how to visualize something that is abstract.

What made you interested in mapping science in particular?

I got interested in scientific literature from a linkage point of view because scientific articles are connected to other, related articles through their citations. It's standard when writing a scientific article to reference other people's work. So I started trying to visualize these relationships by mapping the citations.

How do the maps work?

Well, starting with a single article, every citation is represented as a line connecting the article to other articles it references. If you start to put the articles together, they form a mosaic. You can also think of a citation like a vote—at least one person thinks the article or its conclusions are worth reading. So, the more times an article is cited by other articles, the larger the circle representing it appears.

At the highest level, it becomes like a survey of what everyone in this field is writing about and what contribution or piece of knowledge they think is the most important. So you start with individual snapshots and then you add the element of time, so that the snapshots become like frames in a movie, and you start to get a sense of trajectory—of where the discussion is heading.

Why is it important to understand these connections?

This is a way to get a sense of consensus in the scientific literature. The consensus is not saying that everyone necessarily agrees with the paper they are citing, but that it has value as a reference or discussion point. It gives you a sense of the impact of an idea. You can think of this network as a snapshot of the scientific community's thinking on that subject at that particular time as recorded in the scientific literature.

What do these maps tell us that other methods, such as a survey, could not?

I don't think a single individual would be capable of generating this kind of view—and even if someone could, you would run into issues of individual biases. It's natural to emphasize the things you prefer. This is a problem with the traditional surveys.

How will scientists and scholars use these maps?

It can useful for researchers if they want to, say, decide what articles are influential or also if they want to look for gaps and see what connections haven't been made. Also, when thinking about funding, it may be important to see what areas seem understudied.

How do you see these maps evolving?

There are a lot of different reasons why something might be cited—it could be a negative example or it could be just that it is related to some other social or political issues that don't really have to do with the main focus of the article. Currently, the maps aren't qualitative judgments—they just show what people are talking about. But they do allow you to understand the location of the conversations. The next level is to go down to the text level and try to understand what scientists are actually saying about a given subject. Are they citing an article because they agree with it or disagree? There's a difference between popularity and value. ∎

◀ Reuters at 3 Times Square

Date: 1998–2002. Opened in 2002

Client: Reuters America Holdings, Inc.

Interactive Systems Designer(s):
Luke Watkins, Carson Sloan

Additional Credits: Edwin Schlossberg,
Gideon D'Arcangelo, Angela Greene,
Dean Markosian, Joe Mayer, John Zaia

Project Photography: ©David
Sundberg/Esto

©ESI Design 2007

CASE STUDY

Signs of the Great White Way

Angela Greene, Edwin Schlossberg Design, New York City

When designing such monumental signs for an architectural project, what are the key design considerations?

For this particular project we had to consider the many angles, truncated vistas, and distances that this sign would be seen from; pedestrians and cars up and down the avenues and side streets, multiple distant cityscape views, people at direct street level in Times Square, people entering the building lobby. Other considerations were different demographics of pedestrians, day versus night, and the limited attention span of a viewer in Times Square.

And how does the Reuters project differ from more conventional motion-driven signs?

We set out to create a self-updating dynamic signage system that engages the entire building that was symbolic of the activity within the building and demonstrative of how Reuters gathers, processes, and disseminates information. The sign is composed of multiple animated templates that display live Reuters data feeds as they are generated—financial info, images being taken just minutes before by photojournalists around the world, coverage of special events, to name a few. The templates themselves have a scheduling program that varies the order based on time of day, sponsors, special events (think New Year's Eve)—even the predominant color of each segment. Weekends are different from business hours, which are different from pretheater.

Times Square is zoned for advertising spectaculars, but was there a larger over arching concept behind this cascading sign?

The guiding principle was to externalize what Reuters does in an informative and visually exciting way—that is, gather news, images, and video, and distribute it to the world nearly instantaneously. The motion on the sign is intended to symbolize their news making process; raw information flows down the long vertical panel from the top of the building (in from the world), flows down the building (processing), and when it hits near street level presents itself as a full news story to the viewer on a large display, and then travels to left and right—out to the world. The sign is made up of eleven different-sized LED segments that roughly form an inverted T, covering 7,700 square feet and wrapping around a corner—but we wanted to treat the sign as a single visual field.

Designing for a moving sign is also designing for moving people. Must you be conscious of traffic flow in designing this venue? And how do you do that?

This sign is not so much about moving people as engaging people moving through Times Square and delivering a coherent message for what may be at most a ten-to thirty-second glance. Everything there has an enormous amount of visual competition. We designed the sign to have a unique form and type of motion to help it stand out from the cacophony—and to deliver a message that would always be engaging, no matter how many times you pass by.

Who is more critical to the creative team, the technologist or the design? How do you interact?

From day one, this truly was a collaborative process between designers, technologists, and newsmakers—it could not have worked any other way. The first step was understanding Reuters, news feeds and how to access them—then creating dynamic animated templates that covered the eleven uniquely shaped panels (which run both inside and outside the building) as a single surface, and creating the back-end software and scheduling system to run it. That is a gross oversimplification.

It required an insane number of meetings, phone calls, and hours standing on the street in Times Square tweaking colors, point sizes, animation speed, sequencing, and brightness levels.

Aesthetically speaking, what contributes to a successful result?

It's been running continuously for five years and has evolved to include new templates, interactive games, revenue-generating advertising, and modifications of the original templates to accommodate new content and branding. It now has its own life—yet is still true to the original visual and informational intent. We couldn't ask for a better success than that.

What kind of background did you need to do this project?

Motion graphics, animation, digital typography, logic design, software production strategizing, and the ability to speak the language of the software development team. ∎

This sign is not so much about moving people as engaging people moving through Times Square and delivering a coherent message for what may be almost a ten- to thirty-second glance.

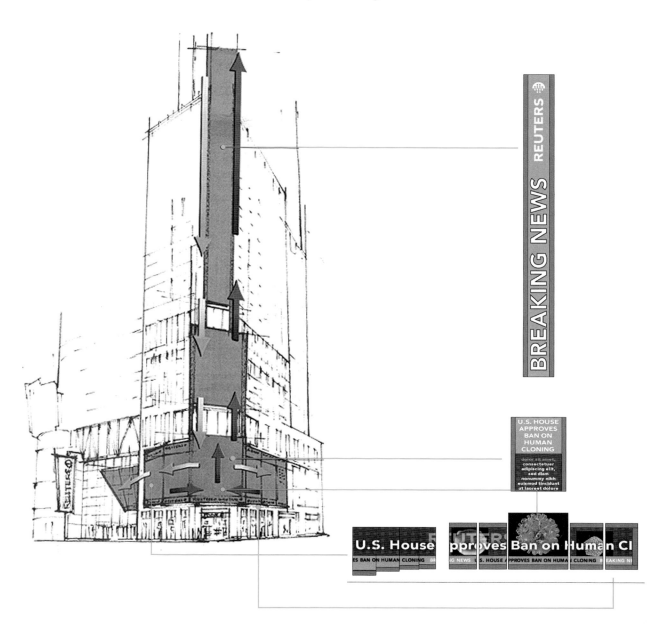

CASE STUDY:

Complexity Made Accessible

Jill Martin, Duarte Design, California

Describe your work creating the graphics for Al Gore's presentation in the film *An Inconvenient Truth*.
Duarte creates graphics at the request of Mr. Gore, on topics that are usually identified by him. We read the available research and information on those topics and suggest which particular points may be the most relevant to the overall discussion. We then translate those points into information graphics that use standard design conventions to establish a hierarchy of ideas. Once they are approved, Mr. Gore incorporates them into his narrative.

What can a graph or chart show that other means (a verbal description, for example) cannot?
An audience, especially a lay audience, may have difficulty accessing raw technical data, but an illustrative graphic is compelling and will be more easily recalled later. Generally, the more simple or metaphorical the graphic, the more important it is that it be accompanied by a strong verbal explanation of what is being shown or symbolized. The combination of a visual example and a verbal explanation cements the idea for both visual and verbal thinkers in the audience. On the other hand, complex information graphics correlate many data points in a way that conveys the overall message without sacrificing the nuance of detail or oversimplifying the concept. Rather, they strike a balance between "thesis" and "data" levels of an argument and thus present a more robust and interesting case.

What is the most important thing to keep in mind when you're designing an information slide?
You want to keep the visuals minimal and eliminate background noise to emphasize your point. Depending on the sophistication of the audience, you might include related data. But generally, the goal is to communicate instantly. You're looking for impact.

How does seeing and hearing the information at the same time work together?
People are either going to read or they are going to listen, and your brain is hardwired to process visually first and then verbally. So you need them to either be listening to your voice or looking at your slides, but not both.

The combination of a visual example and a verbal explanation cements the idea for both visual and verbal thinkers in the audience.

What's the difference between designing presentations that will be seen by scientists and the general public?

A scientific audience that is well versed in the subject being discussed often possesses the ability to digest dense, unillustrated data easily. A mixed audience, made up of people who are informed on the subject but for whom it is not their life's work, will absorb the major points of the discussion more readily if the presentation incorporates graphics. The more foreign the information is to the audience, the more it becomes important to find a way to break it down and present it visually.

How does Mr. Gore approach creating the presentation?

Many presenters make the mistake of assuming their audience is as fascinated as they are by the minute details of the topic under discussion. Generally, unless an intentionally technical presentation is being given to a technically savvy audience, the opposite is true. If the goal is for the audience to come away from a presentation with a greater overall understanding of an issue, presenting clear, factual information in a concise and compelling manner is key. This means incorporat-ing visual explanations wherever appropriate. Mr. Gore inherently understands this concept and is passionate about ensuring that the information he presents is both factually accurate and as visually articulate as possible.

What, if any, were the particular challenges you faced on *An Inconvenient Truth*?

Well, we're talking former vice president here. So you can imagine the travel schedules, requirements associated with presenting in diverse venues, last-minute changes phoned in from the road—you get the idea.

How long have you been working on that presentation? From a visual/presentation design perspective, what if any improvements have you made along the way?

Since 2003. The presentation is constantly being both expanded and refined (seemingly contradictory, I know) as new research is released and new informa-tion becomes available. Since our team is well versed in the data, we're often able to suggest ways to in-tegrate newly released information into the existing presentation. ■

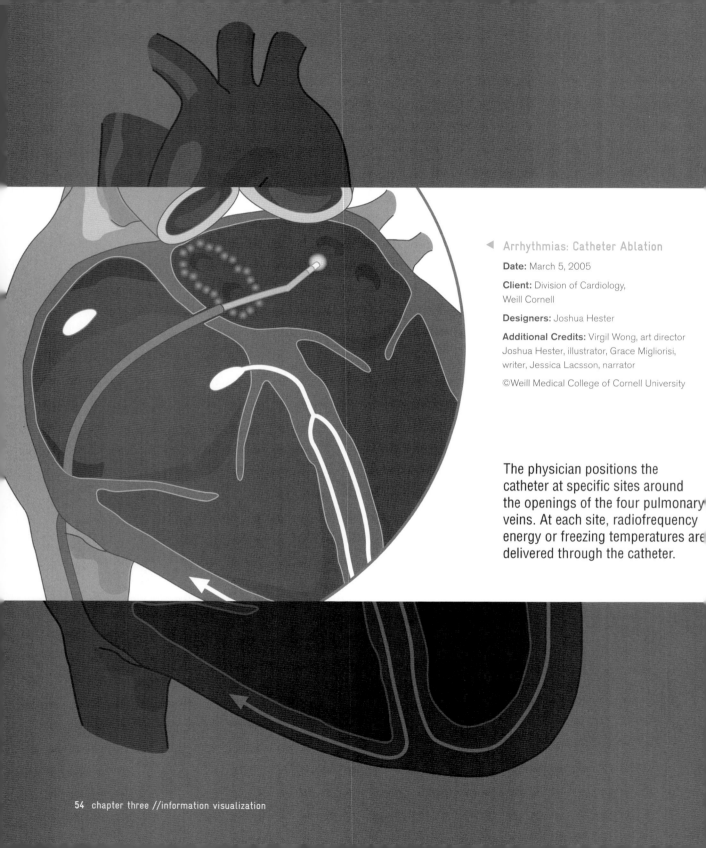

Arrhythmias: Catheter Ablation

Date: March 5, 2005

Client: Division of Cardiology, Weill Cornell

Designers: Joshua Hester

Additional Credits: Virgil Wong, art director Joshua Hester, illustrator, Grace Migliorisi, writer, Jessica Lacsson, narrator

©Weill Medical College of Cornell University

The physician positions the catheter at specific sites around the openings of the four pulmonary veins. At each site, radiofrequency energy or freezing temperatures are delivered through the catheter.

Cardiology Web site/
Cornell Medical Center

Joshua Hester, designer

How did you become a Web designer? Were you trained as a graphic designer?

In the beginning, it was total luck. Back in the spring of 1999, I was finishing up my degree in computer science from Virginia Tech and was still trying to decide what I wanted to do. My classmates were landing jobs as junior software engineers and the like, and I was still trying to find a way to combine my art and computer skills into something other than coloring spreadsheets. I actually had an interview with a firm that suggested that I could express my creative side by coloring spreadsheets.

So you were smitten by the Web?

The Web was really starting to come into its own, and I remember seeing a Macromedia Shockwave animation on a site and I was completely blown away. Just a few years previously, colored backgrounds on Web sites were the new thing. I chanced on an interview while still in college with a software development firm in Richmond, Virginia, that was looking to hire another Web production artist. I had taught myself how to build Web sites, and I think

I had built two—one for a random engineering firm and one for myself. When I graduated that summer with a BS in computer science and a minor in studio art, I went straight to work for the firm in Richmond with a week off in between. I thought for sure they'd discover that I didn't know what I was doing at some point during that first month. I only had the faintest of ideas of what a graphic designer even was at that point.

Describe this cardiology project and the audience it is meant to reach.

This project was done for the Division of Cardiology at Weill Medical College of Cornell University, from summer 2005 through spring 2006. The concept was to create a series of animations describing the condition of atrial fibrillation (a type of irregular heartbeat), and one of the possible solutions, catheter ablation.

The intended audience was the patient, who was either considering or would be undergoing catheter ablation. The animations were part of a larger set of medical illustrations I was asked to create. I worked with our

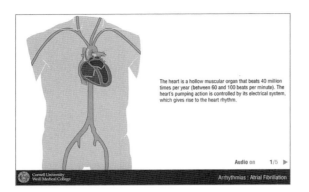

The heart is a hollow muscular organ that beats 40 million times per year (between 60 and 100 beats per minute). The heart's pumping action is controlled by its electrical system, which gives rise to the heart rhythm.

Audio on   1/5 ▶

Cornell University
Weill Medical College   Arrhythmias : Atrial Fibrillation

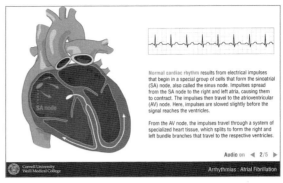

Normal cardiac rhythm results from electrical impulses that begin in a special group of cells that form the sinoatrial (SA) node, also called the sinus node. Impulses spread from the SA node to the right and left atria, causing them to contract. The impulses then travel to the atrioventricular (AV) node. Here, impulses are slowed slightly before the signal reaches the ventricles.

From the AV node, the impulses travel through a system of specialized heart tissue, which splits to form the right and left bundle branches that travel to the respective ventricles.

Audio on ◀ 2/5 ▶

Cornell University
Weill Medical College   Arrhythmias : Atrial Fibrillation

copyriter, who is a former professor of anatomy, and the doctors in the division to ensure that the illustrations and animations were accurate.

In working for a hospital where the site must appeal to doctors and patients, how much detail must you know to provide the most accurate information?

Our main purpose in creating content for the various Weill Cornell Web sites is to tailor it first to the nonmedical yet still well-educated viewer. But true, the sites must appeal to doctors, and in most cases we rely on them and their staff to provide most of the information. Our copywriter usually has to restructure and rewrite that information to make it as accessible as possible for the nonmedical layperson. We work to provide enough detail to not misinform, but keep it from becoming too overly technical where we can. In terms of the medical images I created for this project, this meant adopting a straightforward illustration technique that was still anatomically correct. I frequently referenced medical illustration textbooks and had the doctors point out any corrections that needed to be made.

What are the design parameters? Are there limitations in terms of illustration and typographic technique?

The overall airplane safety diagram style originated from earlier animations done by our former art director. I refined the style a bit to work for these new animations, but kept as much of it the same as possible to maintain consistency across our sites. The use of Helvetica Condensed, the banner at the bottom with the "Cornell red," and the dimensions of the animation all had to remain the same. This helps anyway because, as one would expect, it allows the user to focus on the specific topic of the animation and only have to familiarize themselves with the layout once.

What software works best in this kind of project, particularly so there is no room for error?

Adobe Illustrator and Macromedia Flash are necessary, mainly to produce the animations, and less for the room for error involved. Illustrator was used to create the comps, which were shown to the doctors. They would then have me make corrections, which was infinitely easier with Illustrator being a vector-based program. I would adjust the curves of the organic forms as precisely as I could to

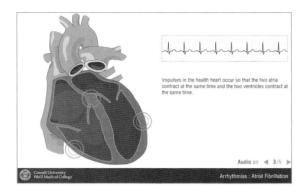

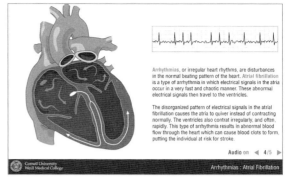

make it look as accurate as possible, within the adopted flat-color style we were using. Vector art also allowed me to port the illustrations over into Flash with little effort. Flash is invaluable as an animation tool for a project such as this because I could quickly create motions, such as the heart beating, and send it to the doctors to review. That kept the room for error small because I wasn't investing weeks on animations that would need to be radically changed later, so I could produce many more iterations if necessary to get the motion just right. With this type of animation and visual style, there will always be some room for error, which is fine as long as the users understand what they're seeing.

How uniquely special is working on a medical site, compared to other Web projects you've done?

Working on a medical site is in many ways completely different than any projects I had done before. The animation side of my work is completely unique to my time at Weill Cornell. I had created illustrations before that were used in sites, but never when it was as much of a focus as it is on these sites for the hospital. The structure of the work is also different, mainly in the relationship to the client.

The web team at Weill Cornell is an internal department, funded by various divisions within the hospital. As such, there are no bids for which design firm will get the work, nor are the time and cost estimates as strict. Of course, we would as a team create estimates for the work involved, and stick closely to our schedule, but the clients seem less concerned with the time it takes to complete a project than they would if they had to see cost adjustments based off of scope creep. My view as a Web designer of the specific costs and estimates is limited, but my perception has been that clients within the hospital would sometimes change their mind mid-project if they thought that the final result would make for a more accurate, better presentation. In most cases, we were willing to make those changes, because we want our work to be as accurate and clear as they do, if not more.

Did you enjoy the process?

I feel that my effort is making a difference in people's lives. It's almost sappy to say, but it feels much better to be creating animations to ease someone's fears than to be making a site to help someone buy a couch.

Designing for Growth

One of the fundamental principles of digital systems is that they have the ability to expand and grow. If you can master the art of facilitating this growth, your career will grow as well.

Designing digital systems is about counting chickens before they hatch—something my grandmother told me never to do. But then, Grandma was notoriously slow to ramp up.

As a digital designer, your job will be to anticipate, accommodate, and even encourage change. According to a report commissioned by the Australian government, the average life of a Web site is forty-five days. There are insects that live longer than that. Many digital designers' portfolios are a graveyard of defunct projects that have been redesigned or are no longer online—a screenshot is all that remains of their blood, sweat, and tears. It doesn't matter how lovely your design is if the system you build gets chucked out because it can't keep up with the demands of the project or business. To survive, a digital system needs to be able to grow.

Doug Lloyd of Flat compares digital design to gardening: "What fascinates me is that I get to play with living systems," he told me. "You're never exactly sure where the system may go, and as a designer, my role is to 'seed' the future, and guide its direction. Systems are brought to life by their use. I'd say my job is done when the site takes on a life of its own."

Creating a site or system that can grow is no easy task. It requires carefully balancing short- and long-term needs. Clients—like designers—get excited by the possibilities offered by technology and tend to overestimate the amount of time they will have to update their system. It is easier to add content and sections than to remove them, so don't design a system that requires updating unless you're sure there will be time and resources to maintain it.

Blogs are a particularly seductive sinkhole. Literally millions of blogs have been created by ambitious people with good intentions who simply don't have time to maintain them. And few things look worse than a "Latest News" section that hasn't been updated in months.

However, digital technology offers ever-expanding opportunities to get other people to create content for you. When you find yourself waking up in the morning and logging on to see what other people

Digital Dark Age

The Internet has made more information available to more people than any other technology in history. There are now about 11.5 billion Web pages. Every day, 7,300,000 new Web pages are published, adding up to 250 megabytes of information produced a year for every man, woman, and child on Earth.

Even though information is now being created at an unprecedented pace, however, it is being forgotten almost as quickly. Web pages, on average, exist for only about hundred days. Unlike printed material, Web pages often disappear without a trace. They go dark. The templates and databases are discarded, dismantled, or overwritten. As a result, all the mindless ramblings of bloggers, the recipes for roadkill chili, as well as vital information about who we were and how we thought about ourselves in this new medium disappear without a trace.

And so, as the pace of information creation accelerates, we are remembering less and less about the past. Without this information, we have no means to learn from our success and failures. "Paradoxically," Brewster Kahle, founder of the Internet Archive, has written, "with the explosion of the Internet we live in a digital dark age."[1]

[1] www.archive.org/about/about.php

have posted to your site, then something is going right. In fact, some of the most publicized projects in recent years have not been the result of breakthrough technologies—what was called in the dot-com years a *killer app*—but, rather, of the combination and centralization of existing technologies in a way that encourages community involvement and sharing. MySpace is a prime example of this phenomenon, as are blogs such as Boing Boing and Gawker. The conventional wisdom at the moment is that if you can get enough people to come, then the business model will work itself out. "The future," as Don Delillo wrote in his classic novel *Mao II*, "belongs to crowds."

So how do digital systems grow or scale? If you can answer this question, then you also know why Bill Gates is the richest man in the world. Microsoft creates one application and then replicates it a million times. Once it has paid for the initial cost of developing the application and promoting it, every sale is money in the bank. Think about how different this is from old-fashioned ways of making money—take making cars, for instance. Cars cost a lot to develop, but they cost even more in materials and labor to manufacture. Microsoft's costs are more or less the same, whether it sells one copy or one million. And now Ford is struggling to pay the health care costs of its employees, while Bill Gates can't give away his money fast enough.

The Microsoft kind of growth is based on replication. You make something once and then you sell a million copies. This is basically what a page template does, on a smaller scale. Rather than replicating an entire application or Web site, a page template lets you make copies of page layouts and then populate them with content. Press a button and up pops an identical page, which is already linked up to the necessary applications and is just waiting to be filled with content.

The Good Way versus the Good Enough Way

What if you want your system to do more than replicate itself? What if you want it to evolve? There are two basic ways of evolving a digital system. For simplicity's sake, I'll call them the *good way* and the *good enough way*. The good way, practiced by corporations such as IBM, Yahoo!, and many others, is to do the type of research described in the chapter "Action/Reaction"—you go out and study your target audience, come up with a range of options, and then test them, select the best option, and then test it again.

Until recently, it seemed that, for big companies, this was the only way to go. IBM, for example, has 100,000 or so pages on its site, and even a small change has a big impact. If you want to change the global navigation, you had better know how it is going to affect all of your user groups and be absolutely certain that people are still going to be able to find what they need.

The *good enough way* is to build something, watch people use it, and then fix what seems broken. There are a lot of drawbacks to this approach: You risk losing your audience right away if they don't like what they see when they get to the site. It can also be confusing to repeat users if your site is always changing. This approach does have one big advantage, which may outweigh all other considerations: It is extremely fast, and, in a world where attracting attention is crucial to success, being first is often more important than being perfect.

Before Google, the good enough way was thought to work only for smaller businesses that didn't have much to lose. Google changed that. Instead of having one big site with lots of functions and pages that were all tested and all linked together, like IBM or Yahoo!, Google has lots of small sites that they make public as soon as they can and before they are "finished."

Google's key insight was that, in the rapidly changing world of technology, if you wait until something is finished and tested, it may already be obsolete. In fact, Gmail, Google's incredibly popular e-mail service, is still listed as beta several years after its launch—meaning that the system millions of people rely on every day for their important communications is not really ready yet.

There are three reasons that Google can get away with this approach. The first is that what does work works very well; the second is that the interfaces tend to be extremely simple, so users are unlikely to get confused by changes; and perhaps most important is that Google has made their users feel like they are part of something new and exciting—they are part of the adventure. Everyone knows that adventures include bumps.

The good enough way still requires planning ahead. In order to be able to rapidly launch different iterations of a site or system, you need to have your data in order. In the digital age, databases are far more durable than interfaces. As a digital designer, your design options will largely be determined by whether your data is clean, consistent, and accessible. For example, are all of your products and pages tagged in the same way? Does your customer information include first name and last name, and have the e-mail addresses been verified? If you have good data, then you can do almost anything with it. Redesigning a Web site can be as simple as changing the style sheet.

Getting It Together

We've talked about how to design systems that grow, but what about your growth as a digital designer? As Doug Lloyd observes in his interview, "Most of the really exciting work being done in digital design is beyond the ability of any one person to create." Projects are too complicated and move too quickly to go it alone, and digital designers almost always work as part of a team.

Effective collaboration is an art onto itself—one that is seldom taught in design school, where, for a variety of reasons, the emphasis remains on individual achievement. But learning how to get along with others—when to go with the flow and when to dig in your heels and, perhaps most important, how to bring someone around to your point of view—is essential.

Although almost everyone agrees that it is important to work together, the structure of teams remains the subject of debate. The open-source approach favors bringing in as many brains as possible to work on a problem, but others believe that small teams work best. Jason Fried, a partner in the (small) firm 37Signals, has this to say on the subject: "One thing I find interesting is that when big groups really want to get things done, they don't make the group bigger; they make the group smaller. For example, when Congress really needs to consider something important, it forms committees. When the military needs to conduct an operation with absolute precision, they usually call on the best small team they have."[1]

While projects have become more complicated, setting up a design studio has become simpler. It used to be that only a big studio could afford all the equipment that was necessary to do cutting-edge work. Therefore, the standard career path for a designer was to graduate from design school and spend the first few years working as a small cog in a big machine and saving money in the hopes of one day going it alone. Many designers still take this route, and for good reason—if you are a cog in the right machine it can take you places that you would never have go to on your own. If this is your plan, then it behooves you to consider early on what kind of cog you would like to be. Do you like to get your hands dirty with programming? Are you more visually focused? Do you like to organize other people or would you rather work alone? If you don't figure out where you fit in, someone else will put you where they want you—which is rarely where you would most like to be.

More and more often, however, digital designers are striking out on their own or with a few friends and setting up small studios or even designing and marketing their own products. There are even design programs now that are especially geared toward turning out design entrepreneurs. After all, if you can think it up and design it, then why shouldn't you finish the job? The cost of setting out on your own has never been lower. Anyone with a computer, a high-speed Internet connection, and access to a decent copy shop can now hang out their shingle and produce almost everything that a big studio can.

Finding Your Place

Whether you decide to join a big firm or go it alone, understanding how teams are structured is essential. If nothing else, it will help you understand all the functions that you will have to perform to complete a project by yourself. The most basic team structure exists in advertising. At many ad agencies teams still consist of a designer and writer who work together on multiple projects and

[1] Vinh, Khoi. "Getting Real." Adobe ThinkTank, http://www.adobe.com/designcenter/thinktank

sometimes stay together for years. This is changing as advertising evolves beyond a picture and tagline. The interactive version of this simple structure is to have a designer, programmer, and content provider (which may sometimes be the client). In this model, the designer focuses on the *presentation layer*, or what the end user will actually see, while the programmer focuses on the underlying structures that will support the site or system, including integrating with other systems and managing the content. Often, sites will repurpose existing content and/or the client will have a copywriter on staff to help.

On large projects, however, teams can expand to include dozens or even hundreds of people. Here is a breakdown of some of the common roles you find on large digital projects (note that different firms may use different terms for these roles).

■ Engagement manager: This is the primary client contact for the project and is responsible for understanding and representing the client's needs, as well as working within the client's budget. Often, work will be presented to the engagement manager before it is given to the client.

■ Project manager: This person is responsible for the day-to-day operation of the project, including scheduling, taking notes at meetings, and making sure everyone has the resources they need. The project manager is sometimes also referred to as a *producer*.

Why Collaborate?

There are designers who believe that originality means working alone. They cannot conceive of having worth if another person shared in even a minute part of the creative process. "Collaboration" means consorting with the enemy. And in design, the enemy is a collaborator.

Hogwash!

In design—and particularly digital design—collaboration is the heart of creative activity. The interrelationship of two or more people in search of a common goal is about the most fulfilling of creative experiences. Indeed, all of us are the result of collaboration.

Designing is rarely a solitary activity. Just look at the roll call of credits in any design annual for virtually every designed object. Although visionaries create the styles, develop the ideas, and promote the concepts that the majority apply, ultimately even these people are spokes in a larger wheel of process.

No matter how talented, a designer invariably must answer to a client, which in many cases might be a design director, creative director, art director, or other mediator, who plays an integral role in the finished product. In all multiplatform designs—Web, film, television—creativity depends on this promiscuous exchange.

Some collaborations are imposed, while others are divined. However they manifest, collaborations offset weakness and bolster strengths. But collaboration is much more than a simple calculus of X + Y = Z; it is a fusion of chemistries that results in a unique entity. When everything is working well, when ego satisfaction derives totally from pride in the project as a whole, then the collaborators' distinct contributions result in an outcome that only one person could never have accomplished.

Although there are no laws for how collaborations should work, the best are those in which the participants respect one another's turf, while nimbly crossing the boundaries as necessary. One can be controlling or submissive and also be a good collaborator.

We don't think there's room for specialists on a small team. If you have four people, and one person can do only one thing really well, we think they're wasting space.

■ Creative director: This is the ultimate creative position in many design firms. The creative director is responsible for all design and content and usually oversees multiple projects at the same time. Creative directors can either have a design or writing background.

■ Associate creative director: The associate creative director, or ACD, oversees the day-to-day creative work on the project. Often ACDs will define the creative direction, which the designer will then execute. ACDs have either a design or writing background.

■ Designer: The role of the designer in this system is to choose the images, define the color palette, select the typography, and lay out the system. Sometimes they will be working from templates created by the information architect.

■ Information architect: The information architect oversees the entire system, making sure that the necessary content and functionality are included in the finished product. The IA will usually produce a site map, which shows each page of the Web site and how those pages relate to one another. Often, the IA will also be responsible for determining the site's global navigation.

■ Programmer: Programmers come in many forms. Some specialize in Flash and motion, others focus on the back-end architecture and getting various systems to talk to one another.

On big projects, several people may be performing each of these roles, as well as others that aren't listed. On other projects, a few people may do all of them. The advantage of large teams is that they allow people to really focus on a particular problem or area and develop expertise. The disadvantage is that a lot of time is wasted through communication. Stacks of documents are created that serve no other purpose than to keep everybody on the same track. The waste that is inherent when communicating with a large team causes some studios to reject them even for complicated projects. 37Signals designs complicated software solutions that, ironically enough, are often tools for bringing large teams together. Partner Jason Fried says, "We don't think there's room for specialists on a small team. If you have four people, and one person can do only one thing really well, we think they're wasting space. You are better off with someone who can code HTML/CSS, design user interfaces, structure information, and write copy. We think all of that is a designer's job. Not the job of four separate people." ■

Daylife.com ▶

Client: Daylife

Date: February 2007

Designer: Jonathan Harris

Software: Adobe Illustrator,
Adobe Photoshop, Flash

Streaming News

Tom Tercek, partner, Daylife.com

What is Daylife? And what is it doing that has never been done before in the digital world?

Daylife is a new way to explore the world. Today, unprecedented amounts and types of news are freely accessible through the Web. The events and stories that shape the world, along with the insights and perspectives that frame them, are becoming immediate and interconnected. Yet, this surge of information has created a challenge for people to find what they're looking for and make new discoveries. A new method for organizing and presenting news is needed. New tools give people a voice—and for media brands to succeed in this environment, it's important to listen.

This type of media tears down the authority of big media and establishes the authority of the audience. They tell you what they care about and what really matters, and if they don't like established media choices, they'll establish their own. Daylife doesn't create news. We organize it and make it easier for people to find it, collect it, share it, and react to it.

How does this occur?

Daylife gathers stories of all shapes and sizes from many perspectives around the world, and then presents them in a rich, browsable landscape, helping you make connections you never knew existed. Our goal is not just

Client: Daylife

Designer: Jonathan Harris

Additional Credits: John Zipps, Frederico Duearte, Anne Poochareon (photo editors)

Software: Adobe Illustrator, Adobe Photoshop, Flash

to share the top stories; we aim to guide your journey through the events that shape your world. It's also the first news service designed to be distributed. Although we have a destination site, any publisher, large or small, can use our platform and data to add to their own service or build new applications. It's what it means to be a network on the Web. Daylife will also evolve as people engage with it, use it, contribute to it, and shape it.

With so much feeding into Daylife, what is your design scheme or philosophy? Who designed your basic interface?

Jon Harris is our lead designer. He not only is a great information designer, but also understands the relationship between design and people. With so much information presented in new ways, it's important for Daylife to provide a clean, understated design, both on the site and with its distributed modules of content.

While we leverage technology to do a lot of the heavy lifting, it's important that we show a human quality to the brand personality of Daylife. It's not about just having optimal functionality and better lists, or data. We're not designing an airplane cockpit. We're a media company, and for us, that means creating the most pleasurable experience possible. It's a trade-off toward joy, not performance.

Daylife seems to be in the business of branding (and packaging) news for individual users. Is there a design component to this, and what is involved?

Daylife is a media service for people who are curious about the world, designed to give people a view of the landscape and help them explore further. Everyone is different. No two people see the world the same way. Daylife believes that news should reflect this. So we present news on countless subjects from thousands of global sources, reflecting numerous interests and perspectives.

But are there visual components that express or make up this landscape?

Yes. The world is amazing, motley, diverse, thrilling, tragic, and beautiful. We believe that news, as the record of human life, should be more than just headlines. To help express life's color, Daylife includes lush photographs, juicy quotes, interactive charts, and more to help enrich the experience. And that's just the start.

There are so many different kinds of designers these days—so-called conventional designers versus a slew of information, interface, and experience designers—what kind of designer do you need for Daylife? And what are the qualifications you look for?

We're looking for people who understand how to visualize new forms of digital media in entertaining and informative ways. It's not limited to one particular discipline, but quite the opposite. We prefer people who have a passion for developing new ways of seeing and understanding, in a visual context.

◀ Universe

Client: Daylife

Date: February 2007

Designer: Jonathan Harris

Software: Processing

On the printed page, typography that speaks in some conceptual or emotive way to content is usually a good thing. What is the role of type on Daylife?

Typography plays a critical role in the presentation of information, but we're not limited to typography. In fact, we try to stay away from lists and strive to use graphic imagery to help illustrate a concept or topic. Typography is part of the bigger whole.

Finally, you've said you want artists and designers to be involved in the packaging or interpretation of the news on Daylife. How do you see this happening?

We believe artists and designers can utilize our data to conceive of new ways to present the world's media. As I stated earlier, we're interested in showing the landscape, and automated lists of information don't achieve that. Second, we believe part of our role is to entertain while we inform. Just as networks provide programming in different formats, we too intend to offer new types of media for the world to enjoy.

And does intervention on the part of artists and designers enhance journalism, or create an entirely new genre that is something between art and journalism?

The site is a concept space to produce new methods of organizing and visualizing world news, media, and information. But it's just the beginning. As more and more people and businesses interact and adopt Daylife, we hope it will grow in new ways to help people accumulate, disseminate, and consume media and information. ■

Designing for Multiple Devices

Digital design is no longer confined to the desktop. Find out how new technology is climbing the walls.

Imagine your trash can calling to tell your refrigerator not to order any more vegetables because they keep going moldy. And the refrigerator would say, "Don't blame me—all he ever wants to eat is Cheez-Whiz." "Oh, I know," the trash would reply. "He really is a slob. He went three days last week without emptying me." "Do you think he's putting on weight?" the refrigerator asks . . . and so on.

From a certain perspective, the future of networked computing looks pretty grim.

We're at the beginning of what a report to the United Nations termed the Internet of Things. The report, by the International Telecommunications Union, states, "Today, in the 2000s, we are heading into a new era of ubiquity, where the 'users' of the Internet will be counted in billions and where humans may become the minority as generators and receivers of traffic." This means that, rather than communicating with you, computers will increasingly communicate about you: analyzing what you wear, how well you eat, whether or not you're likely to commit a crime.

This chapter will look at how digital devices share information; how observations of your current behavior are used to predict future behavior; and what the very near future holds in store for us when we go to the store. Perhaps we can also figure out where design fits in a world where, as the UN report observes, "Science fiction is slowly turning into science fact."

Speak Clearly

In order for your appliances to be able have a conversation about you, they need to speak a common language. The digital language of 1s and 0s is a good start, but they also need to interpret those 1s and 0s in the same way. The problem is that technology has developed in a landscape of competition, rather than cooperation. Competing companies have attempted to outdo each other in the race to launch the best product and, in the process, have interpreted 1s and 0s slightly differently.

This is why Web sites look different—or may not work at all—depending on the Web browser that you see them through. Internet Explorer and Safari, for example, have no real reason to work together—because both want us to see the Web only through their eyes.

This isn't the first time we've had problems with establishing standards: When railroads were getting started each train company designed their locomotives to run only on their own track. Eventually, a "standard gauge" was agreed on. Train makers would space their wheels four feet eight inches apart. But standards take time. Over 150 years later, still only around 60 percent of the world's railroads have adopted the standard gauge.

The inventor of the World Wide Web, Tim Berners Lee believes that in order for digital information to be accessible to "anyone, anywhere, anytime, anyhow," there need to be standards. He has established the W3C—the World Wide Web Consortium. This group is leading the effort to establish standards for how information is structured and interpreted. But although standards sound like a fine idea, they may have drawbacks for designers.

For example, while you may want people to be able to view your Web site on their mobile phone, do you really want to be thinking about that three-by five-inch screen when you are work-

Sound Design

You know that sound your computer makes when it's starting up? Someone designed that. Most companies now have signature sounds that accompany their logo—a few notes that seem to stick to your brain like Velcro. Sound design has long been an integral part of making movies. The swoosh of a punch followed by that crunching thud. Although sound design itself is as old as church bells, it used to be that in order to make a noise you had to blow, bow, or bang something. With new digital interfaces, however, what used to take hours in the studio can now be made on your computer in the comfort of your own home. Kung Fu fighting, anyone?

Visual interfaces to sound design software essentially allow you to stop time and see notes. So you can visually adjust tone, levels, and rhythms, or mix existing sounds or music by creating new tracks. The ability to re-combine sounds became big news when DJ Danger Mouse made the *Grey Album*—a mash-up of Jay-Z's *Black Album*

and the Beatles' *White Album*—in his bedroom on his computer. *Entertainment Weekly* named it the best album of 2004.

Although these interfaces allow you to modify sound visually, you can also modify your visuals musically. The British design firm United Visual Artists, for example, creates custom interactive systems that bands such as Massive Attack and U2 use in concerts. These systems are capable of modifying and displaying dynamic content pulled live off the Web, so that the visuals are always different and relate to what's happening in the world at that moment.

As networked devices become more prevalent, there will no doubt be new noises to accompany new functions. I predict, for example, that it won't be long before you hear your refrigerator "moo" to let you know that you're low on milk.

ing on your thirty-inch cinema display? And what about blind users? Shouldn't they be able to hear what you have to say? Apple thinks so—it built Voice Over into OSX, a program that will read a Web site to you.

In order to be readable, however, it helps if the site has a simple structure. The interesting layouts that look so good on your wall-mounted monitor will cause a screen reader to stutter. According to Google technologist T. V. Raman, "It turns out that much of the visual complexity that creates stumbling blocks for mobile users also become show stoppers when it comes to listening to a Web page using screen readers."

Will standards condemn digital designers to a future of boring layouts? Not necessarily. The key is separating the information (data) from the layout (presentation).

Are You Looking at Me?

We've touched on the fact that computers are no longer just communicating with you; they are communicating about you. This is nothing particularly new. Search engines and online retailers have been tracking you for years, compiling a detailed profile of the Web sites you visit and the purchases you make. This information is used to predict your behavior and buying habits so that the system can display products and offers that are likely to appeal to you. Sites that present content based on user preferences are often referred to as dynamic. They are assembled almost instantly, based on the profile of the person who requests them.

One of the most common processes used to turn past profiles into predictions of future behavior is called collaborative filtering. Nine out of ten readers agree that collaborative filtering is a process worth understanding. Basically, collaborative filtering makes predictions by matching you up with people who have purchased the same things you have or have expressed similar preferences. Let's say you have purchased albums by Dead Pres, Twisted Sister, and Lil' Boozy online. The collaborative filtering system will look for other people who have bought those albums and ask, "What other albums have they bought?" Now, it turns out that most people who bought these three albums also love David Hasselhoff. So the next time you log on to the music site, you'll see Hasselhoff front and center on the homepage.

The underlying assumption behind collaborative filtering is that people who have behaved similarly in the past will behave similarly in the future. When the system has only a few examples to base its recommendations on, it doesn't work very well. Let's say you buy a Conway Twitty album for your grandma. The next album the system recommends to you might be *Coal Miner's Daughter*. Human behavior is erratic, and just because you buy something doesn't mean you like it (take this book, for example). But after the system has collected a few thousand examples—or a few million—these profiles become increasingly accurate. We are creatures of habit, after all.

Using collaborative filtering, Web pages are assembled on the fly, according to what the system knows about the user. So, instead of thinking of the Web page as a page, it is more accurate to think of dynamic sites as a grid of boxes, just waiting to be filled with content that is selected just for you.

Because you can't put a round peg in a square hole, each piece that goes into the grid must be more or less the same size and composed of the same elements. If your page layout calls for a picture and text, then your description of the David Hasselhoff album needs a picture—no matter how off-putting all that chest hair may be. Not only do the "pegs" need to be the same size and shape, but they need to be described (or tagged) and organized in such a way that the system can find them instantly. In other words, they need to be standardized. This standardization allows Web sites to move beyond just pulling product copy. Any information that is in the correct format can be pulled onto the site. Information on the weather or the price of soybeans can be displayed, if that's what you're into.

Just as dynamic sites make a clear distinction between content (what goes in the grid) and layout (the grid), a similar distinction allows content to move easily between different types of devices. As long as content is consistent, that grid may be a hundred squares across, or only two. The same content may look very different, depending on what device is accessing it. Not all the features available on your thirty inch screen will be there on your cell phone. But that's all right, as long as you find what you're looking for.

Just one more note: While it is important to understand the relationship between data and display, keep in mind that a display is also a kind of data. One nice trick I've been seeing recently are sites that vary their appearance based on your user profile. For example, if the system knows you are logging on from Denver, it will check the weather in Denver. If it happens to be snowing, little snowflakes will drift down across your screen, mirroring the weather outside.

The Internet of Things

So the problem with dynamic sites based on collaborative filtering is that what you do online only gives a clue as to who you really are. If you really wanted to learn about someone, what makes them tick, what would you do? Would you walk up to them and introduce yourself? No way! You would hire someone to follow them and take notes.

A few years from now, your behavior offline will be tracked in the same way your behavior is being tracked online now, only with far more interesting results.

The United Nations report on the "Internet of Things" focused specifically on RFID tags, which are currently a booming business. By the end of 2007, there will be one of these tags for every person on Earth. RFID tags are microchips that have tiny antenna attached. Perhaps its no coincidence that the former head of Homeland Security, Tom Ridge, is on the board of one of the largest suppliers of RFID tags. Because they broadcast a signal, RFID tags can be read from a distance, without the object or person who is "tagged" even knowing. Currently, passive RFID tags (which don't have batteries) transmit a unique ID number that allows a person or thing to be identified. These tags are smaller than a grain of rice and cost a few cents. Active RFID tags, which have batteries that last for up to ten years, are currently three or four times that size and can contain and transmit much more information. For example, active RFID tags are being imbedded in new passports issued in the United States and the United Kingdom and will provide information about your travels as well as a complete profile and even a digital picture.

RFID tags have many potential business applications. Currently, they are used in the fast-track lane of tollbooths. You just drive on through, and the RFID tag sends a signal that is picked up by a reader, which deducts the amount of the toll from your prepaid account. This same logic can (and will) be applied to retail. Soon, you will no longer have to wait in a checkout line to pay. You will just slip on that pair of stiletto heels and strut on out the door. The store's RFID reader will pick up the signal from the credit card in your wallet, pick up the signal from the pair of heels, put two and two together and automatically bill your account.

Your interaction with RFID technology is likely to begin the moment you enter the store and will continue long after you've left it. As soon as you walk in, the RFID reader will identify you and pull up a list of your past purchases. It may also read the tags on the clothes you're wearing that you bought elsewhere. Armed with this information, the salesperson will be able to walk up to you and say, "Do you know that you would have saved fifteen percent if you had bought that tongue stud here instead of Wal-Mart?"

Using the same collaborative-filtering technology that generates recommendations for you on Amazon, he or she will know your proclivities and be able to immediately direct you to the whips-and-chains department, where they will be waiting with your size. Once you leave the store, you will continue to be tracked—at least until you leave the shopping mall (most RFID tag transmissions currently have a range of only about 750 feet—but that's likely to change).

Of course, you won't actually bother carrying credit cards. An RFID tag containing information on everything from your medical history to your bank account balance will be worn as a pendant around your neck or simply implanted. RFID tags have been approved for human implantation since 2004. No more losing your wallet! It will be imbedded in the fatty tissue of your upper arm (the most popular place for implants).

Speaking of losing things, it will probably not come as much of a surprise that the uses of RFID tags extend beyond shopping to things like predicting crime (but act surprised anyway; they're watching). Pilot programs are already under way to use these tags to track prisoners as they move between—or within—institutions.

But what if, using a tool like collaborative filtering, you could predict crimes before they were committed? Why couldn't the same system that predicts what books we'll like predict whether we are likely to commit an act of terrorism? In fact, what if the books we like were actually one of the predictors? Remember Tom Ridge—the nice man on the board of the company that makes RFID tags? While Tom was director of the Department of Homeland Security he used the Patriot Act to force libraries to turn over their records showing what books people had checked out in order to try to spot potential terrorists. Librarians all across the country protested. More recently, search engines including Google and Yahoo! were asked to turn over information relating to Web searches. Google refused. Yahoo! declined to comment.

Design without Boundaries

What role will the designer play in this brave new world in which tiny devices surround you with a cloud of information triggering all sorts of actions and interactions? In the same way that dynamic content changes the way we think about designing Web sites, ubiquitous computing (meaning computing that is everywhere) changes the way we think about other kinds of design. For example, is it still design if you can't see it?

I think it is. The more our lives are shaped and mediated by technology, the more we'll need the compassionate hand of the designer helping us to navigate this strange new world. If you look at design not as a set of skills or products, but as a philosophy—even a mission—to help people understand and enjoy the world around them, then design will only be more necessary as our world becomes more complex.

After all, humans will still have eyes and will still respond to the visual, even if they are walking through clouds of invisible systems. While recognizing the effect that technology is likely to have on how we live, it is important not to lose track of what we find meaningful. Just as photography changed painting but did not replace it, there will still be room in a digital world for beautifully designed posters and print material. ■

◀ Channel Frederator Web Site

Client: In-House, Next New Networks

Designers: David Karp, Timothy Shey

Web site Producers: David Karp, Fred Seibert, Timothy Shey, Halley Hopkins

Show Producers: Michael Green, Eric Homan, Melissa Wolfe

Program/Software: Proteus custom application; running on multiple ITV platforms

©NextNew Networks

CASE STUDY:

Small-screen Television

Timothy Shey, founder and head of network development at Next New Networks

How did you get drawn into the digital world, and into design specifically? Did you train as a designer?
I grew up doing digital design, though I didn't know it at the time.

As a kid in the 1980s, I would design and write software and games on my Commodore 64, and was also pretty active on the BBSes (bulletin board systems) that were a precursor in many ways to the Web. Design then meant working in low-res pixel and ASCII art, but it was good training for what I'd end up doing in the nineties and beyond.

Design for me has always been about doing the best thing possible within the limitations of the media and the scope of the project. In college, I studied English and fine arts, but spent most of my free time in the computer lab, figuring out HTML and designing Web sites for many of the student organizations on campus. By 1996, a friend and I had started our interactive design company, Proteus, in a dorm room, and had signed on a number of corporate and nonprofit clients.

I had a good grounding in composition and color theory from my art education, but I had to learn the subtler points of layout and typography as I went, through close attention to other designers' work and books like yours. I still feel the lack of having an educational grounding sometimes—I don't always know the right terms, and I tend to measure almost everything by eye instead of using tools—but it's probably too late for me now to change my habits much.

You were originally designing for handheld devices; what kind of skills and aesthetics did you need for this curious–indeed, Lilliputian–format?

When we first started designing applications for handheld and mobile devices, the limitations were so extreme that design was mostly about content and user experience. Aesthetic decisions were simply how much copy you wanted to put on a screen, and whether you could use abbreviations or type-based symbols (like a caret for a forward link) effectively on the page.

The devices' download speeds were so slow and processors so limited, you had to think a lot about caching any images you used and reusing them effectively from page to page in a design. At that point, we were getting a bit bored with Web design as it got increasingly graphical, so having such limitations again were fun. Whenever we came up with something really clever that we thought improved a design, we were pretty proud of ourselves, even if no one else could appreciate it.

Were there other challenges?

The other challenge, which continues to this day, was a lack of standardization. As more and more mobile devices hit the market, you found yourself designing for an extremely complex landscape with thousands of permutations of screen sizes, coding language support, browsers, and operating systems, and the trick would be to use flexible style sheets and adaptable layouts to create a good user experience on as many devices as possible without designing for the lowest common denominator.

We were pretty happy with the work we did on HBO Mobile in 2004 for *The Sopranos*' fifth season launch, which supported a wide variety of handsets with a pretty deep amount of content, from games to episode recaps, and looked good on nearly every one.

Do you believe design standards have been established and reached, yet go beyond the basic functional requirements of design for small screens?

It doesn't seem so to me, though I've been less involved with design for small screens in the past two years. For example, I'm nearly incapable of spending my hard-earned money on a mobile phone. Nearly every time I pick one up, I'm disappointed by the user experience.

I don't know what's happening in the industry—maybe there's a lot of churn, or a lot of design by nondesigners, but it doesn't feel like there's been much evolution or progress in the design of mobile apps, but rather, that people are making the same mistakes over and over again. I think that small screens should take context into account, such as a user's previous decisions, their potential distractions and limitations, and present the options that people will most need, with a minimum of scrolling or input needed at any stage. Try nearly any device, and you won't see that happening—and until we have that basic requirement met across the industry, we won't move forward to truly exceptional design. That said, I'm pretty impressed by the new Blackberry Pearl's OS, and Google's apps like their SMS tools and mobile maps, and the iPod experience was nearly perfect, until their capacities got so large that browsing by a scroll wheel became less optimal.

Are the tenets of good design the same for a small-screen format as on a luscious page?

For me, they tend to be. I like my page designs like my small screens, with an economy of design, well-chosen imagery, clean typography, and an emphasis on ease of use. That said, if a graphic artist wants to mess things

Wurlitzer Digital Jukebox

Client: Gibson Audio

Designers: Sunil Doshi, Zaida Jocson, Andres Quesada, Timothy Shey, Vivian Solowey

Creative Director: Timothy Shey

Program/Software: Custom application by SimpleDevices

©NextNew Networks

▲

Callaway Rule 35
Interactive TV Application

Client: Callaway Golf

Designers: Sunil Doshi, Zaida Jocson,
Andres Quesada, Timothy Shey,
Vivian Solowey (Proteus)

Producers: Timothy Shey (Proteus),
Andy Askren (Tyee Euro RSCG),
Kate Ertmann (ADI)

Creative Directors: Timothy Shey
(Proteus), Andy Askren (Tyee Euro RSCG)

Program/Software: Proteus custom
application; running on multiple ITV
platforms

©Next New Networks

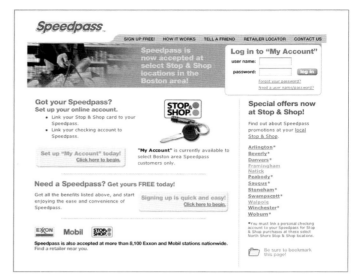

▲

Client: ExxonMobil

Designers: Sunil Doshi, Zaida Jocson,
Andres Quesada, Timothy Shey

Creative Director: Timothy Shey

©Next New Networks

up in either format for aesthetic reasons, I really enjoy that, too. One of my favorite experiences on the small screen in the past year was a game called Lumines for the PSP, which took a while to make sense of, but was absolutely beautiful.

You are now involved in creating video content (TV shows) for Internet distribution. First, tell me what those shows are all about. Then, what are the design requirements for these to separate them from what we usually see on YouTube?

I've been working on online video content with an episodic, serial format—in that way, they're more like television shows than the individual clips and short videos that are making up most of the video viewing on the Web right now. The formats vary—some of them are like newscasts or interview shows; others might compile clips and videos sent in by the audience and wrap them up with an editorial point of view. It's videoblogging, basically, in the sense that what we're doing relates to television in the same way blogs relate to the publishing formats that came before. The content in most cases is fresher, more interactive, and more personal to the audiences' interests and tastes than television has been—and the best people doing it engage in a conversation with their viewers that blurs the traditional line between audiences and creators.

And what about design quality?

The design requirements for these formats are still emerging, but we're starting to learn things that work. Short form works, because it's easier for people to download, view, and share with others. We brand the shows, so that viewers can recognize them in the Wild West of the video landscape, though we do it in different ways from television—the branding is usually an integrated part of the experience, very quick and straightforward. Less post production is a good idea as well—the more

graphics and editing and polishing you do to these programs, the less viewers often like them, and the more it costs, which hampers our ability to move fast and try a lot of new things. The best shows are a pure expression of talent, and pretty close to a first draft, though made as perfect as possible within the limits of time and budget. I like to tell people it's like sushi, or good Italian food—you want to get the best ingredients and assemble them fresh, and serve them quickly—overcooking or too much time on the shelf can ruin the meal.

What do designers entering this digital environment need to know that you, at thirty-two years old, didn't even know when you entered the field?

I didn't know anything when I entered the field—I didn't even know that the field existed—so I would say they should not be afraid of what they don't know. I've worked with dozens of designers now over the years, and I've never seen one that didn't learn more on the job, and faster, than they had in their formal education. I jumped right into projects because they looked fun; I made a lot of stupid mistakes and bad designs; and I stayed humble and kept learning, and at some point along the process, I became a legitimate designer, then a creative director. It was probably helped by the fact that I didn't know enough about the field to be intimidated—so I would say that to anyone just starting: Don't be intimidated—you're young, we're old, and we have at least as much to learn from you as you do from us.

What are you looking for in designers for Next New Networks?

Ambition, critical thinking, and a desire to learn. I'll always rather work with someone who can roll up their sleeves, try ten different approaches to a design, and improve every time than someone with a lot of raw talent and a stunning portfolio who isn't willing to learn how CSS works. ■

PART /

Media and Methods

With a laptop, some software, and a cup of strong coffee, you can design pretty much anything. Over the last twenty years, huge warehouses worth of tools that would have taken dozens of people with years of experience to operate have been reduced to scripts that take ten seconds to download. From your corner seat at the coffee shop, you can create prototypes of buildings, build dynamic systems, or create motion graphics and send them streaming through the lobbies of office buildings. The power and availability of digital tools is breaking down barriers between disciplines.

IN THIS SECTION:

Designers are adapting anvd combining tools in unexpected ways. I recently learned that Adobe Illustrator, a favorite with print designers, has been adapted by product designers to create proto- types of running shoes. In the typography section, Jonathan Puckey talks about how he writes his own plug-ins for Illustrator to create new, dynamic letterforms. Software is what you make it.

Not only are the same software tools being used to design very different types of products, but products are being networked to create systems that would have been difficult to imagine just a few years ago. For example, Nike and Apple have joined forces to create a running shoe that syncs with your iPod. Not only does the shoe broadcast information such as how far you've run and how fast so you can hear it through your earphones, but you can actually sync your music selections to your running pace. Then, when you get home, you can upload the information on your workout to a Web site to race your friends. This is only one example of a micronetwork that is now on the streets. In his interview in "Beyond the Screen," Adam Greenfield discusses what lies in store for us as these networked systems become everyware.

The pace of development of digital devices makes it likely that we'll see more specialization in terms of design roles. Although anyone with a laptop can design a building or financial system, the truth is that the results will vary wildly, based on the experience and training of the person at the keyboard.

Each type of project has unique challenges and different tricks of the trade. In the same way that schools now offer specialized courses in game design and motion graphics, we're likely to see specialized courses in areas such as financial systems and digital communities, as well as crossover programs such as wearable computing and networked appliances.

In this section, we talk to individual designers about what they do, what they like about it, and how they ended up doing it. It is interesting to note that, with a few exceptions, they probably couldn't have imagined their current job when they started school. Cavan Huang, for example, has been out of school only a few years. But could he have imagined that he would be an interactive DJ at the Time Warner Center? Probably not. Like the rest of us, these designers are making it up as they go along, and, in the process, they are shaping the future.

The one thing that seems certain is that the pace of technological change ain't slowing down. So, whatever your particular interest, it is important to be aware of the larger trends that are driving innovation. As Dr. Anthony Dunne points out in Chapter 14, twenty years from now you don't want to be known as "that digital guy"—the one who is hopelessly wedded to an outdated technology. Dunne and his students at the RCA are studying biotech.

A Web Master on Mastering the Web

What does it take to be a solid Web designer? Khoi Vhin, design director of New York Times Digital, gives his wish list.

EDUCATION: So much of the Internet has been designed and built with self-taught knowledge that it would be shortsighted to require a specific kind of degree or schooling before hiring a candidate. If you can demonstrate the right skills, intelligence, experience, and enthusiasm, it doesn't matter to me where you learned it.

SKILLS: Here are the basics that will get a CV onto my desk: Photoshop, Illustrator, OmniGraffle, XHTML, CSS, JavaScript, PHP, MySQL. To get into the door, you need to demonstrate that you can take all of those skills (and whatever else may be necessary) and combine them to create a living, functioning Web site, from the concept through visualization through implementation.

TOOLS/PROGRAMS: Platform ambidextrousness is good; if you can use a Windows machine as well as a Macintosh, that's ideal. But we're a Macintosh shop, mainly because of the exposure that the platform gives designers to much more innovative ways of thinking about design and interactivity. So being an enthusiastic Macintosh user is definitely an advantage, as well as being an enthusiastic consumer of new software of all kinds as the Internet changes and evolves.

THEORY: As the Web becomes more dynamic, we're looking for people who can combine the long-standing principles of graphic design (typography, composition, etc.) with a grounding in design for interactivity. Specifically, we're looking for an awareness of how to design **behaviors** into interfaces, how to make interfaces optimally **usable** for people, and an understanding of how people and groups **respond** to the functionality that interfaces communicate, and how those interfaces should respond to people. This is a constantly evolving field of study; there's no Rosetta Stone for interaction design, so we also look for a vigilant interest in how these principles are changing with new technologies.

AESTHETICS: There's a place for it, but at NYTimes.com we have little use for decoration or wide-ranging graphic expressiveness. Our visual vocabulary lies within a fairly narrow aesthetic range, so we prize the kind of beauty that brings order to chaos, and that can do so efficiently, with the fewest possible elements. Our credo is "maximum elegance with a minimum of ornamentation."

TALENTS: I'm looking for designers who can solve problems with the structural precision of technologists, and for technologists who can create solutions with the qualitative intuitiveness of designers. Most often I find this in candidates who have tackled the wide and varied creative challenges of developing content-rich software, who have rolled up their sleeves and thought through the way real people will interact with their designs. If I had to pick a term for it, I'd say I'm looking for creative **agility**.

PORTFOLIO: I look for a portfolio, first and foremost, to be available online in a presentation that's been conceived, designed, and executed by the candidate herself. This is vitally important, because it provides insight into the candidate's breadth of experience and her editorial skills in selecting and presenting that experience, as well as insight into how she has technologically implemented that presentation. –Khoi Vhin

The Perfect Portfolio (for Now)

Randy J. Hunt of Citizen Scholar (www.citizenscholar.com) has come up with what could be considered the perfect portfolio under various circumstances—at least for now. For online portfolios to be viewed in a Web browser, this is the ideal, in decreasing order of complexity:

▲

CitizenScholar Web Site

Portfolio Web site with custom content management system written using RubyOnRails.

©Citizen Scholar, Inc.

1. Build a custom solution so I could update through a Web interface exactly what I needed.

   This is a great opportunity to learn the basics of more advanced Web development. Essentially, it's like making a two-sided Web site—one with a public side and a private side where you can edit and make changes.

   - I'd select one of the common languages used in Web programming and dive in with some basic online or book tutorials. Sites developed this way can be tested on a local server (one running on your computer), but eventually need to live on a live server with certain features.

   - It is easy to find a Web host that will allow you to configure this and administer some settings. A system that supports PHP and a MySQL database is the most common, but other options are quickly being adopted by most hosts, so any up-to-date tutorials will give you a good starting point. My current preferred method for developing sites is the RubyOnRails framework, which uses the Ruby language. I find it more intuitive than PHP.

   - The most important thing is to be comfortable with what you're doing and take it step by step. It can really be quite fun.

2. Retrofit one of the common blogging platforms and ignore the chronological aspect (just use the "normal" pages); my current choice would be Wordpress, http://www.wordpress.org.

3. Just make static HTML pages with a simple navigation, or even put every image/link/document on a single long page. There's some charm in that.

   - These have the advantage of easily being able to include video, audio, links to live sites, and the ability to show interactive projects that need a database server running in the background.

A portfolio that would be distributed online would need to be downloadable:

Downloadable PDF Portfolio

Multipage PDF portfolio created in InDesign.
PDF preferences set using Adobe Acrobat to
display full-screen when opened. Formatted to
print on 8.5" x 11".

©CitizenScholar, Inc.

Presentation Portfolio

Presentation portfolio created with Apple Keynote.
Can be controlled remotely with an Apple Remote,
Bluetooth clicker, or mobile phone.

©CitizenScholar, Inc.

1. Design it *nice and pretty* in InDesign in a format that would also fit well on 8.5-by-11-inch pages
if someone decided to print it. I'd save it out as a standard-quality PDF, which would be a relatively
quick download. Links to video files and live sites online could be included in the PDF through
Acrobat. The person would still need Internet access to get to those things, but at least they'd have
a reference for them.

2. Make a QuickTime movie if I wanted to narrate it somehow. You can add simple navigation to
QuickTime movies, so the viewer will be in control of what they see, but your description could be
spoken as if you were presenting it in person.

For a portfolio on disc, do one of the following:

1. Include a PDF as described above.

2. Mirror a Web site on the CD, with links to videos or other multimedia files on the disk.

Here are some other portfolio options:

■ My preferred portfolio format, which does require me to be present, is a presentation built in
Apple's Keynote. I usually lay out any text slides in Illustrator or InDesign programs, since the
type tools are more developed in those applications. Working this way allows for quick changes
and easy customization for the audience. Keynote allows embedding of video files, which makes
for seamless transitions to motion/video/film work.

■ I also recommend SnapzPro X, a screen capture tool, to record a Web site in use, so the video
can later be played back during a presentation without Internet access.

Where the Jobs Are

The digital revolution has opened many more opportunities for design and design-related jobs than ever before. For one thing, Web design and Web administration are endemic to almost every business. Although some Web sites are designed and maintained in amateur manners—on the cheap and usually with the aid of a secretary or some other neophyte—most medium to large companies have invested in having significant Web presences, working with everyone from design directors to art directors to designers.

The following is a list of areas in which digital designers at all levels are wanted (for more information it is useful to surf the various job-hunting Web sites).

EDITORIAL (MAGAZINE, NEWSPAPERS, WEB SITES):

The venerable newspaper seems to be struggling with decreasing circulations, but magazines are still being pumped out at breakneck speed, especially those in niche markets such as fashion, home services, and shelter. Web sites are also fast becoming supplements rather than complements to print periodicals, and some are even integral entities not tethered to any mother ships. Designers are wanted in all these areas. While print is not dead yet, having Web in the portfolio is a value additive.

EDITORIAL (BOOKS):

Just as print periodicals are still breathing, so, too, books are as vital as ever. The designer who specializes in books should also have a Web background, but typographically speaking books are a more rigorous genre.

ADVERTISING AND MARKETING:

The traditional methods of advertising—television, newspapers, and magazines—are in trouble, but the field is still very healthy. In addition to new conventional media, such as LED signs and spectaculars, advertisers are increasingly looking to the Web, handheld devices, and what is now called **viral and guerrilla media**. The latter include anything that is out of the mainstream that could involve print or outdoor extravaganzas, but also could include digital formats. In an industry that for so long relied on print and video, the digital designer and art director have untold opportunities.

ENTERTAINMENT:

The main U.S. industry is entertainment—film, games, network and cable television—and the need for designers working directly in these subgenres, as well as for components like the Web, is constantly growing. For instance, every major television station and network has a Web component, just as does every radio station. The need for skilled designers to build the Web presence and maintain its standards has never been this high.

CORPORATE:

Every major U.S. corporation (and minor ones, too) has Web components. And if they haven't already, they are developing interfaces for handheld devices such as phones and PDAs, as well. In addition, they still maintain their print and environmental needs, including logos, signs, and packages.

INFORMATION DESIGN:

This is less a media genre than a discipline that weaves its way through all kinds of media. Interface, user experience, and data organization are all components of this field, which is sought after in everything from corporate to entertainment design.

Being Digitally Indispensable

Being **indispensable** is a useful, indeed, valuable attribute on any job. Yet it's also a double-edged sword. On the one side, for employers to believe that they can't get along without you raises your stature and maybe your weekly salary. On the other, it means that as the go-to person, you become responsible for a lot, often too much, without the requisite compensation.

That said, being the crown prince of indispensability is much better than being a mere knave among knaves. And in the digital design world, being digitally multiskilled and software fluent is the best way to be so knighted. The next is to become the troubleshooter-in-charge, who, with an expansive knowledge of hard- and software, can solve the wide range of problems fellow workers will encounter.

The problem, however, with being a solver of problems is it can too easily pigeonhole you as a technician. Being a digital designer should not mean you focus exclusively on technical matters, but rather, employ technology to successfully execute your design.

So how do you become digitally indispensable, yet retain your design integrity? The answer is to establish yourself, first and foremost, as an indispensable designer. Whatever the extent of your hard- and software know-how, you must exhibit an even greater finely tuned aesthetic, as well as ability to conceptually compose type or image in whatever medium is your particular specialty.

Given all this, to be all-around indispensable in whichever way you chose, you should always follow these steps:

1. Volunteer whenever a problem arises.

2. Anticipate problems and provide solutions.

3. Don't stop at fixing a glitch; offer your talents, and practice what you preach.

4. Show, without stepping on another's feet, that projects move smoothly when you are intimately involved.

5. Show that in addition to working well collaboratively, you can also be a project leader—and that's the ultimate in indispensability.

Java Technology Concept Map ▶

Designers: Hugh Dubberly, Audrey Crane, Jim Faris, Harry Saddler

Date: 2002

Master Class

An interview with Hugh Dubberly

You were a true pioneer in the digital world, when we just called it computers. What made you jump into the breach so early?

When I was an undergraduate at RISD, Chuck Bigelow introduced me to digital type design. Dutch type designer Gerard Unger was also teaching at RISD. They encouraged students to focus on low-resolution type. For me, that led to a summer job with Xerox working on type for some of the first laser printers. Chuck also introduced me to Don Knuth's work on Metafont, a programming language for describing typefaces. As a grad student at Yale, I designed a typeface using Metafont.

Several of my classmates from RISD also got involved in font design. Carol Twombly, Dan Mills, and Cleo Huggins went to work at Adobe shortly after it was founded. They've been able to retire. I took another path. I went to Wang Laboratories to be design director. (This was when Wang was a Fortune 500 company,

and one of the largest computer manufacturers.) My work at Wang led to Apple. Apple led to Netscape. Netscape led to my own design firm, specializing in software design.

Apple was an amazing place. I got to grow up with the technology. My first week, I got to play with a video camera connected to a Mac Plus. It scanned on the fly, one column of pixels at a time. You had to hold very still to get a traditional portrait. Of course, everyone moved, which created fantastic experiments.

At Apple, two moments stand out for me. The first was seeing John Warnock demo the software that became Illustrator. He lugged in a Mac Plus, booted it up, clicked, drew out a line, clicked again, and there was a curve, which he proceeded to adjust. It was an epiphany for me. I'd programmed in Metafont and Postscript, where control of curves had been indirect. But I had enough experience to realize Warnock was showing an application that wrote Postscript as you drew.

My second epiphany was seeing Bill Atkinson demo the software that became HyperCard. I was working in a conference room with a writer. Bill walked in and said, "Oh. This isn't my meeting." My writer friend recognized Atkinson and was smart enough to ask Bill what he had on the hard disk he was carrying. Bill's eyes lit up, and he showed us a slideshow—images flying by faster than anything we'd seen on a Mac or PC at that point. Then he stopped on a slide of a carriage. He clicked on a wheel and brought up a slide of car; he continued clicking on a series of visual links. The only place I'd ever seen anything like it was on a DARPA project at MIT. It was amazing.

Bill's demo led to my involvement in launching HyperCard and to making HyperCard applications for Apple, such as the HyperCard version of Apple's 1987 Annual Report. My work on HyperCard led to working for Apple on "Knowledge Navigator" and a series of other

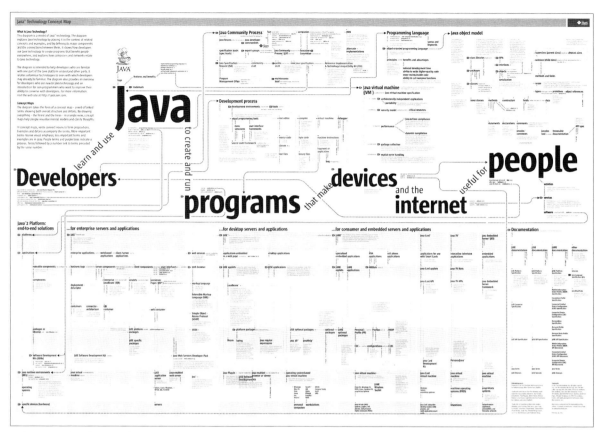

videos on the future of computing. From there, it was a short step to working on multimedia and the Web, which brought me and several other Apple folks to Netscape, where we designed and built large-scale Web-based services.

Do you believe, as many have predicted, that the digital realm will surpass traditional print production and design?

Yes. It already has. Last week, I taught a seminar at University of the Arts in Philadelphia. On the sixth floor, between two computer labs, they still have a giant process camera. It's so big you walk into the back of the camera to load the film. I saw no one use it the whole time I was there. Process cameras used to be everywhere. When I was a student, they were in constant use, and you had to put your name on a waiting list to get a turn.

Twenty years ago we labored through a complex analog process to produce a piece of print. Sending out for type, pasting it up, shooting the pasteups to make film, stripping the film into flats, making plates from the flats. Today everything, including making the plate, is digital. For now, high-end color printing remains an analog craft, but even that is changing. The quality of high-speed digital printing continues to improve, even while costs fall. What's more, every copy can be customized so it's a little different from the next.

Design of printed communications has moved from mass production to mass personalization. We used to think in terms of grid systems. Now we have to think in terms of creating and managing information assets—in terms of databases and content management systems.

Are there design conventions for digital work that are substantially different than for print?

Printed information can still be a little bigger and a lot higher in resolution than information you see on screen. With print, it's possible to show everything at once as on a poster; that's still almost impossible on-screen. (But eventually that will change, too.)

Computers and networks have enabled us to look more closely at how we interact with information and at the role of time in presenting information. Of course, sequence has always made a difference in design. Books and architecture have always been interactive. And opera has long been multimodal or multimedia. But somehow in the last ten years or so, our focus has changed. It's now possible to work as a communications designer without preparing pieces for mass-production printing. It's possible to focus solely on designing for the screen. New design activities have emerged around structuring information (information architecture), around sequencing activities (interaction design), and around creating worlds in which people can play (game design).

The earliest work in this area is only forty years old, and only within the last ten years have large numbers of people been focused on designing in the new media. It's all pretty new. We're still inventing new forms, new language, new conventions.

Pioneers like D. W. Griffith or Sergei Eisenstein adapted film technology to telling stories. We're still waiting for someone to invent the new media equivalent of Porter's *The Great Train Robbery* and Eisenstein's montage.

What are some of the ways in which digital has evolved since you began?

Gordon Moore's law, the fact that processor speed doubles every eighteen to twenty-four months (at the same price), drives the information revolution. A similar law applies to network bandwidth—wired and wireless. Networks introduce another effect. Robert Metcalf's law points out that networks become exponentially more valuable as they grow—every new member can connect to every existing member.

These basic processes have led to profound change:

- Computers used to be rare and expensive. They're becoming cheap and ubiquitous.
- Negroponte will soon deliver a notebook computer for less than $100.
- Google has the world's largest civilian computer, with 150,000 CPUs. And Google is still growing. Quickly.
- Computers have moved from tool to medium.
- From stand-alone to networked.
- When I was a grad student, I had to go to the computer center to work. Now you're always on, always connected.
- Pagers, mobile phones, Palm, Blackberry, and digital cameras happened.
- ATMs and TiVo happened.
- Multimedia, hypertext, and the Internet happened.
- Netscape, Amazon, eBay, Yahoo!, and Google were born.
- Newsgroups, chat rooms, IMs, cams, blogs, RSS feeds, tags.
- Web 2.0 emerged.
- We're soaking in cyberspace.

- The science fiction of Vernor Vinge, William Gibson, and Neal Stephenson has become real life.
- We have become our avatars, working, playing, and living in virtual worlds.
- Making a living as a trader on eBay no longer surprises us.
- Now we're seeing people make a living playing Everquest or in virtual places like CyWorld and Second Life.

Of course, when I started working, the world was black and green. No grays. No color. Black and white was a step up. We worked on a 512-by-342 pixel, nine inch screen and ran the whole OS, application, and data file in 1MB of RAM on an 8 MHz processor. For a long time, we swapped floppy disks to manage applications and data. Jumping to a 20 MB hard disk was a big deal.

Things have changed. Today, for about the same price, you can get a screen that's 2560-by-1600 pixels (30 inches) and a computer running a 2+ GHz processor with 1 GB of RAM and a 120 GB hard disk. (Your processor probably has more RAM in its internal cache than my first Mac had in total.)

In the twenty years since I joined Apple, screens are almost twenty five times larger, processors 2,000 times as fast, RAM at least 1,000 times as large, hard disks more than 6,000 times as big.

Where will we be in another twenty years?

What are the ways digital designers will be used in the next few years as new devices and better programs are developed? Some opportunities for designers are easy to see: More games. More Web sites. More Web-based applications. A proliferation of handheld devices.

Less obvious is the need for designers to help make sense of changing technology: The long-promised digital convergence has arrived. Your phone is a camera, a radio and music player, a game device, a PDA, and a computer. Soon your TVs will be connected to each other, to your stereo, to your game machines, and to the Internet. Computing is becoming ubiquitous: Anywhere. Anytime. Wireless will keep us connected. GPS and RFID will identify the location of everything. The distinction between virtual and physical will fade.

These changes create the opportunity for many new kinds of products. Companies will experiment with different combinations of technologies, services, and business models. They will tinker with variations on organization and interface. They will try new things. They will experiment—and all of these experiments will require design and designers.

At the same time, the practice of design is changing. Design has moved from a focus on form and meaning to a focus on action and interaction. Increasingly, designers are faced with the need to design integrated systems. Systems of systems. Connected sets of products and services. These systems form ecologies that grow and evolve. Their outcome cannot be predetermined. Even the full range of use may be difficult to predict.

The challenge for designers becomes creating expandable platforms. Creating tools for creating tools. Designing for customization. Designing for conversation. Designing for evolution.

Among the biggest challenges for designers will be identity, privacy, and community.

- How should people be able to represent themselves online?
- How do we preserve anonymity while also maintaining community?
- How should progressive disclosure and reciprocating disclosure work?
- How do we encourage diversity without losing a shared center?

Why limit the list to ten years?

- Fall Joint Computer Conference Demo, Douglas Englebart, 1968.
- The mother of all demos.
- ArpaNet, 1969.
- The father of the Internet.
- Unix, Bell Labs, 1971.
- Current versions still run banks, corporations, and our military.
- Xerox Alto workstation, PARC, Chuck Thacker, 1973.
- Alto begat Star. Star begat Lisa. Lisa begat Mac. Mac begat Windows.
- Ethernet, Robert Metcalfe, 1979.
- The foundation of networking.
- VisiCalc, Dan Bricklin and Bob Frankston, 1979.
- The first spreadsheet—modeling with numbers.
- PostScript, John Warnock and Chuck Geschke, 1985.
- The foundation of printing.
- PageMaker, Paul Brainerd, 1985.
- The beginning of the end of typesetting.
- Illustrator, John Warnock, 1987.
- The beginning of the end of plaka.
- HyperCard, Bill Atkinson, 1987.
- Hypertext for regular people.
- Photoshop, Thomas Knoll and John Knoll, 1990.

- Now every kid with a computer runs a Scitex machine.
- Linux, Linus Torvalds, 1991.
- Proof that open source works.
- Mosaic (later Netscape), Marc Andreessen et al., 1994.
- Adding images to Web pages changed everything.
- Amazon, Jeff Bezos, 1994.
- Allowing commerce on the Internet changed everything again.
- AuctionWeb (later eBay), Pierre Omidyar, 1995.
- Universal markets emerge; the net develops its own currency.
- Google, Larry Page and Sergey Brin, 1998.
- A good search engine, an amazing networked operating system.
- Craigslist, Craig Newmark, 1999.
- The beginning of the end of classified ads and yellow pages.
- Napster, Shawn Fanning, 1999.
- A testimony to the power of distributed networks.
- Salesforce.com, Parker Harris, 1999.
- Proof that businesses will lease Web-based services.
- Wikipedia, Jimmy Wales, 2001.
- Proof that collaborative media work.
- iPod, iTunes, and the Apple Music Store, Steve Jobs, 2001—2003.
- The quintessential integrated system of products and services.

- MySpace, Tom Anderson and Chris DeWolfe, 2003.
- The most successful social networking service.
- Flickr, Stewart Butterfield and Caterina Fake, 2004.
- 25 million users tag photos —more collaborative media.

The main thing for designers is to be curious—and to learn how to learn. My ideal curriculum might look something like this:

- Design Theory
- Design Methods
- Research Methods
- Information Structures and Key Models
- Principles of Interaction

Philosophy and Ethics of Design Visual Studies:

- Principles of Visual Perception
- Rapid Visualization Drawing
- Typography (editorial and display)
- Content Management Systems (grid systems)
- Way-finding Systems
- Information Design (visualizing information structures)
- Motion Graphics
- Sound Applied to Motion Graphics
- Filmmaking

Design Practice:

- Information Spaces
- Tools and Applications
- Games and Collaborative
  Authoring Environments
- Interactive Spaces
- Controls and Haptic Interfaces
  (physical interfaces)
- Integrated Systems of
  Products and Services
- Tools for Making Tools
- Systems that Evolve

History:

- of Art
- of Architecture
- of Graphic Design and
  Product Design
- of the Design Methods Movement
- of Science and Science Fiction
- of Information, Computing, and
  Interaction

Computer Science:

- Procedural Programming
- Data Structures
- Object-oriented Programming
- Web and Network Applications
- Data Structures, Building
  Sensors, Displays, and (Acutators)
- Data Structures, Modeling with
  Fractals, Genetic Algorithms,
  and Cellular Automata

Communications:

- Data Structures Writing
- Public Speaking

- Rhetoric
- Semiotics
- Epistemology
- Cybernetics (science of feedback)

Related Disciplines:

- Biology (natural systems)
- Cognitive Psychology
  (learning systems)
- Sociology (social systems)
- Cultural Anthropology and
  Ethnography
- Marketing
- Economics
- Organizational Management

**What was your most challenging
project, and why?**

We are helping Nikon redesign all the software that ships with its cameras. It is a very collaborative process that involves designers, engineers, and marketing people in Japan, the United States, and Europe. They are very smart, very good people. In many ways, they are an ideal client. Yet, working across many disciplines, many cultures, and many time zones makes the process complex and takes time. As our relationship has progressed and we've learned more about how they work and how they manage, we've begun to talk about the design not only of products but also the design of the development process and how development is managed.

This process is far from unique. Sustained software design engagements naturally lead to discussions about organizational issues. Whether for large manufacturers or small start-ups or Web-based services companies, making substantive changes in products—real improvements—sometimes requires changing the way organizations work, changing the process by which products are developed. This type of organizational change can take a lot of time. Often, it requires multiple product cycles. Facilitating organizational change is a new and challenging role for designers.

**Do you have a philosophy or
methodology about design in
the digital environment?**

I believe design should make the world better. It should serve people. It should make things stronger, faster, clearer—and cheaper. It should surprise. It should engage. It should delight.

I believe design is a collaborative process. In that sense, design is political. It is a sort of discussion. And the designer's role is to help facilitate the discussion. The traditional tools of drawing and prototyping are remarkably helpful in this role. Sometimes the subject of the discussion is abstract. In such times, designers must be able to prototype abstractions—they must be able to create models, which are simply tools for thinking.

I believe designers should root their work in the context of its use. We must understand our audience. Who are they? What do they believe? What do they want? At the same time, we must understand the economic systems and technologies which make products possible. All three equations—audience, business, and technology—must be solved simultaneously.

What do you look for when hiring young designers (or technicians)?

I try to hire people who are better at something than I am. I look for people who are curious. People who read. People who try new things. People who are excited about technology. And design. ∎

A Model of Innovation ▶

Designers: Hugh Dubberly, Nathan Felde, Paul Pangaro

Date: 2007

Web Design

Every year, more marketing dollars shift away
from TV and print and move to the Web . . .
about 30 percent more on average.

Online retailing is increasing at a similar rate, and, of course, more and more people are downloading
music, finding dates, checking stocks, and playing games. As of 2006, 70 percent of U.S. households
had broadband access.

If your goal is to keep your fridge full of pizza, you could do a lot worse than learning how to design
and build Web sites. Although tools such as Dreamweaver have simplified the Web design process,
most people would still rather leave it to a professional (or at least someone who can fake it). Today,
designing Web sites is probably the quickest way to keep yourself from starving as a designer.

But, as Khoi Vinh points out later in this chapter, to make the big bucks you're going to need to be
able to do more than just push a few pixels. Web sites are an integral part of many businesses and so,
in order to understand what to design, you have to know how to be able to talk to executives in a way
that inspires confidence—which means having an understanding of business goals and processes.

The other issue is that the Web itself is changing. Social networking sites such as MySpace mean
that it is easy to establish an online presence without the help of a designer. Although many individuals
and businesses still want a custom site that sets them apart from the crowd, that could change as
profiles become more sophisticated. As educator Anthony Dunne points out, it's important to think
beyond a particular type of technology—even if that technology is as important as the Web. We don't
know what the world will be like ten or twenty years from now—but we do know it will be different. So
don't think that just because you've posted a few pages you can rest on your laurels.■

Digital Craft

An interview with Tsia Carson and Doug Lloyd, FLAT, New York City

Many Web sites seem to aspire to be something or someplace else—whether that is a video or a print piece. But the sites that FLAT designs seem to be exactly what and where they are supposed to be. How does designing for the Web differ from your approach to working with other materials (whether that is print or yarn)?

DOUG: Whatever the project, we want to make things be what they are, whether a logo, an editorial treatment, or an interactive experience.

Our approach to designing a Web site is no different than any other medium. However, one way of organizing the kinds of projects we do is to divide into two general types: systems and one-offs. The systems we design, for instance an identity package or a community-driven Web site, will be used over time and are expected to evolve.

Whereas the one-offs will never change once produced—for instance, a book or exhibition.

We approach one-offs with a pretty traditional, linear design process: discovery, design, production, etc. Measure twice, cut once.

However, when designing a system—since a system will never actually be finished—we take an iterative approach. Or, to borrow a software development term, adaptive. The process stresses rapid cycles of development that produce versions and iterate toward, and beyond, launch. The focus is on doing over planning. We start making the thing quickly and adapt it relative to deeper consideration and feedback. We place emphasis on collaboration.

We do this for a variety of reasons, but primarily because with a system everything changes. We have also found, when presenting

systems, that people respond more thoughtfully to the thing itself, rather than to abstract representations of what it will be. Often, speed is a virtue, and getting something out quick is a primary objective. And, as our world becomes more transparent, people are less afraid to do their research in the marketplace and are more willing to experiment publicly.

I know you are both interested in craft, but I'm not sure I know what craft means. Is there a certain set of principles or mandates (or a mantra) that defines your approach to design, regardless of format?

DOUG: Through our Web site about craft, SuperNaturale.com, we've tried to pry open the term craft, give it a broader application, and blur some boundaries. We use the term as a lens to view the world through. To look at things from the

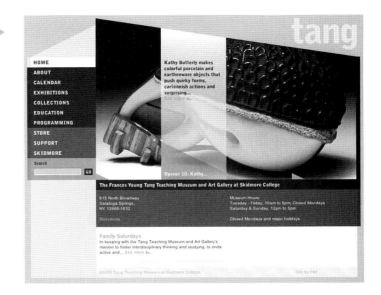

perspective of making rather than consuming, which seems to be the focus of most media, from blogs to magazines, these days.

We make hands-on decisions. We don't divorce strategic planning, research, or creative direction from the process of making something. This means craft, or the art of making, is central to what we do.

TSIA: I'm not sure I know what craft means either. I guess I consider myself a culture maker. So I take a similar approach regardless of medium (art, craft, design), and this allows me to approach a wide variety of projects in a similar way—Web sites, lamp shades, gardens, children.

I don't know what the right term is here—mantra? mandate?—but the place we start with projects is being hyperaware of context. What the project is, where it will go, who the various audiences are, and why they will use it. With our work we try to set up a zone of meaning—understanding that the message (unless terribly stupid) will not be exactly the same to everyone who sees it.

Different audiences extract different meanings based on their context and lived experience. Therefore, we try and create something that can be read clearly on one level within a certain zone of meaning. Then, if we're lucky, we lay in some nuances that the exemplary reader will notice and that will enrich the communication.

How does working with other materials inform or inspire your digital work?

DOUG: I'm currently learning how to garden. We live in a forest. I've been researching the ecological history of the area. The forest here has not been very well maintained over the last 300 years, and as such, is not that productive right now. I want to make the ecosystem more diverse, more productive, and more useful. To do that I'm learning how to design ecosystems—or actually, self-sustaining and fertilizing perennial polycultures.

What fascinates me is that I get to play with living systems. You're never exactly sure where the system may go, and as a designer

EXHIBITIONS
ARTISTS
HISTORY

RESOURCES

SOCIÉTÉ
ANONYME
INC

Exhibition Overview

The Société Anonyme: Modernism for America
brings to light the extraordinary history of the
Société Anonyme, Inc., an organization founded
in 1920 by artists Katherine S. Dreier (1877-1952),

The Société Anonyme: Modernism for America © 2006 Yale University Art Gallery. All Rights...

▲

The Société Anonyme: Modernism for America

http://artgallery.yale.edu/socanon

Client:
Yale University Art Gallery

**Site Concept Design &
Implementation:**
FLAT

Information Architect: Doug Lloyd

Art Director: Pettr Ringborn

Programmers:
Renda Morton, Bart Szyszka

Software: Flash, XML

©Flat, Inc.

my role is to "seed" the future, and guide its direction. This is directly related to my interests in designing interactive systems. Systems brought to life by their use that go in unexpected directions.

TSIA: I don't make distinctions with materials beyond what the material does or doesn't do. A ball of yarn doesn't need a back-end content management system. A content management system can't crochet. Ilook at most things as a system to design. In my life all this stuff feeds into each other.

Some of the things that I like about your sites are that they tend to be colorful without being ostentatious, and they make use of ornament without being ornate or overwrought. How do you know when a site is finished?

DOUG: We do such a wide variety of Web sites. However, for the ones that are truly interactive I'd say my job is done when the site takes on a life of its own.

Most of the Web sites we've worked on have very practical objectives driving the graphic design. This means an easy-to-use interface and a legible reading environment is the best way to engage someone.

TSIA: I think that this question is really about being appropriate with our work. I think in order to understand how we do this we have to go back to the beginning of our approach. When we start to work with a client, I think about it as a privilege—this organization is hiring me and entrusting me with their stuff. If I can't see the work as a privilege, then I can't take the client. Respect is key, and generally beginning in this way creates a good relationship.

I can get excited about the intricacies of almost any project—I see it as all interesting and challenging, so I approach it invested and with a great deal of empathy. I think that, as a designer, if you are a cynic going through the motions then just go ahead and do something else—there's a world of difference between having a critical eye and being cynical. This also means that there are certain clients/design problems I just can't do well for political or personal reasons. So you turn stuff down; life is short.

Because we invest in the project and its content, we tend to be able to step back and not be frivolous—authorship in its traditional sense

http://environment.yale.edu ▶

Client: Yale School of Forestry and Environmental Studies

Site Concept Design & Implementation: FLAT

Information Architect: Doug Lloyd

Art Director: Pettr Ringborn

Programmers: Bart Szyszka, Renda Morton, Matthew Kosoy

Software: Flat E-mail and Content Management Systems

©Flat, Inc.

isn't where my head is. I think this is why our work is so measured in this regard. We really put the project first. Of course, this is not the approach that wins you many design awards (she says as a bitter aside).

How did you first get interested in making Web sites, and what, if anything, has kept you interested?
DOUG: I started designing interactive experiences as a fine artist, influenced by performance theory. I was creating situations that would start as one thing, something easily accessible and conventional, but whose structure allowed it to transform into something else, something unexpected and driven by the participants. I looked for situations that had emergent properties.

In effect, the designed situation, for example an ice-cream social, is the interface that facilitates the experience—for example, falling in love. What interests me is how people use incredibly simple, open, designed tools to organize and facilitate life. Interactive tools that enable new and unexpected experiences to emerge.

TSIA: Once upon a time, for our master's thesis, Doug and I created a haunted house in Columbus, Ohio, called "The House of Cruelty." It was a temporary 7,500-square-foot maze where people had to find their own way through. We designed the space and inserted other artists' installations in the environment. There were very dark, dense spaces

(like a fifty five room triangle maze), followed by large lit spaces (like a doctor's waiting room). People became totally disoriented.

It was a massive undertaking. We had a small crew of builder-thinkers, fifty employees, and we opened for six weekends. Eight thousand people came through. There were people in animal suits who took their roles very seriously—vice squad investigations with hidden cameras, patrons wet their pants, there were a lot of tears. This taught me all I know about interactive design.

What advice would you give a student who was thinking about a career in digital design? What do you think is particularly important (or frequently lacking)?

Most of the web sites we've worked on have very practical objectives driving the graphic design. This means an easy-to-use interface and a legible reading environment is the best way to engage someone.

◀ **www.isaacmizahinyc.com**

Date: 2006

Client: Isaac Mizrahi

Site Concept Design & Implementation: FLAT

Information Architect: Doug Lloyd

Art Director: Pettr Ringborn

Programmers:
Bart Szyszka, Matthew Kosoy

Software:
Flat E-mail, Content, and
Commerce Management Systems

©Flat, Inc.

DOUG: Students should think bigger—beyond what they can do on their own as a student. Most exciting work being done in digital design is beyond the ability of any one person to create. As students, they should understand how they will be situated within an industrial framework and position their work properly.

TSIA: Just to expand on what Doug is saying . . . I don't think programs are very good at teaching students about how collaborative their future work environments will be. There are a few that really try

and do this—University of the Arts comes to mind here—but I think this is mostly learned via internships.

I also think there is a strange divide between the old-guard graphic design programs and the new digital technology programs. Depending on the lean of the program, the students' eyes glaze over when you say database or when you say typography. I think this divide does not benefit students—who then tend to come out as either technology wonks or graphic stylists—neither of which are particularly employable profes-

sions. We need a more integrated future.

DOUG: The graphic design community dropped the ball. It's embarrassing how insignificant our role has been in shaping how people communicate over the last ten years. And there is still no meaningful academic discourse in the graphic arts concerning information technologies. Because of this, I generally tell my students to learn typography, to learn semiotics, to gain a broad liberal arts knowledge, and to, most importantly, learn how to learn new things quickly. ■

Defining Feel(ing)

An interview with Eric Rodenbeck, Stamen Design, New York New York

Given the balancing act between look and content, you seem to value clarity. On the Web, is design different than in traditional media?

I'm not sure that I'd say we value clarity above look, or that there's necessarily a conflict in our minds between them. It's that we're more interested in building things that grow and change than we are in applying a specific style to the things we build.

Having said that, we're deeply invested in the way things look, and even more in how they feel. We stick with fairly basic design techniques because almost all of what we make is *template-driven* (in the sense of being programmatically generated). The clearer we keep the basic structure of a piece, the more leeway we have for the presentations to get really wild. When there's not much happening, say, in the patterns generated by taxicabs driving around San Francisco, our visualizations look really calm. During rush hour, though, they begin to look quite hectic—and we're very interested in things that reflect these changes in the real world.

As far as traditional media goes, that's a big question. I think there's *definitely* a big difference between, say, what we do and what generally happens in print design or other static media, mainly because what we do is generative and changes all the time. Print doesn't really accommodate this. So it's not so much that design is different on the Web, but that for certain kinds of things on the Web, the media is so different as to require a different way of thinking and talking and making.

The term feel is common in Web design. Can you define feel?

When we talk about it, we're usually talking about making the work as free as it can be from things that don't have some kind of real-world referent. If it doesn't *mean* anything, then it doesn't belong in what we're doing: "Does this feel like it's real?"

Information is the word, and information architecture is the mantra, of today's Web design. Can you explain how aesthetics are introduced into information presentation?

If they have to be introduced, it's too late. *Introducing aesthetics to information presentation* sounds like putting lipstick on a pig. It's something that needs to be present from the outset.

But would you agree that some pigs are more attractive than others? And some information is poorly designed?

Absolutely. Our industry owes a lot to Edward Tufte, who more than anyone has started to canonize the ways that aesthetics play a part in making information comprehensible. Once you've read his books,

it's almost impossible to make the kind of graph where a drawing of a woman's leg is used to show panty hose sales changing over time, or use a thick black outline where a gray one will do.

The challenge for us as a studio, and I think for our industry in general, is to start to understand the principles that emerge from information design in the digital environment, which is a much different kind of space than the print world that Tufte has done so much brilliant work in explaining. There's very little common understanding of the effect that motion and interactivity, for example, have on information design.

How important is typographic fluency in the Web environment? Is it as key as it is in print design?
It's not so important for us, at least

not in the sense that we think it's very important for people to have designed their own fonts and spent a lot of time really understanding the minutae of how all the different font issues work together. So much of that stuff is taken care of by the computer now—it cracks me up when people still put two spaces after a period in a sentence, which is a holdover from being taught to type on a manual typewriter. We mostly use Helvetica in any event; it's a great font, everyone has it, and if we can cut out having to decide what fonts to use, it frees us up to think about the thousand other things that go into a design.

What we mainly look for is an understanding that type, and everything else actually, flows differently in the digital environment. While you can sort of control what the presen-

tation is going to look like, you can never be really sure that the careful crafting you've done to ensure that you keep widows and orphans out of your paragraphs is going to go right out the window once someone changes their font size in a browser. *Typographic fluency* for us means that your design looks good in a very wide range of environments, from a tiny monitor to a projection on a wall. It's not always possible to do this, but if you understand that your designs are going to be seen in many different contexts, you can start to plan for it and make better choices.

When the term experience design is applied, what does it mean? Whose experience are we talking about?
I've never really understood it, honestly. It seems to be a phrase that's look-

◀ http://backchannel.stamen.com

Date: 2006

Client: Self-initiated

Designer: Mike Migurski

©Stamen Design

ing to contain the hugely proliferating range of things that designers do, without really being able to wrap itself around the activity. I read recently that MBAs are starting to talk about "designing businesses." Humans are almost designers by definition, if you think about it this way—and I think there are worse definitions of what it means to be human.

You are a ten-year veteran. What has changed in that time and how has it impacted your design? When I first started doing this I knew next to nothing about the Internet or how it worked. CSS and flash weren't part of the landscape, and I pretty much picked up everything that I needed to know by trial and error (and by stealing other people's JavaScript when I needed it). So my designs came out of a sustained desire to investigate the space that I was working in to try and push things in directions that were innovative but also were true to their medium, if that makes any sense. I wanted to make things that were *inherently* Internet-based. I wanted to discover what this medium could do that only it could do, working within the intense limitations that the medium imposed.

I still want to do this. There's a part of the industry that continues to allow this kind of investigation, and we fight hard to find it, even though things have settled a bit and the Net isn't quite so new anymore. At the same time, I don't feel like people have a particularly broad or deep understanding of the role that motion and interactivity can play in data visualization, for example. So there's still plenty of interesting work and investigation to do.

There's definitely a much broader understanding of the role that flows of data can and do play in design now; things like blogs and APIs and RSS are starting to percolate out into the broader culture in a much more substantial way than they were even two years ago. When I started working online, the issue of not being able to control fonts and leading was really freaking designers out; that's just not so much the case today. So I feel a lot freer to explore issues of generative media and data-driven storytelling than I did ten years ago. There's just so much more data out there to work with.

You have five members of your firm. What do you look for in a designer—technological skill or design talent?

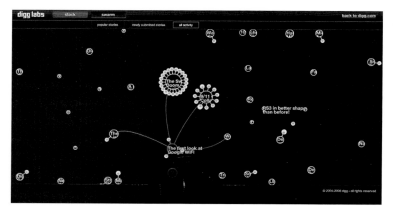

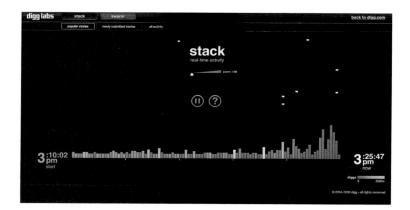

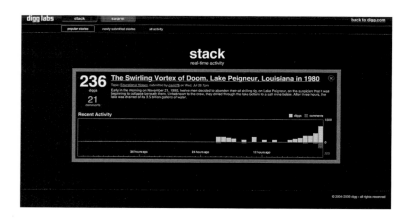

Date: 2006

Client: Self-initiated

Designer: Mike Migurski, Shawn Allen

Creative Director: Eric Rodenbeck

©Stamen Design

We recently started looking to hire someone new, so this question is very much on my mind. We definitely look for both.

I'd say that what we are mainly looking for on the technological skill side is someone who's shown that they're willing to learn new things, who isn't afraid to pick up new tools as they become available or relearn older tools as they become necessary. This is *much* more important to us than any specific set of technological skills.

On the design side we look for someone who can think ahead on their own and who can shift gears rapidly from thinking about the tiniest animation details to the overall direction of what they're working on. We definitely look more for people who seem to have an intuitive sense for what's clear and clean and beautiful than we do for someone with a specific design style that may or may not be appropriate for a given project.

It's hard to find people who are really strong in both these areas, which is why we're so small. ■

Loving the Limits

An interview with Geoff Allman, Flash Designer and Action Script Master

▲
www.bionicpower.com

Design and Flash Programming:
Geoff Allman

My portfolio site includes fictional New York skyline image and sky that change relative to the current time and weather conditions in Brooklyn, NY.

You've worked a lot with classically trained print designers. What's that like, and how does the way they think about design differ from the way you think about it? What role(s) do you play in these projects?

I think the primary difference is that the print designer has the expectation of a final, visually static product, while designing for the Internet (in most cases) requires some flexibility within the design to allow for differences in display settings from user to user, and changes in content over time. Often it's the finer details that you lose control over on the Internet—where lines of text break, specific font control and positioning, finite alignment of objects on the page—and with print design, it is elegant control of those details that often distinguishes the average from the exceptional.

In my experience, more classically trained print designers view Internet design as a series of compromises. My job in working with them is to help translate the design to the Internet, which means subjecting their design to Web-specific situations and standards where "does this work visually?" isn't the only question.

You talk about design that is responsive and context sensitive rather than fixed and static. Design that is a verb rather than a noun. Can you expand on this? How do you think your approach differs from the approach of a print designer?

As a Web designer and programmer, I'm comfortable with the indeterminacy of the Web, and I judge aesthetic success of a project in large part based on the flexibility

*. . . my principle interest is at the intersection of design and programming—
using code for design, or at least to customize design tools.*

of the design, and the efficiency and thoughtfulness of the logic that drives the display—that is, design and display elements that can modify and replicate themselves to accommodate changes without further input from me. (Interestingly, though, the beauty of this behind-the-scenes logic is rarely exposed to the user, or at least only as an intangible part of a successful user experience.) What's exciting for me about designing for the Internet is creating an intelligent framework for information, which includes composition and decorative elements, as well as thinking about information architecture and user patterns.

Much of your work is based on what I'm going to call the mathematics of movement. How has ActionScript affected the way you see the world?
Beyond creating data-centric application interfaces, my primary interest in Flash as an animation tool is in creating what I'd called atmospheric animations: scenes or objects that change gradually over time (i.e., an outdoor scene that accurately por-

trays the sky according to the time of day and current weather conditions, microorganisms that replicate and/or interact, or simple shapes that create detailed patterns when they are duplicated and randomly positioned). In that vein, I'm also interested in developing algorithms to re-create organic shapes. I think there is a way to train your eye on the world to find the underlying patterns and movements that contribute to an object's thingness—those characteristics that allow us to recognize it. Cézanne had said that he was "looking for the rules behind the spontaneity of Impressionism," and I think that is an interesting way to think about this as well.

There are really two divergent paths here, although they both spring from using a more code-based approach to design. You can use Flash as a tool to establish structure and organize information for browsing and display, and you also use it to exploit a computer's ability to duplicate and randomize very quickly to create complex, unexpected and often highly organic-looking design. These are

not necessarily at odds with each other, but serve different design goals within the medium.

How did you first get into programming and designing for the Web, and what interested you initially? What interests you now?
Originally, I think I got into Internet design mostly through a fascination with computers and wanting to develop some mastery of the tools (namely Photoshop). At the time (in 1996), the Internet was pretty new and it was relatively easy to teach yourself. However, as a self-taught designer, I never formally explored the history of graphic design, and it's only in the last several years that I've become more conversant in the language of design and aware of a greater context. For me at least, that is increasingly important as Internet design emerges as a distinct craft with applicable rules, a sense of history and shared standards for success.

Currently and moving forward, my principle interest is at the intersection of design and program-

Coach CD-ROM

Client: Coach

Design and Flash Programming:
Geoff Allman

Software: Flash

◀ **www.colorstrology.com**

Client: Pantone, Inc.

Site Design: Third Mind, Inc.

Flash Programming:
Geoff Allman

This site contains 365 daily colors that serve as a kind of horoscope for your birthday. All of the color information comes from a database, so the site is in black and white until it connects to the live data.

Good design isn't always the answer to a question. Sometimes good design works the way the wind blows, and if I ever feel like there is something missing in my work, it's a visceral, sense-of-purpose feeling.

ming—using code for design, or at least to customize design tools. I'm not suggesting that in the future we will just hire robots for graphic design, as much as I am placing myself in a growing group of designers that are at least as interested in defining a logic for design that is then generated by the computer, as making beautiful things firsthand.

Can you talk about your philosophy and approach?

I think of myself as a pragmatic designer. That is to say, I feel it's easy for me to be unemotional about my work, to look at it in the context of a particular project (with unique goals and contraints), and not view it personally. I think that makes me a good problem solver and also a good collaborator, but it also has a downside. Good design isn't always the answer to a question. Sometimes good design works the way the wind blows, and if I ever feel like there is something missing in my work, it's a visceral, sense-of-purpose feeling.

I think my style of creativity is more experimental, more plodding. I view an empty Photoshop docu-

ment as an opportunity for design to happen, not a place where I bring a specific design vision to bear. The more I can disengage my active (theoretical) mind, the more I can create a space for something interesting to happen, or bubble up. I'm not sure if any of that struggle is really reflected in the work I do (it's somewhat heady for a Web page, perhaps), but that's part of what's going on beneath the surface. I also think, from a philosophical standpoint, that this touches on the difference between being a designer and an artist, the different modes of creativity, and that has always been a fascinating topic for me.

You've run your own business, worked for big agencies, and now you are solo. If you want to, discuss the differences between these modes and what you've learned from each.

I think all are valuable experiences. Working for a big agency is nice because there are major accounts and you can see how bigger business happens. But I find that the work I like best—designing and

developing Web interfaces—at a big agency (and here I really mean ad agency) is often an afterthought. Ad agencies are interested in the pitch, the messaging, which is fine, because it sells dog food and cell phones and Mercedes, but it's not really my focus.

I also really enjoy being a part of the whole life cycle of a project; concepting, client interaction, development, and project management. This is what you get when you run your own studio. You certainly have the risk there of being a jack of all trades, master of none, but it's fun and fast-paced and there's a lot of variety in the work. Moving forward, I certainly aspire to have a smallish studio again, but the last few years of freelancing in New York have been great for my personal growth. I've had a chance to work with a lot of different designers and developers and thus been exposed to a lot of different styles and processes. Just as an observer, I find all the social interaction and struggle of business interesting, but it's also given me a bit of a design education. ∎

An Advocate for Users

An interview with Khoi Vinh, Design Director,
New York Times Digital, New York City

So what do you do all day?

My title is design director, so I'm the main creative authority for the way the Web site looks, and a key player in the way the user experience is shaped. I spend most of my days shepherding various design-related projects: That includes the design of promotional areas on the Web site, the restructuring of various topical verticals like our Travel area, to participating heavily in the design and development of entirely new online features and products.

A really big part of my job is being an advocate for how users experience the *Times* content online and communicating the best practices that I've seen in my past experience and on other sites to my colleagues and superiors.

It sounds like you spend a lot of time talking about design: in meetings, e-mails, and reports. How often do you actually design something?

It's rare. I spend most of my time in meetings, going over design issues at a strategic level, and not so much time actually sitting down and designing. But I'm still responsible for being close to the actual act of designing. I work with the designers in my group pretty hands-on, reviewing their comps and mock-ups, and talking tactically about the most effective designs. That means lots of sketching. I do more sketching than Photoshop work, because it's faster, and I feel like part of my job is training the designers to think at a more advanced level, so sketching helps set them down the road for a solution without precluding their own ideas.

So instead of pushing pixels you're pushing people?

Yes, it's definitely the craft of design that I practice. I like to draw a distinction between actually designing (moving pixels around, as it were) and art directing (setting a vision for design and inspiring people to fulfill that vision) and managing design (creating the conditions for good design). Of those three activities, I would say it breaks down to 10 percent designing, 40 percent art directing, and the remaining 50 percent managing.

▲ subtraction.com

Date: 2005

Client: Self

Designer: Khoi Vinh

Software: XHTML, CSS

What advice would you give students as what to study—or what to pay attention to? Should students focus on perfecting their pixels and assume they will pick up the management skills along the way? Or is there some way to prepare oneself for operating well in a collaborative environment like the *Times*?

I think I would have the same advice for digital designers as I would for any other kind of design, which is that wake up early to the idea that design is a tool of business. I don't mean that in a cynical way at all, but I think it's an important that designers recognize this sooner rather than later. Becoming comfortable in a business environment—learning about design's implication in business and how it reaches out and touches so much in commerce—is the best way to get the designs that you want to happen to become a reality.

Especially with digital design, where it's so closely married to technology, which again is so closely married to business goals and strategy, it's an enormous help to understand what the impact of a design solution is on an organization like the *Times*. Students should read *BusinessWeek* and the *Wall Street Journal*. And digital design-

ers should spend as much time at TechCrunch.com as they do at A List Apart.

It seems to me that sometimes designers are the only ones in the room who haven't taken any business classes. Which sometimes means that designers think of things that others don't or say things that others wouldn't. Could this uninformed perspective actually lead to innovation?

Yeah, I see where you're going with that, and I would agree. I wouldn't advocate that a designer go out and get an MBA and become a business strategist who knows how to use Photoshop. I think there's a group of design managers who really push that direction, and I think that it can undermine the innovation that a designer can bring into a room

My take is that the constraints that define any design problem—How big? How much advertising? How will it be distributed?—are essentially business questions. There's absolutely a place in this industry for the designers who want to work with their head down, and just turn out good work in as close an environment of isolation as they can. But those slots are getting fewer and fewer. They'll always be

around, but they're not multiplying like they are for designers who know how to handle the business factors that confront them; those are the designers who will make great design happen in the next few decades.

What do you look for in hiring an entry-level designer?

As much emphasis as I put on business savvy, I definitely look for design skills, a very strong portfolio, before anything. That usually means a fine eye for detail, evidence that the designer thinks problems through at small and large scales, suggestions that they understand what's happening in the world of design right now, but also proof that they know how to resist the trends and styles that don't make sense for them and/or their clients.

Then I look for good written communication skills. Designers who can write are rare and very valuable. The ability to communicate with the written word shows me that they have a rigorous thought process and that they can translate the intangible qualities of their design solutions into concrete terms that real people can understand. I also look for personality, when I interview: You don't have to be an outgoing, class-president type to work with

AIGA Gain 2.0

Date: 2002

Client: AIGA

Designers: Khoi Vinh, Behavior LLC

Software: Flash

◄ NYTimes.com

Date: 2006

Client: The New York Times Co.

Designer: NYTimes.com Design Group

Design Director: Khoi Vinh

Program: XHTML, CSS

me, but you have to show enthusiasm and interest in the work you're hoping to do. You have to be proactive, and have good questions, and you have to do your part in making me understand your value—because you'll need to do the same thing to my bosses or my clients.

Any thoughts on the future of digital design that you'd like to share?

We've been seriously doing Web design for arguably fifteen years. That's just the beginning, obviously, but because the technology changes so rapidly, we can sometimes be lulled into assuming we're very advanced in the way we work on the Web, and especially the way we design. We have a long way to come in terms of the tools we use: We still do things in a very indirect method, through code or content publishing systems, and there are lots of constraints.

One day, the tools will allow much more design flexibility than they do now. They'll bring new kinds of constraints, but they will dramatically shift the way we do design online. That doesn't mean that, in the meantime, embracing the current technology's constraints—XHTML, CSS, browsers, bandwidth, etc.—is unnecessary. It's absolutely necessary to make great design today. I just want to be careful we don't get so wrapped up in the constraints and so pleased with how well we've learned to work around them that we stop being ambitious, that we stop demanding more direct, more expressive methods of making design happen. ▪

TheOnion.com ▶

Date: 2005

Client: The Onion, Inc.

Designer: Khoi Vinh, Behavior LLC

Software: XHTML, CSS, Adobe Flash, SiFR

www.hilllmancurtis.com ▶

Client: hillmancurtis

Date: 2003

Designer: Hillman Curtis

Additional Credits: Scott Debney: html, php, JavaScript

Software: Photoshop, Flash

Cutting Web Films

An Interview with Hillman Curtis, Inc., New York City

You came to recognition being the "grand master" of Flash advertisements on the Web. How much of this mastery is still part of your practice?
I definitely use Flash, but in different ways now. For example, I use Flash more for prototyping interactive studies for larger non-flash site design like Yahoo! or AOL than for advertising. Most of the site design I do does utilize Flash as a component, but besides the Sideshow site (www.hillmancurtis.com/master), which I did two years ago, I haven't really designed a full-on Flash site in years. As far as advertising, I have designed a few Flash ad spots for Adobe but that's about it. I also use Flash to play back some of the video and film work I now do.

The digital world has enabled you to be mobile. You've had small studios in New York and California. As a designer, do feel place is important to creative output?
No. I'd like to say it does, but give me a laptop and a tabletop and I'm in business. I have cut films on a New York–to–San Francisco Jet Blue flight, taken over a cubicle in Yahoo! for three months and helped design their home page, and I cut the Pentagram documentary in the Sierra foothills in a garage on a table made from two sawhorses and an old piece of three quarter inch plywood. I'm answering these questions in a café in the Sierra foothills.

You started your studio in 1998. The Web bubble had grown and burst. But you are now producing some well-trafficked Web spaces. How has the field changed since then?
The excitement has leveled off, as have the budgets to a certain extent, but what has replaced them is a recognition of the Web as a defining medium of our age. I think there was so much hype back then that some looked at the Internet as this cute little toy populated by

Yahoo! Homepage Redesign

Client: Yahoo!

Date: 2003–2005

Designers: Hillman Curtis, Brian Salay, Lowell Goss, Brian Buschmann, Keara Fallon

Additional Credits: Tapan Bhat

Software: Adobe Photoshop, Adobe Illustrator, Flash

wacky scooter-riding geeks, which I guess it was briefly, but I have always seen it as this wonderful communal medium where I could express myself and as a viable alternative to some of the traditional mediums for creative expression.

I think now the recognition amongst advertisers, ad agencies, film studios, networks, political machines, and corporations is that this is a very powerful way to reach your audience. Perhaps the most powerful. And this brings more opportunities and increases expectations.

At this stage, what is the most challenging thing you are working on today? Why?

The work I do with Yahoo! is extremely challenging because it's so huge, and everything you do as a designer has the potential to reach millions. It's superanalytical and research based: Your design has to work within all of these restraints.

It's also being exposed to innovations taking place at the forefront of Web technology, in that there are teams of people there who do nothing but figure out what exactly is happening online; what innovations

are floating to the top in both interactive design and technology. So it's extremely challenging trying to take in the research, the new technology and trends, and then work that into a page that has to extend across many different user profiles—from an advanced user with a loaded computer and the latest browsers to one with a six-year-old computer and Netscape 4, all while never losing sight of the business objectives, search revenue, promotion of the network, relevance, and advertising.

Then there's the film work, which is challenging in a different way.

▲ Adobe Home Page Animations

Date: 2006

Client: Adobe

Designer: Hillman Curtis

Software: Photoshop, Flash

◀ **Met Opera Web Site**

Client: Met Opera

Designer: Hillman Curtis

Software: Photoshop, Flash

Additional Credits: AdamsMorioka, additional design and project management

Most of the films I make have time limits assigned to them, either from me or from the client, and since much of what I do is documentary, it's superchallenging to first find and then piece together a cohesive story line and fit it into those time-based constraints.

In addition to your commercial work—which includes a fair amount of branding online—you make short digital documentary and theatrical movies. Why did you start, and where has this taken you?

I've always wanted to make movies. In fact, that's why I gravitated so strongly to Flash early on. It afforded me the ability to investigate motion graphics and explore time-based design. As soon as affordable cameras and good editing software emerged, I naturally made my way toward digital filmmaking. And since my medium is the Web, I naturally identified that as the place I would show the films. Since I was making movies for the Web I knew the films should be shorts, since the experience of watching something online is very different than on TV

or in a theater, and I also let the medium inform my camera work, which relies heavily on close-ups and avoids long shots, since the viewing area is small.

What appealed to me was being able to make films and have people see them without having to negotiate some shark-infested system. I liked the fact that I could improve as a filmmaker by responding to feedback from whomever watched and felt compelled to write me. I love the fact that I can interview someone like Milton Glaser with just a camera and a tripod and a decent shotgun mic; that I didn't need a crew or lights or a producer or a deli cart.

It made for a real intimacy and allowed me to think on my feet during the shoot. I also knew that video would become extremely important to the Web. It's been extremely satisfying to get into this. And it's opened up a whole new avenue for business, as the very companies I design sites for are now testing the waters with video.

What have you learned from making movies for the Web? And is this different from other kinds of filmmaking?

I'm not sure, never having done any other type of filmmaking. In fact, I have never shot film, only DV tape. What I am learning is that there are no rules except the universal rule—across all arts—of editing everything out that doesn't absolutely support your theme. And that goes across all aspects, from pulling fancy lines out of my script to yanking a beautiful shot from the edit that doesn't move the story forward. I do think the type of filmmaking I do online does consider the size of the playback window (small), and also the need

to compress—and by that, I mean not only the actual compression of the footage to make the file size smaller and provide a better stream online, but also the compression of the story line.

I am always aware that my viewers are not sitting in a big dark theater, having set aside an hour and a half and paid ten dollars to do so. I know that they are most likely taking a break from some other task online, which they will return to immediately if I don't move things along. I know that while watching one of my films their e-mail alert may sound or their phone might ring. I want the films to be good enough so they ignore those things—even just for a few minutes.

You've long been ahead of the pack with your digital practice. How do you stay in that position? What kind of skill (and talent) is necessary to be out in front?

I work really hard and still do most of the work myself. I have to think that helps. Being forced to solve problems, both design and technical, allows me that frustration of banging away at some obstruction—creative

or technical—long enough to quickly recognize something coming down the line that might help.

That aside, I have to use the default of "I follow my intuition." I know that has been said many times before by many people, but what made me buy a video camera was that I wanted to take pictures like Bill Viola, Avedon, or Thomas Struth. In the back of my mind, I knew learning video filmmaking would probably lead to business opportunities, but the first important step came from a very different place.

I know you don't work with a lot of staff, but when you do, what is the prerequisite? Must they have technical expertise or creative know-how?

I look for a clean design style. I want to see that the designer has struggled with what to leave in and what to take out in their work. I don't look at résumés; I look at online portfolios. Most important is the absence of attitude. I don't mind someone who quietly knows how good they are, just so long as they also know they can get a lot better. ■

A Screen's a Screen

An Interview with Chris Capuozzo, creative director, Funny Garbage, New York City

You are an animation maven. Was it a leap from TV screen to Web screen?

Eight years ago I was working on "Gary Panter's Pink Donkey and the Fly" for the Cartoon Network's "Web Premiere Toons" section of its Web site. This interactive show was one of the first of its kind on the Internet. It was my first big project with Gary Panter. We had completed the redesign of the entire site and were starting to create more and more original content. At that time, broadband Internet did not exist; it would take twenty minutes for a two-minute cartoon to download, and it would play and sound like crap; all our design decisions were governed by size issues. We had so many limitations to deal with—we were trying to make something that could work with modems; everything about the show had to be paired down. We were constantly dealing with download issues. It was all about compressing the various file elements to within a breath of their life. Everything had to be compressed. At that time Flash was a program meant for interactivity, not animation. The animation team knew we were pushing things forward. The more animation and motion graphics work we did, the more we could see what was on the way. To a large degree the technology has caught up, so it's actually a fun experience to "watch" the Web.

You teach Web at the School of Visual Arts MFA Design program. It is not about doing HTML but rather what content to put on a Web site. What do you want from your students?

I want them to see how revolutionary the Web is as a communications tool. You can create your own reality. They must understand they're creating an experience. They need to see how important the underlying architecture of a Web site is.

Do you mean clear navigation? Or is there some other, less obvious aspect to the architecture that they need to be aware of?

This is the stage where you create the blueprint of your Web site. You are creating a visual diagram representing an overview of the structure of the entire Web site. You identify the different sections and determine how things will be categorized. They must spend time looking at and using the Internet. There's so much incredibly crafted "fluff" out there.

Can you give some tips for getting past the fluff?

When I'm surfing the Web, I ask myself if what I'm being asked to do (or click on) has anything to do with the information being expressed. I want to get where I'm going. Sometimes it's just a waste of time to click on something and launch an elaborate animation that brings me to a new page. Fluff city.

Intro animations for Web sites drive me crazy—I never want to see them no matter how clever they are; it always ends up feeling like an invisible barrier to what I want to see. Loading screens are differ-

All Images On This Site © 2005 Savage Pencil   Contact Us:

◄ **SavagePencil.com**
www.savagepencil.com

Client: Edwin Pouncy (a.k.a. Savage Pencil)

Date: 2006

Designer: Chris Capuozzo

Studio: Chris Capuozzo Studio

Animator: Devin Flynn

Typographer: Edwin Pouncy
(a.k.a. Savage Pencil)

Software: Photoshop, Illustrator, Flash

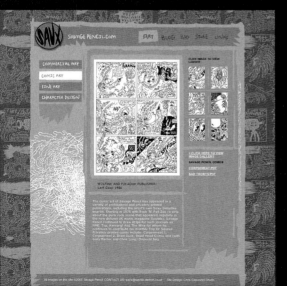

There needs to be a fundamental change in the perception that the Web is this cheap medium to work in. It's hard work to make a good Web site.

ent—at least you know you're waiting for something cool. They need to understand which part of the fluff they should ignore.

I want a student to *feel* the connection they want to make with their audience. I want them figure out what's appropriate for any given approach. There's a lot riding on a button click these days. The button click must deliver.

But how does the Web allow you to create your own reality in a way that is different than a comic book, album, TV show, or other type of entertainment medium?

The audience expects and is able to immediately connect with you through comments or e-mail. One on one. There's no need to deal with an outside distribution system. If you get it together enough, you can have your own store.

Do you practice what you preach? Do you view the content before the frame?

Studying, understanding, and knowing content will usually generate the best framing devices. For the redesign of the *National Geographic*

for Kids Web site (kids.nationalgeographic.com), I created a large, dense interactive collage for the home page. It's basically a way to link to deeper content in the site, yet the frenetic collage approach was a visual metaphor to show the spirit of how exciting and varied the content of *National Geographic* is. When I was younger, *National Geographic* magazine was a way I connected to the outside world, and I loved the magazine for the "trips" I could go on by reading it.

What do you say to the criticism that the Web is full of bad design? Isn't Web design a different animal than traditional design?

There needs to be a fundamental change in the perception that the Web is this cheap medium to work in. It's hard work to make a good Web site. It takes a lot of people working very efficiently to make a "real" site work. Web budgets are still microscopic compared to other media—and yet, Web sites can get more eyes on them than other types of media.

What does concern me, though, is poorly designed sites that are really important—like news, transportation, institutional, government sites . . . sites

that people really need to use—some of them are so awful, and that's where bad design hurts. Most likely, that bad design can be traced to a low budget. If you want quality, you need to spend some money to get quality. There's no way around it. Is that idea different anywhere else?

Do you think that it's also because it's a new media beast?

Every type of media has it's own inherent language. Once you've got that particular language figured out, it's all about the approach to design solutions.

Do you tend to go overboard or restrain yourself when designing for the Web?

It all comes down to what's most appropriate. One of the last sites I made was for an obscure yet important underground illustrator/comics artist/noise musician. I think the site could melt the eyes out of your head. It was a great success.

What are the biggest faux pas when doing Web design for the Web?

No thought to the information architecture. Hidden navigation . . . exploratory

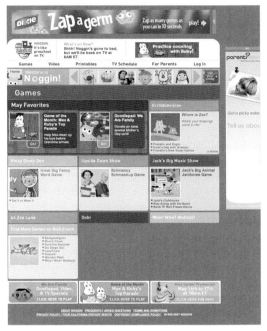

▲

Noggin.com redesign

Client: Viacom International, Inc.

Date: 2003

Designer: Chris Capuozzo, Andy Pratt, William Randolph

Other Credits: Producer: Robert DelPrincipe.
Game Development: Fred Kahl, Colin Holgate

Software: Photoshop, Illustrator, Flash

navigation . . . making someone guess about site navigation. It's obnoxious.

Conversely, what is the biggest asset when designing a Web site? Original content. Well-curated, edited passion. *Otaku*-like obsession.

How to you plan out what you do? Since you are a cartoonist at heart, do you still draw everything? I do sketch out my design ideas all the time. I work out things like the page layout, how the global naviga-

tion fits, and figure out image relationships. This is part of my process. I have a big connection to drawing stories and creating characters. Lately I've been drawing directly into Flash using a Wacom monitor—whew. It's awesome. ■

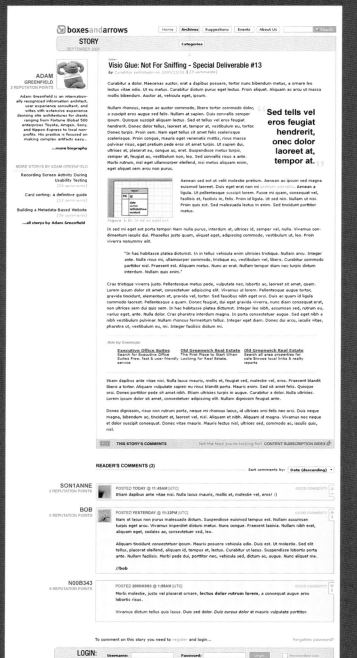

Boxes and Arrows Redesign Web Site

www.boxesandarrows.com

Date: 2006

Client: Boxes and Arrows

Designer: April 3rd, Alex Chang, Matt Titchener

Software: Adobe Illustrator, Photoshop

Control Over Technology

An Interview with Liz Danzico, Senior Development Editor, Rosenfield Media;
Information Architect, Happy Cog; Editor-in-chief, Boxes and Arrows

How did you become so deeply involved in digital media? Was it design? Technology? A combination? Or were you just good in math?

I suppose it was the technology that got me there, but the design that got me to stay. Most of all, what's never failed to fascinate me is the autonomy that digital media affords individuals. In the late 1970s, for example, I used to visit my father's office on my way home from school. Heading directly into the Computer Room (whose capacity could hold precisely one computer), I would sit at the keyboard of this room-sized Hewlett-Packard machine. I'd type simple commands into the, I'm guessing, twenty-character LED screen and watch my stories print out on the painfully slow dot-matrix printer.

This, I thought, is control. I can make technology do what I want it to do. I was eight. This idea of autonomy and control has evolved over the years so that now I'm studying people, trying to understand how to control technology to meet needs they have. What's been fun is now I can include design in the communication or adoption of that technology. It's still control over technology, but it's control with a purpose.

You've managed various big sites, which means immersion in information architecture. How did you train for this role?

It's true that managing large Web sites is made easier by having a background in information architecture (IA), but the two are fairly different skill sets—one a generalist, and the other a specialist.

How do you describe this differentiation?

Information architecture is the ordering and structuring of information so that people can better navigate through a site. An IA's role is to be the user advocate in planning and designing a site, helping the team understand how to structure the navigation system, site labels, and content so that people can use it easily.

And the managing?

Once the site is in use the managing begins. As the editor in chief of Boxes and Arrows (*www. boxesandarrows.com*), for example, I see people using the site in both expected and unexpected ways; with that comes the kind of wear and tear that happens with other kinds of products. People get lost; things don't work the way we had anticipated. And as the site's editor, it's to my credit when the site works, but mostly it's my fault when it doesn't. Having a background in IA helps because I'm already the user advocate, so I can better assess how to come up with the solution.

So, how do you train for something like that?

There are a number of good resources to turn to—both formal

and informal. People can turn to formal education: Colleges and universities all over the country are adopting information architecture courses and entire curricula. You can study information architecture for four entire years! People can turn to mentors: Some professional associations, such as the Information Architecture Institute (*www. iainstitute.org*), offer mentorship programs that help shepherd people already in the field who may want to learn about IA. People can turn to communities: There are rich and lively discussions that go on in online mailing lists around the topic. Not only can a lot be gained from reading and participating in them, but the connections go beyond just the online groups.

Then training is very important, right?

My advice: Don't train for it; try it. Or, I suppose, try first, train later. One of the most valuable skills in managing a site is an understanding of people—the people who use the site, the people who maintain the site behind the scenes, the people who need to use the site, but don't yet know it. By taking a deep dive into it by helping out with either the planning or managing of a Web site,

one can gain a real insight into how to observe real people. Then, choose one of the more formal training methods and do it on the side.

What about the design of a multifaceted Web site is the most challenging?

Anticipation of the unknown. Not that long ago, many of the Web sites we designed were intended as one-way communications. I'm generalizing, but the process went something like this: Figure out what to say, design a set of pages, write the copy, build the pages, launch the pages. People then came to the pages, quietly viewed them, and left. We were designing ways to push information from a company to a person, so we didn't need to worry much about the interaction.

Compared to traditional design, has the direction of this push changed?

Yes. The content, the ideas, even the design of sites can now come (and often largely comes) from the site's visitors. Visitors—visitors with no background in writing or design—are helping to contribute to the process. And it's good. But it's changing the way we're thinking about information architecture

and design. So the real challenge in designing a multifaceted site is that we've shifted from designing sites to designing *frameworks*. We're designing frameworks for people to add their own content and images, and to do that takes a lot more planning about how people will behave. Because we're designing for active rather than passive participants, it's a lot more fun, but also a lot more of a venture into the unknown.

Is there an aesthetic trick to designing for a multilayered digital environment? Or is it more about logic and planning?

I wish there were a trick, but it's more about planning and iterating. In my experience, the most successful approaches have balanced planned and well-communicated brand attributes, while giving designers latitude for interpretation.

How do you address the need to continually refresh and update the look and content of a site?

It depends on what kind of Web site—the good news is, you may not have to. With an editorial-driven site, such as Boxes and Arrows, it's a matter of having strong editors who are keeping pace with what the site's visitors need.

Once content is published, it launches a new opportunity for even more content with the ability for people to comment or add to the content. Many times, a comfortable dialogue develops online with each article published. Authors and readers—refining, arguing, developing ideas further. On Boxes and Arrows, the readers themselves refresh the content and keep the quality high. In fact, the 2007 redesign was done by readers as well.

How do you get people to the content of a site?

Until fairly recently, a large organization's content was relegated to its own limited audience. Findability was not the priority—the priority was about scale rather than access. I think we've moved away from focusing on scale (or quantity) and started finding new ways of facilitating access.

Google has certainly been leading the way there for quite a while, while sites such as Digg (*www.digg.com*) and even Flickr (*www.flickr.com*) have begun changing the way we think about context, expertise, and "the right content." Large organizations still struggle with getting the right content online to the right people, but by providing the content in a semantically sound, standards-based way, more and more people can participate in getting the content where it needs to be seen.

In hiring designers to work on your sites, what are the key most important talents and skills?

When hiring designers to work on sites I've managed, I always look at two things: Do we understand each other; can we have a successful conversation about the design problem at hand? And if so, does their work show that they get it? So much of a good relationship with a designer depends on the dialog between us, and making sure that works is critical. To get there, I typically start out with a conversation with the designer about the problem we're trying to solve. If that initial set of conversations doesn't go well, it's usually a red flag that there may be bigger obstacles down the road. So, the first talent or skill is the ability to articulate design approach and solutions.

What evidence do you need?

Of course, client or portfolio work that demonstrates a solid knowledge of the craft is important. I tend to work on a lot of online publications or editorial-driven sites, so I look for designers who have a solid understanding of the editorial process—whether that be online or off—and the ability to design a system, rather than just design pages. That's the second talent or skill—the ability to think of design as a system, and to do so in the context of a given vertical, such as publishing. ∎

▲

AIGA

www.aiga.org

Date: Redesign 2006

Client: AIGA

Designer: Happy Cog, Jason Santa Maria

Web Point One, Web Point Two

An Interview with Mike Essl, proprietor, Eat Lightning, New York City

You were at the crest of the first Internet wave (web.1), as a designer. Why did this appeal to you?

The Web felt brand-new, ripe with opportunity. It had an almost voo-doolike trance on me as a young designer. It's a medium I could dive into without any of the *dues paying* that a career in print seemed to require. After building one Web site I was considered an expert. Also, I'm a technical person by nature, so learning how code related to the graphic display was relatively easy.

I was never once afraid of it as a tool; in fact, I landed my first Web job by lying. There was a posting at Cooper Union that read, "Do you know Photoshop and HTML?" At the time, 1995, I had no idea how to write HTML.

I just knew that it was the code you made "home pages" with. I called the number, went to the interview, lied and said I knew HTML, and got the job. On the way back from the interview, I bought a book on HTML and learned it that night.

The Web also appealed to me because it gave me a way to quickly get my work in front of lots of peo-ple. I had a tilde domain in 1995, and in 1996 I registered essl.com. The entire time I've been online I've had a portfolio of my work, a few rotating splash pages, and some experiments with short films, etc. It became clear that the Web was a place you could prototype ideas and not worry much about their life

▲
Mr. T and Me

Designer: Mike Essl

Photographers: Mike Essl and Greg Rivera

Illustration: Mike Essl

Client: Mr. T and Me

Date: November 2003

Software: Adobe Photoshop, Adobe Illustrator, BBEdit

span. If I wanted to do a piece about Mexican Luche Libre wresters one day and a Mr. T splash page the next, I could. No one could stop me. Theoretically, there was nothing stopping me from getting the same amount of traffic as Yahoo!.

You were a cofounder of a hugely successful Web design company, the Chopping Block. How did you start this right out of school?

When I was still in school I met two very successful Web entrepreneurs, each with their own companies. I met them both through lying about my HTML skills (see above). In early 1996 I was hired to design the Web site for Duracell USA by Sitespecific and by iTraffic to create the advertising for Duracell. The site and advertising were really the first of its kind.

Duracell.com was the first corporate site to have a game, and the ads were the first takeover ads on the Internet. This led to numerous awards, including a nomination for the first Cleo in Web design. (We didn't win.) The attention the site received sometimes turned on me, and a few stories about the "blue-haired kid that was still in school" that designed Duracell.com made it into a few big industry magazines. After that I had so much freelance that I had to call my mother and tell her not to declare me as a dependent on her taxes!

On the strength of that freelance work, and the print freelance that my partner, Thomas Romer, had, we decided to start the Chopping Block.

Logistically, we started with my high-paying clients and Tom's savings. We never borrowed any money. We started in my East Village apartment and eventually we used Tom's savings to buy some computers and get a studio near Wall Street. After one month of being in business I was able to pay back Tom my half of the money he laid out for us.

The project that really launched the studio was a Web site for the band They Might Be Giants. With my professor Barbara Glauber, we designed, illustrated, and programmed the site. TMGB.com ended up winning a ton of awards, and that got us some great press, which led to more work, etc. It also set a tone for all the work we would later get.

Despite your success, you became disillusioned with the Web design world. Why?

I think I was more disillusioned with running my own business. I felt like our company existed in a style bubble. After a while, the Block got known for a certain look, and

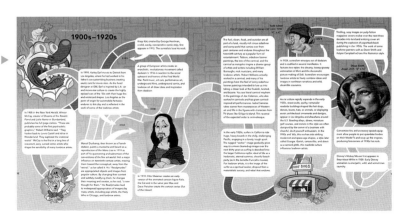

Weirdo Deluxe: The Wild World of Pop Surrealism & Lowbrow Art

Author: Matt Dukes Jordan

Designer: Mike Essl

Illustration: Brian Romero

Client: Chronicle Books

Date: 2005

Software: Adobe Photoshop, Adobe Illustrator

if I tried to do something outside of that look my clients became uncomfortable. By the time 1999 rolled around I wasn't really getting along with our clients or my partners. I felt stuck in a style that we had created in 1996 that I couldn't find a way out of.

Our clients were constantly coming to us to do that thing we do, and I just didn't have it in me anymore to do another ad banner or microsite for *You've Got Mail* starring Meg Ryan and Tom Hanks. It got dangerously close to an ad agency.

Also, I think when you grow to fifteen employees you don't have the luxury of picking and choosing your clients once you have other mouths to feed. We started taking on bad work that I knew would bring in a lot of money. Have you ever designed a site for a minivan? This wasn't the kind of work I was hoping for when I started my own business.

I ended up resenting my colleagues because they continued to work on the cool projects while I swallowed the high-paying clients (my own fault, I know this now), and I became really disillusioned with our focus on entertainment and youth clients. You can only do so many sites for a company that makes plastic building blocks.

Were you also tired of playing with bells and whistles?
When I hear "bells and whistles" I immediately think of Macromedia (now Adobe) Flash. I hate Flash. Hate it. I feel like it sucked the life out of what I loved about the Internet. It wasn't as immediate or as easy. Granted, you could do a lot of really cool stuff with it, but I couldn't stand the closed format or how it was abused on the Internet.

My company began to use Flash early on, and eventually almost every project in the shop used Flash. It got to the point where every single little thing on a page animated or made noise. We overembellished every site in the shop. Mind you, this made us really well known for making amazing illustrative sites, but it also took a lot of time, and as we all know, time is money. I use to make jokes that eventually HTML will win out over Flash.

After selling your company—which has remained very successful—you became an educator. What else did you do to clean your head of the cataclysmic past?
For a year after the Chopping Block, I took almost no commercial work and focused all my time on reeducating myself. I believed that the future of Web design was in

accessibility. I wanted to learn how to make pages that could work on a cell phone or for the visually impaired. I took that year off to learn XHTML, CSS, and a tiny bit of PHP. I also taught myself how to use blogging and content management systems while building my Mr. T memorabilia site, mrtandme.com. I took that year to remind myself that I love the Internet and tried my hardest to contribute something to that mix. I also started a blog that I've been posting to, irregularly, since 2003.

Like many who were on the Web early on, you moved—some might say technologically backward—to book design. Is this because you prefer the temporal, rather than the virtual, realities of designing with tangible materials?
There is something incredibly satisfying about specifying the color of the headband to match the endpapers of the book you are designing. Holding that object in your hands after working on it for so many months is amazing. The other thing that is appealing about book design is that, unlike a Web site, you can't really revise a book after it's printed. Granted, there are second editions, but with Web sites you are constantly adding sections, editing content, and playing the role of

◄ Tools

Designer: Mike Essl

Illustration: Mike Essl

Client: Personal/Graduate School

Date: 2000

Software: Adobe Photoshop,
Adobe Illustrator

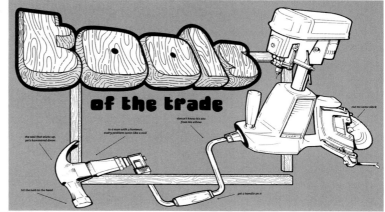

support technician. A book can't call you on a Saturday and say, "Hey, my pages aren't showing up in the AOL browser."

I really do love print and Web equally. I get paid a lot more to do Web design, so I still do a bit more of that than print.

You maintain a Web site with a blog, so you're not entirely divorced from the Web. What interests you about the digital world today?

I love that I can put up a site about my Mr. T collection and get over a 100,000 visitors in one day! Or that I can use MySpace to get in touch with old friends. That I can use Basecamp and Backpack to get real work done. I'm interested in the Web as a platform for personal expression and personal empowerment.

I'm working on a site right now with Robb Irrgang of Thirst called 2.0much.info. The site will let you keep a running tally of anything that you do. You could keep track

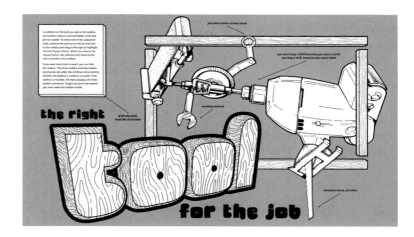

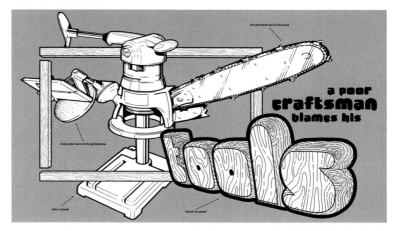

◀ **The Chopping Block Nascar Version**

Designers: Mike Essl and Thomas Romer

Illustration: Mike Essl and Thomas Romer

Custom Typeface Design: Thomas Romer

Date: January 1997

Client: The Chopping Block

Software: Adobe Photoshop, Adobe Illustrator

of your daily soda intake, how many cabs you've taken, how many days it's been since you showered, etc. We want to make a bit of joke about all the personal information that is out there, but also make a fun tool to keep track of these things.

I'm also interested in the Internet as a community. I know that is cliché, but I think we are finally seeing some things that connect people in interesting ways. Like Meetup.com helping people get together offline, or even the site wesabe.com that helps people with their finances. Hell, I met one of my best friends on eBay!

What has changed since those early days to today, both technologically and aesthetically speaking?

The technology is obviously more complex now. There are more choices. In 1996 when I got started you basically had perl. Now you have PHP, Ruby, Asp, etc. Also, the things you can do with JavaScript and AJAX are now very Flash-like. As a developer, you have more choices, so there is automatically more technical overhead than there ever was. For designers like me that know, some tech sites have gotten a lot easier to build.

Thanks to the hard work of other developers I can build small sites that are dynamic and run from a database without knowing exactly how to do that. Users also have it a bit easier now with turnkey solutions for blogs and stores.

Aesthetically, I would say the Web is not that different from ten years ago. Most things look terrible. Ugly MySpace pages look exactly like the free Geocities Web sites from the nineties. There is also an antidesign movement that makes me crazy. People point to a site like Craig's List and say that it's an example of how antidesign will make you profitable. What they forget is the organic way that those pages evolved *IS* design.

There is also some wonderful design going on in the blog space. Designers are making templates for WordPress and Moveable Type that are well designed and free to the public. And design-focused blogs are a great resource for finding great design on the Net.

You've started a new studio. What do you look for when hiring designers—or those who'd like to be designers?

An amazingly designed résumé with all the correct quotes and ligatures, a lot of white space, and a real design consciousness. If the résumé isn't well designed, I won't look at the portfolio. Drastic, I know, but it just isn't worth my time. A well-designed résumé is a window into how much a designer actually cares about typography.

I'm also looking for a self-starter, a designer that can manage the client and get the job done without me being involved in every single step. I look for people that I can partner with on a job rather than someone that would be below me. ■

Print Is Alive on the Web

An Interview with Jason Santa Maria, www.jasonsantamaria.com

How did you become interested in the Web?

I became interested in the Web through animation and publishing, and both for the same reason: the wonderful attainability of creating and communicating without needing anyone else. At the time, a healthy interest (obsession) was all one needed.

You are a specialist in turning print into Web. Other than words and pictures, where do these two platforms intersect?

The Web and print intersect on many levels, and not just on concrete matters like imagery and content. Both forms are mediums of visual communication, and because of this, centuries of design history and theory are vastly usable on the Web. In much the same way artists could work with paint or charcoal to convey their message, the means to the message are related and cross over in their use. All of the design lessons we've learned from the past, like typography, grid design, and just basic fundamentals, all translate over to the Web, and they still work just as well. Every medium has its strengths and weaknesses; it's only a matter of bending each to your advantage.

Print can be nuanced—minimalist, complex, often elegant. Can you achieve the same nuance on the Web? Do you want to?

Absolutely! And for the record, there is plenty of bland print design out there too. Oftentimes, design is a practice of restraint; making the choice not to include all of

A List Apart Web Site

Date: 2005

Client: Happy Cog Studio

Designer: Jason Santa Maria

Illustration: Kevin Cornell

Client: Chronicle Books

Software: Illustrator, Photoshop

The Web is a particularly difficult design medium for this very reason; as technology advances, the lowest common denominator is stepping higher all the time.

your content on the home page, or animate every element on your site. Nuanced design stems from a good understanding of the message and content you are trying to convey with your site.

When designing for the Web, must you get into the head of your prospective audience? Must you design for a high or low denominator?

The Web is a particularly difficult design medium for this very reason; as technology advances, the lowest common denominator is stepping higher all the time. I like to research as much as I can before designing, by finding out what users' needs and capabilities are, while pushing for progressive enhancement (which could also be viewed as graceful degradation).

There is a tendency to put a lot of stuff on Web sites. One might call them entry points or portals to more information or entertainment. In doing this, what are the challenges in making an experience look good?

The fact remains that even if you dump everything onto one page, there is no guarantee that people will actually take the time to look at it all. Most sites I see that put so much online do so out of fear in the place of smart design. Just because something isn't huge or on the first page someone comes to doesn't mean they won't find it. It comes down to smart editing and architecture, which the design should serve to reinforce.

Do you foresee the day when print—as doomsayers have predicted for decades—will be obsolete in terms of the daily consumption of information?

Yes, but I think it's still quite a ways off. Print is alive and kicking; the Web has just made it become more self-aware and forced it to further play to its strengths, like tactility, portability, and history. The Web may be faster to gather information, but the interface to convey it, a screen, still doesn't touch print for long-term legibility and consumption.

Since the Web has become such a "fireplace" of ideas and data, do you think designers should continue to study conventional design?

A resounding, emphatic yes! We are still designing for similar types of information, and everything we've learned from the past still applies to all design. Period.

What do you look for in a designer to hire or help you in your projects?

A solid understanding of design fundamentals, appreciation for content and legibility, and strong typographic skills. Lastly, and I feel it's worth mentioning separately, the ability to write and talk about your work. I want to hear the reasons for a design looking the way it does, and I want to know that thought and consideration were a part of everything. ■

Traditional No More

An Interview with Doug Powell, Schwartz Powell Design, Minneapolis

You are what is now called a traditional designer who, in addition to serving your conventional clients, has created an entrepreneurial design-based product, Type1Tools—a teaching aid for parents of and children with Type 1 diabetes. Did this start in a digital way or in a traditional way?

The development of the original line of Type1Tools products was very much rooted in our experience as print designers. All of the pieces in that line were print pieces. There were several reasons for this: First, and most importantly, this is what we knew how to do and this was where we had the most developed network of production resources. Second, this allowed us to have complete creative control over the designs—we weren't dependent on other creative professionals to develop the line. Finally, we were able to get the products out and to market very fast—again, not having to depend on others. The whole process happened within our professional comfort zone.

In order to communicate your wares, the Web has become very important. What did you have to learn about this platform to be effective?

Once the products were complete, we had to find the best, most effective, and direct way to bring them to market. In 2004, Web-based e-commerce was just hitting its stride, and this was clearly the best option for our new business.

The process of building this site was very much out of our comfort zone, hence we leaned heavily on Web development partners as collaborators. The Minneapolis firm IdeaPark has been our primary Web development partner throughout the evolution of Type1Tools and HealthSimple.

Currently, we are collaborating with our key business partners to develop new products that will be delivered through the Web and other online technology. Truly, the

◄ FlashCarbs®
Designers: Lisa Powell, Doug Powell

Client: Type1Tools®
Photography: Various stock

Software: Adobe Illustrator,
Adobe InDesign

◀ **Type1 Tools® Web Site**

Designers: Lisa Powell, Doug Powell, Brigette Peterson (with IdeaPark)

Client: Type1Tools®

Software: Adobe Illustrator, Adobe InDesign

most important skill I have in this area is how to find the best, most talented collaborators and how to work effectively with them.

I understand that you've become so successful with this product you are giving up many of your service-based clients. Does this also mean you have to become more interactive-savvy?

Increasingly so, I suppose, but I must admit I don't have a very intuitive sense of the Web. I would consider myself a novice in the professional sense.

In producing materials for the Web and PDAs, is there a fundamental design shift?

Yes, I think there is both a shift in design and in complexity of content. The experience of interacting with information on a cell phone or a Web site is dramatically different from that of a printed piece. Certain components must be *dumbed down* for these applications, like typogra-

phy, color, and imagery. However, other pieces can actually be more sophisticated—for instance, motion graphics, sound, and other time-based media.

Is it inevitable for a designer to move more into this time-based and motion-based medium to succeed?

I think it's a bit early to tell how this will all look after the dust has settled. At the moment we're very much in a time of rapid transition. I suspect that new areas of specialty will continue to emerge over the next decade as (presumably) the pace will slow. I think it is unrealistic to expect that the designer of 2020 will be an expert in all media, but I also think it will be less clear-cut than simply *print* versus *new media*. I do think that the clients of this next-generation designer will have very complex needs and expectations and the designer will have to find a way to service those needs.

You must rely on collaboration more than before. How is this collaboration accomplished? Is there a hierarchy of creativity, skill, etc.?

We've got a tight group of trusted collaborators with whom we've worked for years. They tend to be senior-level creative professionals or small, specialized firms. These relationships have been developing since we founded our design practice in 1989. In fact, I would consider our network of collaborative resources to be one of our greatest assets.

Now that you have a business that requires more media platforms, what do you look for in new employees? Is it mostly design or technology?

At the moment we are still a three-person firm, but growth of our internal staff is right around the corner. We will continue to work with collaborative teams—especially for specialized skill-based roles—but we will also need to add staff in the areas of content development, research, as well as traditional design and production. I think any new employee we hire will need to be connected to contemporary culture, will need to possess a deep curiosity about the world around them, and will need to be highly motivated and capable in a set of basic operational areas. ■

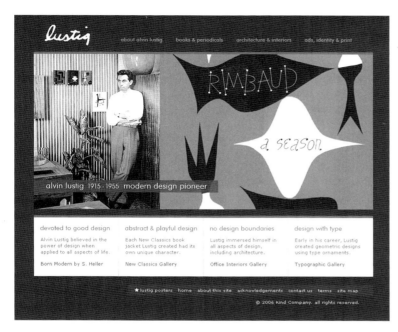

◀ **Alvin Lustig Archive**

www.alvinlustig.com

Date: 2006

Client: Self-initiated

Designer: Kind Company

Software: Illustrator, Photoshop, Dreamweaver, Flash

Additional Credits:
Images: Elaine Lustig Cohen
Text: Steven Heller

CASE STUDY

Alvin Lustig Web Site

Greg D'Onofrio and Patricia Belen, Kind Company, www.kindcompany.com

What prompted you and your partner to create a Web site devoted to the curiously little-known design pioneer Alvin Lustig?

For precisely that reason—Alvin Lustig is a little-known, yet hugely important design pioneer who needed to be brought to the forefront of graphic design. We had seen some examples of his works from the books we were collecting, but when we tried to find out more, it wasn't easily available. At that moment, we felt as if an opportunity was in front of us. We figured the best way to educate ourselves and others was to develop a comprehensive Web site of his work. As a result, we've been able to make his work widely available to an inter-national audience. We like to think of it as our small but important contribution to the design community.

Was this your first Web site?

No, Kind Company has been in business for just over three years providing identity, print, and Web design solutions to other small businesses like ourselves (we're only two people). In regards to Web sites, we've been fortunate to have worked on small static sites, as well as complete branded solutions, including e-commerce. If all goes well, the Alvin Lustig Web site would be the first of several self-initiated projects dealing with graphic design history.

How did you assemble and decide upon the content for this site?

The only way we wanted to present Lustig's work was as a complete solution. We've always believed that if a project is worth doing, it's worth doing well. Initially we had delusions of grandeur, thinking we could collect everything ourselves—fueled partly by motivation and craziness. Fortunately, we were able to contact Elaine Lustig Cohen, who not only provided us with digital images but also generously supported us in this effort. It would have been nearly impossible to do something this comprehensive (the archive includes more than 400 images) without her full support, assistance, and guidance.

In addition to the content, what were your primary concerns in making this accessible?

We didn't want the site to just be a collection of images. We knew we needed some supporting text that would put Lustig's work in context. We had read some articles you (Steve Heller) wrote and decided to contact you to see if we could use some of these articles on the site. Your articles help tie the works together and bring cohesion to the site—something we would not have been able to do, considering we're not writers or academics. So, along with Elaine, we have to thank and give credit to you for bringing this important element to the Web site.

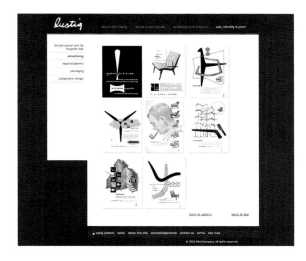

Were you limited by any technological constraints? And if so, how did you compensate for them?

With technology, the possible solutions to a problem can be endless—which is a constraint unto itself. We decided to keep the site simple using basic HTML code and cascading style sheets (CSS). We thought Flash was a smart solution for the image galleries, allowing comfortable transitions between numerous images without unnecessary pop-ups or a secondary navigation system. Finding a balance between function and aesthetics was important to us from the very beginning.

The number one goal of the site, above any design style, is to allow the user to access Lustig's work in a quick, clear, and pleasant manner. If the Web site accomplishes this, then we've succeeded as designers—it's very user-centric.

From a design standpoint, did you want the site to underscore Lustig's methods, or were you seeking a counterpoint to his brand of modernism?

We didn't go into this thinking we would design the site in a Lustig style, which we couldn't do even if we tried. We always intended to highlight Lustig's designs, not the Web site design. We were inspired by his work, ideas, and modernism in general, but wanted to maintain our own ways of designing—clean, simple, usable, and functional. The number one goal of the site, above any design style, is to allow the user to access Lustig's work in a quick, clear, and pleasant manner. If the Web site accomplishes this, then we've succeeded as designers—it's very user-centric.

What were the biggest challenges—aside from time—in making this work?

The organization of the site and images were a big challenge. We had to identify categories that Lustig's work could fall under. And, since he worked in virtually all design disciplines, this was not easy. Elaine was extremely helpful in classifying and understanding Lustig's work, much of which we'd never seen. We ended up with a clear navigation system and used your articles as an introduction to each section—"About Alvin Lustig", "Books & Periodicals", "Architecture & Interiors" and "Ads, Identity & Print". This worked out well, since the articles go into detail about very specific aspects of Alvin's short but prolific career.

Unlike a book, the site can be altered and corrected over time; what are the aspects that you most want to change?

Overall, we're very pleased with the site, and feel it's served its purpose well. Since we're not professional writers, we're always finding new ways of improving what we'd like to say and how we say it—that's the beauty of a Web site. Eventually we'll edit some of our minor text and add a few articles written by Lustig. In addition, some of the sections—like the New Direction, New Classics Gallery—have the option of seeing all the images on a single page. We'd like to add this to some of the other sections. It's great to see Alvin's work side by side.

The other side of this mutability is maintaining the site. It's like having a young child. How do you plan to steward the project from here on?

Hopefully, as more people become familiar with Alvin's work, there will be more written about him. It would be useful to add these new perspectives to the site. It's very important not to think of the site as the end-all, be-all—a full-scale monograph about Alvin Lustig would be better suited for some of the items we've missed, as well as many other reasons. Overall, this project has been a labor of love for Kind Company, and anything we can do to improve it and make people more aware of Alvin is well worth the effort. ■

lustig

about alvin lustig   books & periodicals   architecture & interiors   ads, identity & print

the book jackets
of alvin lustig

industrial design
magazine

catalogs/brochures

knopf

magazines

meridian books

new directions

new directions:
modern reader

new directions:
new classics

noonday press

ward ritchie press

other publishers

the book jackets of alvin lustig

by James Laughlin, New Directions - Print Magazine, Oct/Nov 1956

The first jacket which Lustig did for a New Directions Book - the one for the 1941 edition of Henry Miller's *Wisdom of the Heart*- was quite unlike anything then in vogue, but it scarcely hinted at the extraordinary flowering which was to follow. It was rather stiff and severe - a non-representational construction made from little pieces of type metal chosen from the cases in the experimental printing shop he had set up in the hinter regions of a drugstore in Brentwood. A less fecund talent might have been content to work that vein for years, but not Lustig. A few months later, I remember, he was showing me how he made extraordinary forms by exposing raw film to different kinds of light in a friend's darkroom.

Whatever the medium, he could make it do new things, make it extend itself under the prodding of his imagination. What the true nature of that imagination was I never fully understood until the last year, when he had lost his sight, and when, to our amazement, he not only continued to work, directing the eyes and hands of his wife and assistants as if they were his own, but produced some of his finest pieces, such as the final cover design for the magazine *Perspectives USA*.

In the middle years, when opening each envelop from Lustig was a new excitement because the range of fresh invention seemed to have no limits, I had supposed that his gift was a purely visual faculty. Or, watching him play with a pencil on a drawing pad, I thought that he had some special magic in his hands. Only at the end, when I knew he could not see the forms evolving on paper, did I realize that his creative instinct was akin to that of the poet or composer. The forms took shape in his mind, drawn from a reservoir seemingly as inexhaustible as that of a Klee or Picasso.

Wisdom of the Heart, Henry Miller   Perspectives USA   Mallarme Poems   Nightwood, Djuna Barnes

Lustig's solution of a book jacket problem was seldom a literary solution. He was no verbalizer; as a matter of fact, writing came hard to him. His method was to read a text and get the feel of the author's creative drive, then to restate it in his own graphic terms. Naturally these reformulations were most successful when there was an identity of interest, but it was remarkable how far he could go on alien ground.

In discussions of values in art the positiveness of his assertions occasionally suggested egotism; he would submit himself to it fully and with humility. I have heard people speak of the "Lustig style" but no one of them has been able to tell me, in fifty words or five hundred, what it was. Because each time, with each new book, there was a new creation. The only repetitions were those imposed by the physical media.

I often wish that Lustig had chosen to be a painter. It is sad to think that so many of his designs must live in hiding on the sides of books on shelves. I would like to have his beautiful *Mallarme crystal* or his *Nightwood* abstraction on my living room wall. But he was compelled to work in the field he chose because he had had his great vision of a new realm of art, of a wider social role for art, which would bring it closer to each and every one of us, out of the museums into our homes and offices, closer to everything we use and see. He was not alone, of course, in this; he was, and is, part of a continuing and growing movement. His distinction lay in the intensity and the purity with which he dedicated his genius to his ideal vision.

VIEW BOOK & PERIODICAL GALLERIES

→ catalogs/brochures   → new directions   → noonday press
→ knopf   → nd: modern reader   → ward ritchie press
→ magazines   → nd: new classics   → other publishers

back to top

★ lustig posters   home   about this site   acknowledgements   contact us   terms   site map

© 2006 Kind Company. all rights reserved.

Understanding Duchamp Web Site ▶

Date: 2002, 2003

Designer: Andrew Stafford

Photographers: Man Ray, Philadelphia Museum of Art, Biblioteque National, MOMA, Arturo Schwartz

Software: Flash, Photoshop

CASE STUDY:

Understanding Duchamp

Andrew Stafford, www.understandingduchamp.com

What inspired you to create such a complex online document as understandingduchamp.com?

It started with *The Large Glass*, one of the world's most baffling works of art [properly known as *The Bride Stripped Bare by Her Bachelors, Even*]. I had an idea or two about how to interpret it, in a way that could readily be understood by all (props to Calvin Tomkins and Richard Hamilton, without whom the site would never have happened), and an idea about how to present that interpretation: with a concise, coherent narrative description accompanied by an interactive animation. This Web site could not have been made without Flash.

It wasn't until I was almost done with The *Large Glass* section that I reckoned that, if I wanted to do this job right, it would have to be put into the context of Duchamp's entire oeuvre. So I undertook the rest of the site. If the whole has an organic feel to it (I hope it does), that's because text and images/animation/interactivity coevolved, each closely informing the other.

I notice that your copyright stretches from 2002 to 2006. Did you take that long to conceive, create, and ultimately design the site?

The first version slipped out the dock in 2002. Each year after that saw one or two significant changes—mostly new interactivity and animation—in two instances, significant rewrites of narration. But I honestly think I'm done with it now. Seriously.

What about this site, apart from the movement, could not have been achieved in a print version?

Interactivity, and one instance of audio (1915, frame six). The interactivity is especially important because participation by the viewer—sometimes in a physical way, more usually to engage the viewer's own imagination—is the very essence of Duchamp's art (one point—the main point?—of *Bicycle Wheel* is to incite the viewer to manhandle it). And don't forget: On the Web, distribution is virtually free. "The hell with commerce" is my motto.

1887-1903   1904-11   1912   1913   1914   1915

Marcel Duchamp (1887-1968), the painter and mixed media artist, was associated with Cubism, Dadaism and Surrealism, though he avoided any alliances. Duchamp's work is characterized by its humor, the variety and unconventionality of its media, and its incessant probing of the boundaries of art. His legacy includes the insight that art can be about ideas instead of worldly things, a revolutionary notion that would resonate with later generations of artists.

Three Paintings

Chocolate Grinder

Family Life   Student Days   *3 Standard Stoppages*   Bicycle Wheel

---

1924   1925   1926-34   1935-45   1946-66   1968   notes

Behind the door is a three-dimensional construction, like a museum diorama. There, in mid-day lighting a naked woman sprawls on a bed of dry twigs, face turned away, with her legs spread, exposing her vagina. She holds aloft a glowing gas lamp. In the background is a landscape of forests amid mountainous terrain. In the distance, a tiny waterfall shimmers.

The full title comes from one of Duchamp's notes for *The Large Glass*: "Etant donnés: 1. la chute d'eau 2. le gaz d'éclairage." In English: "Given: 1. the waterfall 2. the lighting gas." Water and gas are the elements animating both *The Large Glass* and *Etant Donnés*. But from these common premises the two pieces proceed to astonishingly different ends.

Etant Donnés, interior

◀ PREVIOUS   NEXT ▶

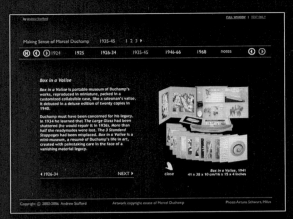

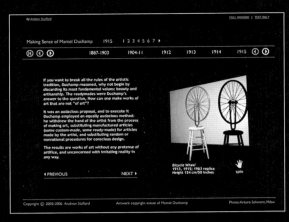

Photographer: Arturo Schwartz

Photographer: Arturo Schwartz

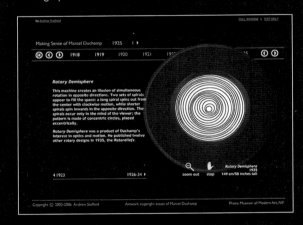

Photographer: Philadelphia Museum of Art

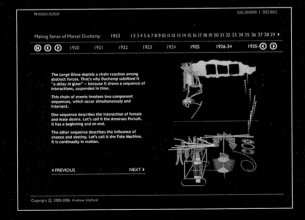

Photographer: Eadweard Muybridge

Date: 2002, 2004

Designer: Andrew Stafford

Illustrator: Andrew Stafford

Photographers: Misc. (as indicated)

Software: Flash, Photoshop

The interactivity is especially important because participation by the viewer—sometimes in a physical way, more usually to engage the viewer's own imagination—is the very essence of Duchamp's art

What is your own design background, and did it begin in the digital world?

Self-taught. I am emphatically not a graphic design guy; I'm a content guy. For me, design success is hard-fought, achieved only through much trial and error. (Shout-outs to Muller-Brockman, Allan Haley, Tschichold, especially "Form of the Book," Tufte, *National Geographic*, Frank Capra's "Hemo the Magnificent" and the 1959 animated film "Donald in Mathemagic Land".) The Aspen Web archive (ubu.com/aspen/) gave me a lot of practice with layout and HTML.

Building a site like this requires some sophisticated understanding of coding and programming. What did you bring to the project? What did you have to learn? And what did others do for you?

What I brought: Like I said, I'm a content guy, so I hope I was able to bring the ability to explain complex concepts with clarity and economy. Also: a vision of what I wanted to accomplish; good problem-solving skills; and great software (Flash). What I had to learn: Flash, from scratch. Also, how to write in short, discrete chunks of about one hundred words per page. What others had to do for me: special shout-out to friend and editor Nick Meriwether, who, when I was stalled on the text, reviewed my notes, identified omissions, and interviewed me to fill them in.

How much of your day is now devoted to "Making Sense of Marcel Duchamp"?

A few minutes to review access logs, a couple of times a week. I'll continue to give the whole site a thorough review a couple of times a year.

Have you done, or are you planning, any further documents of this depth?

I would love to find another project I could plunge into in a similar way. I have some ideas.

How would you define good design on the Web?

To me, good design depends on meaningful content. For me, design is about finding the underlying structure of information, which exists apart from design. Uncovering that, and using it to guide decisions about layout, type, color, etc., makes for good Web design. ▪

CASE STUDY:

The *New York Times* Tablet Project

Nick Bilton, an art director for the *New York Times*

You started as a print designer, working with digital tools. How and when did the on-screen world become your passion?

I got my first computer in 1982 when I was about six years old (a Spectrum Sinclair ZX), and have had a computer, or more than one, ever since. I also had a passion for drawing, painting, and pretty much making a mess on canvas and paper. I originally went to school for fine art, and one day in college, while waiting for a friend in the computer lab, I discovered the fonts folder on one of the computers. That was a major turning point for me. I was amazed at how quickly I could change the design and art of a page just by picking a different typeface.

How did you learn the skills you needed to become expert in this world?

I have always been able to get on a computer and figure out a new program just by exploring. Some of the basics I learned from professors in college, but the advanced program usage I mainly learned from trying to solve a problem and toiling over how to do it. I also had a couple of college friends that were very interested in a suite of digital design tools, and we would share new tricks and tips with each other daily. We were—or should I say we are—design nerds.

Did you have to teach yourself, or were the fundamentals available to you in school?

Like some people can play a sport well, computers and programs are an intuitive process to me.

What similarities are there between what you do on paper and on-screen?

I learned basic techniques that you can only really understand from getting your hands dirty with a paintbrush or piece of charcoal. I can re-create any technique I see on paper using Photoshop, but I never would have understood such a thing if it wasn't for executing the real medium first and understanding the principles that come along with a hands-on technique. I think it should be a prerequisite for all computer artists and designers to take hands-on courses in college, especially drawing and painting.

And what are the key differences?

One of the most frustrating things as a designer today is seeing people try to design for interactive without a traditional design background. How can someone design moving images and typography if they haven't mastered the art on a constrained flat page? A lot of designers that have worked for me on Web projects don't

Date: February 2007

Client: The New York Times

Designers: Nick Bilton, Kelly Doe, Tom Bodkin

Design Director: Tom Bodkin

Programs: Adobe Illustrator, Photoshop, InDesign, QuarkXpress, Microsoft Sparkle, Macromedia Flash and Dreamweaver

Programming: Microsoft and Nick Thuesen, Dreamweaver

Nick Bilton – The New York Times

*I can re-create any technique I see on paper using Photoshop, but I never
would have understood such a thing if it wasn't for executing the real medium first
and understanding the principles that come along with a hands-on technique.*

understand grids, or balance of a page. These are just a couple of the integral parts of being a great designer. When I work on an interactive project, I always solve the problem in my head, then move to a flat surface before making things move and become interactive.

Do you think differently as a designer when you're working on the *New York Times* tablet project—which transforms a once solely paper medium onto the screen?

The challenge with the tablet project has been to design for screens of all sizes, and for people of many penchants as to how they read the news. It has to be a pellucid experience for every user, from the novice to the online news junkie. I think the tablet project is ahead of its time, which is also a factor when designing for such a project. In 1998 I started working on some initial designs for PDA and Palm applications, which turned out to be an equally difficult task, but like the tablet project, a lot of fun, and challenging.

If you were to start your education over again, would you devote yourself entirely to interactive design, or does print still hold a fascination?

No. I would still take the road I took. I may have explored even more digital realms, like more programming and exploration of manipulating the hands-on computer experience—controlling objects through design. Today, there is a small collective of people that try to integrate design

and devices, which is a fun challenge within itself. The Graffiti Research Lab is an example (see http://www.graffitiresearchlab.com).

Do you feel that you're still a designer? Or has the technology you are working in made you more of a technologist?

I definitely still feel like a designer. But I am a *geek-designer*. I love technology and where it can take you, but I think without design most technology would fall on deaf ears. An example is the film title designers of the 1960s. They were traditional designers but had to understand film and the different types of negative, developing, and filming to understand how to apply their design to the moving image. For me, it's the same with the digital projects I work on. I don't want to just design a pretty cover for a book; I want to read it and understand how the book is made and the type of paper it's printed on and what you can do with the ink.

What should students and others who are entering this realm of design know now that was different from when you entered the field?

When I was entering the field, most students would pick a design genre and aim to go into that field. Today, even if you want to specialize in book design, you must understand how to make a Web site to showcase your work. Students should understand the basic principles of design before trying to design for an interactive or moving experience. ■

Business Day 'China Oil'

Date: Wednesday, August 3, 2005

Client: The *New York Times*

Designer: Nick Bilton

Design Director: Tom Bodkin

Software: Adobe Photoshop, Adobe InDesign, Adobe Illustrator, and CCI

Nick Bilton – The *New York Times*

Business Day 'Overhauled Housing Market'

Date: Saturday, May 28, 2005

Client: The *New York Times*

Designer: Nick Bilton

Design Director: Tom Bodkin

Software: Adobe Photoshop, Adobe InDesign, Adobe Illustrator, and CCI

Nick Bilton – The *New York Times*

CASE STUDY:

Web Comics

Jesse Willmon, www.com-mix.org

How did you become a Web designer?

I applied for the job at comedycentral.com, having only designed one Web site. I learned about Web design on the fly, and about a year later the art director left and I was the only designer. The Web site kept growing, and now we have nine designers, which I art direct. We work on things like minisites for TV shows, portal sites, cell phone applications, set-top box applications, online games, animations, and broadband video players. I oversee all of these things and make sure that they match up with the style of the TV network and adapt that style in a way that takes advantage of interactivity.

You have a keen interest in comics. Is this what drew you to your current job?

Not initially; what drew me to Comedy Central was that all the TV I was watching was on Comedy Central, so I wanted to be involved in something I liked. As I grew in my job, I found a way to incorporate most of my interests, like comics, into the design of the Web site. Comics are

a big part of how I think about design, and I think it really helps at Comedy Central because it keeps all the design relaxed and ultimately entertaining.

As your master's thesis for the School of Visual Arts MFA Designer as Author program, you created a Web site called COMMIX, an interactive site that enables users to create their own comics using other artists' artwork. First, what was the inspiration for such a site?

The initial inspiration came in a Web design class by Chris Capuozzo. During the class, I was reading a lot of Krazy Kat, and I thought that it would be fun to write my own versions of that. So I made a make-your-own—Krazy Kat Web site that was fun but not that interesting. When people used the site they either copied Krazy Kat dialogue or made Tom and Jerry comics. So I expanded the idea to letting people mix their favorite comic characters together. Like, what if you could write your own strips where Popeye fell in love with Veronica,

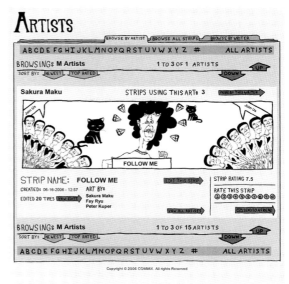

or if it was Calvin and Garfield, or what if Charlie Brown got shot by Dick Tracy? From there it just came down to finding artists who would let me put their work on my site.

In addition to the work involved in getting over a dozen artists to agree to have their work used by others, what were the design and technical issues you had to grapple with?

One main issue was to make sure that all of the art could be combined into one comic strip. To accomplish this, I put a few limitations on what the artists could do. All the art is black and white, so that at least the strip has a consistent color palette. Also, the proportions they can draw things in is fixed, so that the art fits into the user interface. File size became a big issue with some artists who had very detailed work. I had to find a happy medium between keeping the spirit of the artists' work and making sure that art could be used to make strips online.

How is this done?

Everything in this site design revolves around the database. All the art and text needs to be stored, as well as the position of all these things in a strip. Then everyone who visits the site needs to be able to change all of these things. The important thing for the design of the site was that the complex database had to be totally hidden from a user. It just needed to look like it was the easiest process in the world to create a comic on the site.

Making the site look hand-drawn is consistent with the theme, but did you have other user concerns? Did you design with the user's aesthetics in mind?

I think I always had the end users' aesthetics in mind. It's a basic drag-and-drop interface at its core, but you have to make sure that people who aren't designers or don't use Photoshop find the site easy to use. So part of that was to make the site very hand-drawn so it didn't look like a complex piece of technology.

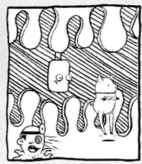

I also think the design actually covers up some of the technical limitations of the site. If it was designed clean, organized, and looked very technical, people would expect it to do everything perfectly. But since it looks very relaxed, people are willing to be a little more patient with it. If you have a design that looks like a million bucks, it has to work like that, but if you have a design that looks like a hundred bucks and works like a million bucks, then people are happier with it than with a really fancy design.

What about testing COMMIX? It's one thing to design according to your tastes, another to make sure it is usable in such a way that your audience will return. So, what did you do to ensure this?
Well, the testing of COMMIX was done mainly on my co-workers at Comedy Central, who spend all day thinking about Web sites. The big thing Web people constantly think about is always having new content; people will come back to your site if they have something to come back for. So it's a constant thing for me to find new artists to contribute, to highlight new writers on the site, to add ratings so people can find the good out of the bad, and also to make it easy to share the comics they write. A site like COMMIX really relies on someone creating a comic, then showing it to all of their friends, who, in turn, create comics of their own.

This is an entrepreneurial business. What did you have to learn to prepare you for creating this business?
Making money off of a Web site and treating it like a business is a fairly difficult thing to do. It takes a long time to build a user base for your site that is consistent enough to make advertising money. The main thing I had to learn is how the business of comics works. How comics are created, what artists know each other, how to approach groups of artists, how to make sure that artists keep their copyrights but also allow me to use their work on my site. All of these things I had to figure out on the way. Any Web site you build like this, you have to know everything not only about the business of the Web, but also everything about the content you are featuring.

How collaborative is the production of this site? Did you have to employ a team, or did you accomplish what you wanted on your own?
Making a Web site of this kind is always a collaborative process. Basically, I do all the design, artist contact, production on the artwork, wire frames, and user interaction design. After I do all of this work, then there is some complex programming that you have to get done. So I have a Flash/Action Script person who does all the programming of the Flash pieces, and I have a database programmer who does all of the back-end

work making the whole thing run. They are constantly telling me what is working and what isn't, so the site changes depending on how it's programmed. Eventually, though, these two people will run out of work to do on the site because they are programming it so that it builds new pages itself. So eventually I will be the only person working on the site.

What do you foresee as the future of COMMIX? Is it a viable property? Or is it more a testing of the waters?

I think that in the future COMMIX could be a viable property. The response from artists and visitors to the site is positive. The level of experimentation that is possible on a site like this is what makes it possible to think about it as a business in the future. Giving people simple tools and then seeing what they do with them is what is exciting; it's really up to users of the site to make it a success. If it does not become all that I hope, I have gotten to work with and talk to some of my favorite artists. That alone is a reason for me to keep COMMIX going.

With the skills you've acquired while at Comedy Central and now with COMMIX, what do you now need to learn to enhance your control of the Web and Web design?

▲

www.com-mix.org

Client: SVA MFA Thesis

Designer: Jesse Willmon

Artists: Ivan Brunetti, S.Y. Choi, Molly Crabapple, Patrick Dorian, Caroline Gould, Gabriel Gutierrez, Tom Hart, Paul Hoppe, Nora Krug, Peter Kuper, Mike LaRiccia, Alec Longstreth, Sakura Maku, James McShane, Sarah Perry-Stout, Fay Ryu, R. Sikoryak, Mark Stamaty, Maggie Suisman, Gary Taxali, Jack Turnbull, Britton Walters

Software: Flash, Teamsite, Dreamweaver, PHP, Illustrator

The one thing about Web design is that the technology to do it is always changing. The technology and programs that I used for COMMIX and at comedycentral.com are top-of-the-line, but tomorrow they will be obsolete. So you have to keep up with the technology, but always remember that Web design is really about how you get people who don't know each other to interact, whether directly or through an interface. So the thing I need to focus on in the future is more of how people get together and learn more about that; then my Web design skills will follow behind that. ■

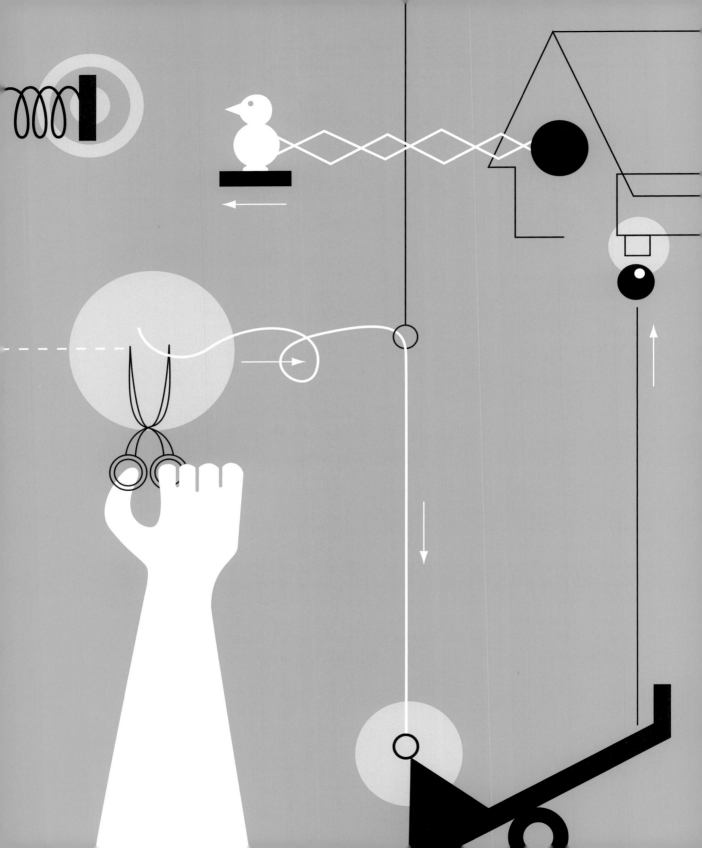

Motion Design

In its primordial interactive form, motion design dates back to around 1914, when Winsor McKay performed live with his animated cartoon creation Gertie the Dinosaur on vaudeville stages throughout America.

Unlike earlier, even more primitive animation techniques, this breakthrough invention was interactive insofar as McKay simulated play with his virtual friend. The film was synched to follow McKay as he walked and talked to the dinosaur onstage as though it were real (and who's to say it was not?). The audience, in turn, was given an unprecedented user experience. Since then, scores of animated films—from Gene Kelly dancing with Jerry Mouse in *Anchors Aweigh* to the sexy vamp in *Who Framed Roger Rabbit?*—have integrated live action and animated characters (and it wasn't easy in the days before digitization).

Motion picture title sequences—whether live-action, animation, or collage and montage—are another popular design discipline. In 1955 Saul Bass created a genre-defining title for Otto Preminger's *The Man with the Golden Arm*, a marriage of expressionistic graphics and modernist typography, which introduced abstraction and symbolism to the precincts of contemporary film. Bass produced dozens more signature titles in later years—*Vertigo, North by Northwest*, and *Walk on the Wild Side*—and was copied by scores of other title designers.

Yet another true original was Pablo Ferro, who, using time-consuming optical technologies, created moody, narrative preludes for scores of films, including the inventive multiple-screen technique for the 1968 film *The Thomas Crown Affair*, which was adopted by other filmmakers of that era as a means to make their films look contemporary—and so it did for a decade or so.

The magical confluence of type, image, and motion has long inspired graphic designers to create beyond the mere conventions of the flat printed surface. The ability to make otherwise static elements jump, prance, tumble, and contort is one of the joys of any design process. If this sounds overly prosaic, just wait until your first attempt at motion comes to life. You'll understand.

But until the computer, and really only over the past decade of the digital revolution, it was rather difficult to do motion without a large, powerful, expensive computer, or without software like MAYA. Over the past ten years the software has become more democratic. In fact, iMovie has made even the amateur into a virtual pro—and offered considerably greater potential for everyone, especially designers, to produce motion design in various media and on numerous platforms. Sites like YouTube have further made motion as common to create and distribute as print and picture documents. Even handheld devices are capable of making and showing motion works.

For the longest time, motion design—at least the high-end variety—was the province of trained professionals. Today, fluency in motion tools is essential at even the beginning levels of design practice. Thanks to interactive design, the distinction between graphic design and motion graphics has blurred.

In the mid-1990s, many designers got a taste for designing motion graphics by creating CD-ROMs that combined audio and video in a designed environment. With the advent of Flash (first called Futuresplash) the Web was soon full of bouncing buttons, menus that bulged and rippled, and animations of every description. These animations began making their way from the computer screen back onto the silver screen. In 1996, Matt Hanson founded onedotzero, the first festival of digital filmmaking. David Lynch, famed director of *Blue Velvet,* made his most recent film entirely in digital video.

As more designers have embraced motion and animation, the film and television industries have begun to embrace design as a matter of course. These media awoke to the fact that designers could do more than just the title sequence when music videos began combining live action and animation. It started with music videos in which colors and erratic scratches covered the screen, or animated flowers sprouted from saxophones. As Chris Dooley of National Television tells it, directors began inserting design into their scripts with instructions like, "Awesome graphics swirl around the artist."

At the same time that more graphic elements were making their way onto the screen, graphic designers such as Mike Mills began to make names for themselves as video directors. It became clear that not only could designers make visual flourishes, but they could also bring a new perspective to telling stories visually.

The increasing integration of motion components—from high to low end—into all kinds of on-air and online entertainments, information graphics, and environmental kinetic spectaculars (i.e., huge Times Square billboards) has changed the definition of communications design, and radically altered the staffing of graphic design firms and studios. Now, traditional designers are hiring motion design experts, while younger organizations are hard wired to combine static and kinetic into seamless entities. The introduction of motion also blurs the boundaries between traditional rivalries. Once only ad agencies made commercials. Today, design firms have assumed the role of commercials and videos. In short, the media world is flux and motion design is the flux-o-matic. ■

From Disk Jockey to Motion Jockey

An Interview with Jakob Trollbäck, proprietor Trollbäck + Company, New York City

What prompted a graphic designer to become expert in motion—film and video?

I find graphic design very formal when it is static. There can be an amazing energy in a printed piece, but it is what a physicist would call potential energy. It is what makes print design hard—to find the expression that hits the energy level where it works just right. Motion, on the other hand, is all about kinetic energy. It moves within the linear passing of time, and creates tension and rhythm patterns in its flow. In my twenties I was a music freak and a DJ, and used graphics to promote events. Ultimately I realized that I was even happier when I could apply my skills as a DJ and mixer to a flow of images.

What is the most challenging aspect of creating visuals in time and space?

Ninety percent of all graphics that I see doesn't mean anything. It's frivolous and ultimately bores me.

Do you tell stories or make design?

If you want to make people feel in a special way, you have to be very particular about what you design and how you present it. For anyone to understand what you try to say, you need to work inside (or outside) a set of social and cultural values. This is why good motion design is a close relative to storytelling.

There are times when a client just wants something new, and the whole idea is to create something that nobody has seen before. This can be a great challenge and forces you to search all kinds of cultural expressions for unique voices. But in the end, without the story (however convoluted), it will never really move anyone.

How did you learn to work in this medium? How much is craft and how much is design intuition?

I was always pretty good with technical things, and felt at home with all kinds of software that helped tremendously. I spent years learning to move things around on a screen. This is the craft, to understand how to shoot, animate, and edit something in order for it to feel in a certain way—heavy, doughy, airy, cold, angry, happy, etc. Then you need to invoke some magic to find that unseen angle that makes it unique.

What is the most satisfying piece that you've done?

This is a hard one. There's a lot of work through the years that I am very happy with, but obviously, running a company means that I'm not always as much hands-on, which in the end is most satisfying to me.

I'm very happy with the live-action spots that I directed for Lifetime, and some recent branding work, like AMC and TNT. I still like the numerous openings that I've done for the TED conferences, and for some reason I keep looking back on the main titles for *Night Falls on Manhattan* with joy.

Given your trajectory, how would you suggest that designers enter the motion field?

With passion. There is no substitute for it.

But specifically, what are the necessities that a motion designer must have?

Rhythm. Syncopation. Listen to Bill Evans' piano on Miles's *All Blues*. Especially what he is doing under the solos. You've got to try to be totally in tune with the piece. And at the same time be as joyfully unpredictable.

It's a true gift, and I believe that the link between music and motion is imminent.

Once you understand this and can feel the rhythm, you take your idea and go to work with your toolbox of images, color, type, art, culture, and patience.

P.S. Magic is very rare, but it does happen, too. ■

▼ TCM Menus

Client: Turner Classic Movies

Date: 2006

Designer: Nathalie de La Gorce

Director: Jakob Trollbäck

Creative Director: Jakob Trollbäck

Software: Final Cut, After Effects

NEXTgencode.com ▶

Client: HarperCollins and Michael Crichton

Date: Fall 2006

Designer(s): Jon Milott, Cary Murnion, Matthew Cooley

Software: Illustrator, Photoshop, Flash, After Effects, Final Cut Pro

Full of Ideas

An Interview with Cary Munion, coprincipal of Honest, New York City, www.stayhonest.com

You began as a print designer. How easy was it for you to segue into Web and motion?
Jon [Jonathan Milott, coprincipal] actually started more as a Web designer. At least, that was his first job out of school, and I worked at a company that had Web and motion design departments, so I had opportunities to work on those kinds of projects to get some experience. Plus, we had both studied motion and Web design while at Parsons School of Design, so we knew all along that we didn't want to stick to just designing for print.

It was easier getting Web projects for our own studio because the Web site that we designed for ourselves proved that we could do Web projects, and people really responded

well to it. We also were given a great opportunity very early on by Paola Antonelli at MoMA to design a Web site for one of the shows she curated, so having a Web site for MoMA gave us instant credibility. Getting motion design work was a little more difficult, so we kept on doing our own personal projects—animated shorts, work for friends, work for our Web site—and sending out new reels until various networks started trusting us and giving us work.

How deeply involved are you in the techniques versus the aesthetics of digital design?
To really be able to get the most out of these mediums you should be pretty up-to-date on the technical advancements and limitations. But

on the other hand, there's almost always a way that something can be done, so sometimes it's better not to be concerned with what can and can't be done and let your imagination go wild without any constraints. With our clients we're usually the ones that have to explain the technical aspects of a job, along with our aesthetic approach, so we always have to know enough about each to be able to explain it to them clearly.

Honest has a very complex Web site (www.stayhonest.com). Many bells and whistles, with much content. What is your goal in doing such a maximal site?
Our goal with our Web site is to have fun and be creative. Our minds are full of ideas, so we think that

*. . . if we're not totally committed to what a client is asking us to do,
then we won't work on the job.*

our Web site should reflect that. We also think that instead of a Web site just being a framework that displays the work we've done, it should be the work. We want people who come to our site to immediately get a sense of who we are and what we can do *before* seeing examples of work we've done in the past. But the simple answer to this question would be that me and Jon are maximal people, so we have a maximal Web site.

By creating a site that has so many surprise features, do you appeal to one audience while filtering out another?
Oh, most definitely. It seems that people either love our site or hate it, and that's exactly the way we want it to be. If people contact us wanting us to work with them, we want them to be passionate about us, not on the fence about whether or not they think we're a good fit. It's a waste of our time and theirs if there's anything less than total commitment. Moreover, if we're not totally committed to what a client is asking us to do, then we won't work

on the job. Our Web site seems to attract people who are committed to the same goals as we are, and it's not an aesthetic thing, because people may not like the style of our Web site but are still drawn to the enthusiasm and innovation that we bring to the site, and, in turn, would bring to their project.

In addition to graphics that invoke a mechanical, almost futuristic veneer, you use sound to great effect. What is the importance of sound design?
With the experience we've had in film projects we've learned that sound design can be 50 percent of the success of the project, and sometimes even more.

It's a little bit different for a Web project because you can't always depend on people having their computer sound turned on or having good enough speakers to really pick up on all of the nuances, but we want to reward the people who do. We want our Web site to act almost like an interactive animated film, so sound design is very important in bringing that goal to fruition. Our goal

is to create a fully interactive experience with our Web site, and without sound we would never be full.

You do Web work for some very hip companies—Kate Spade, Issey Miyake, etc.—do you subliminate your design personality to their needs, or are yours in sync with theirs?
They're usually in sync, because what makes those companies so great is that in their respective markets they are innovators, and that's what they see in our work and it's what they want us to bring to the table when we work with them. They want to do something that pushes their brand in a slightly new direction, sometimes less dramatically than others, but pushes it nonetheless. They don't want to bring our *style* to their project; they want to bring *our way of thinking*.

What dominates an approach—do you let the print side of things influence the Web and motion, or vice versa?
It's strictly about the idea. Whether it's a print, Web, motion, or all of

Honest Magazine Issue 2 ▶

Client: Honest

Design Studio: Honest

Illustration: Christopher A. Rufo

Software: Adobe Illustrator, Photoshop, InDesign

those combined (which we actually love the most), all that matters is communicating the core idea of the project. We do that first and then start working on how it will be applied through the designated media.

What don't you do that you'd like to do with your firm?

We haven't directed a feature film yet, which we want to do and are working on scripts for right now.

What do you look for when seeking out new employees? Must everyone have digital fluency?

Great ideas are the most important thing we look for, because that's rarer and harder to teach. If they're a super tech-nerd in addition to having awesome ideas, then that's a major plus. Liking video games, working their ass off (like we do), good typography, an odd sense of humor, strong personalities, and an interest in things other than design are also added bonuses. ■

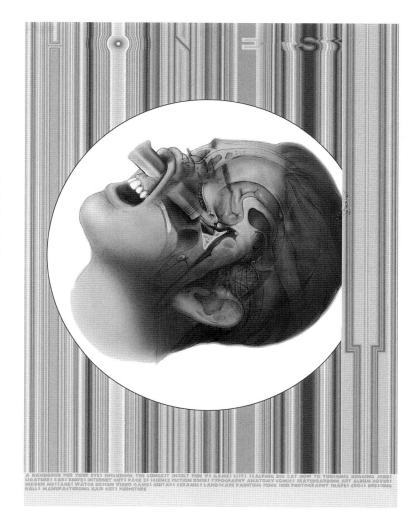

◀ www.stayhonest.com

Client: Honest

Date: Winter/Spring 2005

Designer(s): Jon Milott and Matthew Cooley

Software: Adobe Illustrator, Photoshop, Flash, After Effects

Pushing the Limits

An Interview with Beatriz Helena Ramos, found/creative director of Dancing Diablo, New York

▲ PBS

Client: PBS

Direction: Beatriz Helena Ramos

Producer: Diego Sánchez

Art Direction and Design:
Adriana Genel/Beatriz Helena Ramos

2D Animators: Vanessa Rodriguez—
Germán Herrera/Mariana Capriles/
Beatriz Helena Ramos

CGI Animators: José Luis San Juan/
Germán Herrera

Editor: Beatriz Helena Ramos

©Dancing Diablo

You were an illustrator; how did you become interested in animation?

As an illustrator, you learn to tell stories. Whether it's illustrating comics or doing storyboards for advertising, all you are doing is telling stories visually. In a sense, animation is illustration in motion, so the leap seemed like an obvious one to me.

In our particular case, our animation relies strongly on illustration. I would say that we first illustrate and then we just give life to that world.

How did you become a member of Dancing Diablo?

I worked in the animation industry for years. The more versatile you were as an artist, the more competitive you were in the industry. I specialized and became an expert in color. However, in time I felt the need to do other things, not just color. I wanted to be engaged in all aspects of the process, as well as being able to decide how to tell the story and the final look of the piece. I thought I could only achieve that by starting my own company; thus Dancing Diablo was born.

How much has digital technology impacted the way you work with your medium?

In a huge way. Fifteen years ago it would have been impossible to do the work that we do, and as many projects as we handle, with only a few people in a small studio. Also, new technology allows for new ways to solve creative issues and can directly set the trends for new styles. It can also affect the way schedules and budgets are calculated.

As a general rule, we try a new approach in every project. Experimenting plays a big part in our creative process. We are always exploring new territories and new challenges.

Still, I consider digital technology a tool, not a medium. Stylistically, we try to do as much as possible with our hands: drawing, painting, making puppets, building miniature sets, etc. We do everything we can traditionally and use digital technology for practical reasons.

What is now possible using digital tools that you could not have done before they were available?

What is amazing is how fast you can see results thanks to digital technology. The process has become immediate, just like technology has made communication immediate. What would have taken weeks to fix now only takes hours.

More specifically, we can now re-create a three-dimensional environment completely digitally using the Maya software, and we can manipulate the camera in that 3D environment just the way you would in real life.

For stop-motion animation, we can shoot directly from a high-resolution still camera to an inexpensive software on the computer that captures the image, allowing us to see instantaneously how the animation looks and to make changes right on the spot. It gives us more control over the final product. In the old days it used to take weeks just to be able to see what you had shot.

Two-dimensional animation can also be done these days directly on the computer. We can draw with a pressure-sensitive pen on a digital tablet or directly onto the screen, using software instead of an animation lighting table. We can even let the computer do some of the animation for us through mathematical calculations.

Another interesting aspect of digital technology is the fact that it allows us to communicate easily with our studio abroad. I can direct a project done entirely in Venezuela from my office in New York. I manage the team through instant messaging, give directions through the optical camera, have conference calls via Skype, and transfer heavy files through our FTP server. All of it at very low costs.

Of all your projects, which one has been the most challenging, and why?

As a general rule, we try a new approach in every project. Experimenting plays a big part in our creative process. We are always exploring new territories and new challenges. We are always pushing our own limits. I can't think of any particular project as the most challenging; every project has its own particular issues.

Animation is such a collaborative activity. How much of your time is spent on technology versus being creative?

Although I've always tried to use the latest technology and I'm not afraid to embrace it, technology is definitely not as important to me as the creative is.

For me, technology is at the service of creative, and not the other way around.

I spend time learning new software or new digital tools only if they will allow me to achieve my creative goals.

Is it necessary to know the intricacies and nuances of digital technology to produce the kind of work you do?

Definitely to some extent, yes. I think it's important to understand the digital world. However, I don't think you need to be an expert on software or know 90 percent of specific software to do the work that we do. Software can be very complex, and many times all you need to know are just a few specifics.

When hiring for a project or as a member of Dancing Diablo, what do you look for in a candidate?

The most important thing to me is artistic qualities in people. I'm looking for sensibility and taste. I want to know how well developed are their drawing, sculpting and painting skills. I want to see if they have a sophisticated sense of color, composition, and design. Imagination is very important to me; therefore, I'm particularly interested in their own projects. That gives me a lot of insight into their ideas, discipline, interests, and influences. Lastly and secondarily, I ask about their knowledge of the specific software we use.

It's easy to teach anyone how to use software, and with enough time, most people can eventually be efficient at it. But it's a lot harder to teach people about coming up with great ideas and developing a sensibility. ∎

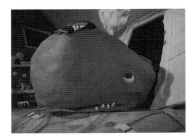

Making Graphic Videos
and Videos Graphic

An Interview with Chris Dooley, principal, National Television, Los Angeles

What is National Television?

National Television was founded by directors Chris Dooley, Brumby Boylston, and Brian Won as a creative studio, with emphasis on storytelling through design and animation.

We turned on our computers in the middle of 2004. But despite each of us having a huge body of work created during the four years prior to that, we opted to spend our first year creating a reel of entirely National projects in order to avoid having a reel comprised of work from other shops. This became pretty important for us in terms of developing a tone or voice for the shop. We did a lot of work in a very short amount of time and were able to launch our Web site and show reel in June of 2005.

How did you train to be a video director? Did you start with this goal in mind, or did you evolve into the practice from another discipline?

While in school I did some shooting, but my primary focus was always on graphic design. Directing music

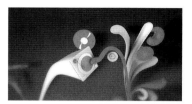

videos was a direct result of being at a great studio where we were doing some really influential work. Around the same time a couple things happened that helped blur the line between live action and motion graphics. First off, with digital filmmaking becoming more prevalent, small-scale live-action shoots became a more accessible solution for designers. And while music video budgets shrank, the need for

▲ Coke and iTunes "Free Music"

Client: Mother, London

Direction: National Television

Executive Producer: Jared Libitsky

Art Direction: Chris Dooley

3D Animation: Kevin Walker, John Nguyen

them grew due to an increasing number of outlets.

As designers continued to make low-budget highly graphic videos for indie bands, labels and directors began to take notice, and in turn, legitimate music video directors were writing graphics into their treatments. Sometimes it was just a single line ("Awesome graphics swirl around the artist"), and other times I was fortunate to work with a director like Chris Applebaum, who was legitimately interested in the collaborative process between live action and graphic design.

And then . . .

After this, record labels began approaching motion graphics shops directly to write treatments and direct our own music videos.

On a side note, an early collaboration between the partners who would become National Television was an entirely animated music video for a band called Beulah in 2001. We had no idea what we were doing, and we drove to San Francisco, where we shot the band performing with a DV camera in the lead singer's living room. That video should have made us famous.

In looking at your reel, I notice a collage sensibility at play. Would you call this National Television's signature style?

I think the biggest compliment we've been given about our reel was the lack of a singular distinctive style. In my experience, connecting your problem-solving process to a specific look or trend is the fastest way to make yourself obsolete. I would agree that there is a sensibility at play in our work, but I would argue that it is more of a humorous tone or attitude that defines our work and makes our reel stand out.

You have done work for Virgin Digital, Comedy Central, and MTV—each a highly popular "youth" company. Is National Television set up to cater to youth market? If so, how do you reach them?

Again, I feel like it's our sensibility that connects our work to any market, youth-oriented or otherwise. I think clients recognize the humor and wit in our work, and they understand how those qualities can be applied to their product or service. The leap from what we do to selling networks like MTV or VH1 is a relatively easy one to make. What's exciting is when a potential client sees the same work, and they understand how it could be used to market things like high-end athletic shoes, potato chips, health bars, or long-distance service. Over the last few years the work hasn't dramatically changed direction to attract clients, but clients have definitely become more willing to try something new to appeal to their market.

How do you work as a director? Do you conceive, create, and fabricate? Or do you put the pieces together and watch as it happens? In other words, is this a hands-on job?

We're a small shop that people come to for a unique take on their problem. And to a large degree, that is a sensibility that we've built around ourselves, which is why we feel like it's important that we creative direct every project. I think because it's our own shop, we feel even more pressure to control the quality of work and as a result find ourselves spending a even more time on the box, and occasionally doing the heavy lifting ourselves.

In some cases, projects are completely insulated between the three of us (with us writing, designing and animating a complete piece), while in other instances we bring in designers or animators to help out when the creative calls for it. We all believe in hiring the best person for the job. Part of that is finding people we enjoy working with who understand the attitude of the shop. Since day one we have been extremely fortunate to have surrounded ourselves with talented and good people.

▲ **G4's Late Night Peep Show**

Client: G4 Network

Direction: National Television

Executive Producer: Jared Libitsky

Art direction and design: Chris Dooley and P.J. Richardson

2D Animation: Preston Brown, Earl Burnley

3D Animation: Hansoo Im

A traditional project generally follows a schedule like this: After we get a brief from the client, we have an initial brainstorm where everyone discusses possible directions the project could take. At the same time, a producer is working on scheduling and budgeting of the project. Realistically, this is also a part of the creative process, as limitations with time or money could potentially impact how we solve a problem.

Occasionally, we're asked to write treatments for live-action spots or music videos, in which case we'll work up potential directions the idea could take and design style frames to accompany the treatment. Once the job awards we design proper storyboards that represent the spot from start to finish. There are designers we like to collaborate with who will usually come in around this time to help in the design phase.

If there is a single idea we all feel strongly about we'll present only that. However, more often than not, what happens is that we present a number of potential design directions to the client and they will choose one, or have a revision on a couple directions before we enter into animation. We build the animation team specific to the boards the client chooses, and bring in whatever resources necessary to get the best-looking final product.

What is the most challenging job you've done to date, and how has this tested your mettle?

As a general rule, the jobs with the most protracted schedules tend to wear you out the most. One of the things that attracted me to this industry was the fast turnarounds and short production time lines. Aside from embracing my ADD, it also allowed me to learn to trust my instinct and not second-guess what could be the right answer to a client's problem.

As with any client-based industry, another thing that can complicate or make a job harder is a ton of people that need to approve aspects of a project. So much so that we'll usually ask going into a project how many levels of approvals there will need to be, even if it's only to protect ourselves against a lot of downtime while things get signedoff on.

In terms of most challenging, I feel like the campaign that I directed for Orange during my last year at Brand New School. Because Mother is a British advertising agency, and Orange a British corporation, my whole team and I offered to invert our work schedule (sleeping days and working overnight) to accommodate client approvals and conference calls. Totally unhealthy, but totally worth it.

Another thing that can make a job difficult is an unwieldy amount of deliverables. In that case it becomes both a production challenge as well as a design challenge. We recently finished a modular tool kit for Fox Sports Net for the entire Major League Baseball season. Because of the numerous regions, potential team matchups, and accounting for player

◄ Virgin Digital
"Exercise Your Music Muscle"

Client: Ground Zero

Direction: National Television

Produced by: National Television

Art direction and Design: Brian Won, Chris Dooley, Brumby Boylston, Ben Lee

2D and 3D Animation: Brumby Boylston, John Nguyen, Kevin Walker, Wonhee Lee, Camille Chu

injuries throughout the season, we had close to five hundred separate elements that needed to be delivered prior to the start of the season.

Since National Television has television in the title, how do you define television these days? Are you solely producing for the cathode ray (or plasma screen), or have you found other venues?
I don't understand when people say they don't watch television. To me, what's happening with TV right now is infinitely more fascinating than almost any other artistic outlet. Television needs a new publicist, because I always find myself convincing other people that TV is fantastic.

Not to say that it will always be commercials, but personally I would be thrilled to make good television for the rest of my career.

We have directed projects that live exclusively on the Web, as well animations for in-store displays. These present an interesting challenge from the perspective that they require a different kind of storytell-

ing. If it's a viral or Web campaign, they need to remain interesting upon repeated viewing, which was one of the many successes of the Virgin Digital piece. And in the case of some in-store displays, the animation needs to be loopable, ending where it began, as it does in the Nike "Nature" spot.

I will say there is a level of pride that prevents us from providing content for cell phones or PDAs. For no other reason than it's so much work for something that is ultimately very small and ephemeral. I imagine it's the same way record album designers felt when they were told that their work was going to be put on cassette tapes or CD sleeves.

In hiring for National Television, what qualifications do you look for? Indeed, what kinds of jobs do you need?
The quality we look for first is problem-solving skills. The ability to look at a problem from a different angle than any of us would is key. If someone gives us something we could've done

ourselves, there's almost no reason to employ them. If you have a unique take on a client's needs and you're able to sell them, you will find yourself busy all the time.

Another key quality we look for is personality. We are and will most likely always be a small *boutique* shop that works very closely with our clients and each other. If you don't mix or you're someone other people don't enjoy working with, you most likely won't last long.

Finally, I think the final and most rare quality in people we look for is the ability to lead. Having ideas is great, but if you have to shout for people to hear you, no one is listening anyway. Finding people who can make other people listen is a rare find.

From a very practical standpoint, we hire the best person for each job. If a job requires heavy 3D modeling or animation, we build a team of 3D artists. The same goes for every aspect of design and animation. Over the last few years, all of us have developed a core group of talented friends who we like to work and hang out with. ■

Nike Free "Nature"

Client: Nike

Direction: National Television

Producer: National Television

Art direction and design: Brian Won, Chris Dooley and Brumby Boylston

2D and 3D Animation: Brumby Boylston, John Nguyen, Robin Roepstorff

Pre-MTV, Post Motion

An Interview with Graham Elliott, Optic Nerve, Inc., Brooklyn, New York

▲ Greyhound to Cuba Poster

Date: 2006

Client: Optic Nerve Productions

Designer, Illustrator, Photographer: Graham Elliott

Software: Photoshop, Illustrator

How did you become a music video and short film director? Were you a designer before this?

I came out of the Royal College of Art, with a master's in Illustration. I was doing psychedelic computer collages on a pre-Mac sixteen-bit Artron, the first one in London. Vernon Reid, the front man from the rock band Living Colour, asked me to do his record sleeves. After pestering him to do a music video I ended up on a set for the first time directing the "Glamour Boys" video.

Your work is rampant with collage elements and quick cuts. How did this style develop?

I grew up pre-MTV, so I can't blame that. After a stint as an illustrator and too much agonizing over a single image, I think I reached a critical mass and reacted by going the other way.

Are you telling stories or providing sensations?

I am now trying to be more narrative, and storytelling excites me. I always wanted to be a stand-up comic, so I'm excited to get more humor in my work. I know my earlier stuff was more visual eye candy.

Is your style a response to the current technological options, or is this the way your mind/eye sees?

I don't think my style is influenced by the new tools. Much of my work starts off quite organically. But the democratization of moving-image production has been an incredibly empowering and exciting event. I just fin-

www.opticnerveny.com ▶

Date: 2007

Client: Optic Nerve Productions

Designer, Illustrator, Photographer:
Graham Elliott

Software: Illustrator, Painter, Photoshop,
Flash 8, After Effects, Cinema 4d, Maya/
Final cut Pro/Poser

ished my first feature film and was basically able to do everything on the Mac. Edit, record voice-over, make music, produce opening titles and end credits. Then author-interactive DVDs, design, and print the covers. And spit out a cover letter!

You say on your Web site that you are making motion for the youth market; how do you know what that segment really wants? I teach the music video class at the School of Visual Arts. My students are my toughest critics—they haven't learned to bullshit yet or be afraid to burn bridges. I show them my work, and if I'm patronizing the demographic they tell me straightaway.

You've mastered the short-form—commercials, music videos, etc. Your most recent film, Greyhound to Cuba, while maintaining your signature style, is a longer film. Other than length, what is the difference?

This project gave me the chance to tell a meaty story. It was a self-initiated project, so I had to learn to edit it myself. Simply the scale of putting together a ninety-minute piece from fifty-four hours of film needed a completely new way of working. I had to develop systems of recording and tracking all the media, as well as trying to keep my creative head going. It took six years to realize—nine months solid in the edit . . . I usually get bored with things if they go on too long, but I knew I had to complete this one. So I guess the scale of the piece and the discipline to com-

plete it without client involvement were the main differences.

What does a neophyte need to know about making youth-oriented films? Should they follow the pack? Or find new methods and styles? As much as I hate focus groups and too much research, I really think you have to get out there to find out what's really hip and happening. I did some research films for Nike and hung out with skateboarders and realized they were into things that I had absolutely no clue they would be. ∎

Abstract Data Adjusters

An Interview with Terry Green, director, Twenty2product Studio, San Francisco

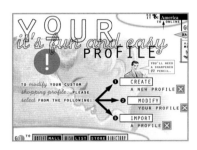

▲
AOL Market Place

Client: Colosswal Pictures
for America Online

Date: April 1995

Designers: Terry Green and
Nori-Zso Tolson (Twenty2product)

Illustration: Eric Donelan and
Bob Aufuldish (Big Cheese and
Zeitguys fonts)

Software: Adobe Photoshop
and Illustrator

Some of your work has a very abstract sensibility—kinetic patterns made from overlays for color and form—while other work is fairly straightforward interfaces (like the work for TiVo). How do you balance the two? And what determines how you will solve a digital problem?

Clients drive the nature of our product, and we don't presume to know more about their business than they do. The fun is trying to get up to speed with a client's highly contexted way of talking about their world, and then using our ability as communicators (paraphrasers?) to try and make their intentions more universally understood. That's what's common to all the projects.

We love the process of making images, and our craft is very much about recognizing success in an existing communication and trying to extract why it worked, figure out how that specific treatment satisfied the needs of both the communicator and their audience. We are safe assuming that there isn't a single right solution for any design problem, and so we present many and then listen when a client tells us what's working for them and what's not.

When you design for an interactive purpose, do you start out with an aesthetic plan, or do you need to determine the goal of the site?

A client usually has a clear set of goals, but as consultants we're paid to make suggestions about how to refine the focus or, if necessary, add to the capability set of a site. The hope is that a visitor will have a memorable experience, but our objective is always to quickly satisfy the initial impulse for coming to the site. The destination may look like a poster, but it's really software and should function as a tool.

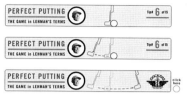

◀ Dockers Golf

Client: Phoenix Pop Productions for True North / Levi Strauss

Date: April 1997

Designers: Terry Green and Nori-Zso Tolson (Twenty2product)

Software: Adobe Photoshop and Illustrator

How much of what you do is determined by the nature of the information you must convey? For example, you did datagraphics for Fox Sports Net on the San Francisco Marathon; was the visual component based entirely on the nature of the event?

Viewer expectations mostly; there is anticipation toward a certain way of presenting statistical data during sporting events, and the knowledge that when those graphics take over the screen there's less time to watch the action. That's why these graphics are mostly minimized and positioned at the edge of the screen when possible—as they are in video games.

Despite those conventional ways of showing statistics, designers are relentless tweakers (adjusters?), and we personally love the challenges that informational graphics present. We do remain mindful that the client/broadcaster's objective for these graphics is to present a fast and comprehensible snapshot

of the relationships in play, allowing a nearly instantaneous return of attention to the actual game, and this keeps us sane and our client happy.

In designing for the Web, can you be too image-based, or too aesthetically driven?

Absolutely; that's why the Web design discipline is now split into both visual and interaction design practices. Our company predates this convention, and our sense of proper/natural information flow comes from a desire to satisfy a passive viewer's evolving expectations, conducting their attention with graphics and animation. Motion graphics and interactive projects are really similar in that goal.

The shopping application for America Online seems to have so many options that a user can get confused. Where do you draw the line in terms of density and complexity?

Yes, that sketch was very much about chaos, the flea market experience expressed as a UI (user interface). Sometimes complexity is the communication, not individualization of the component parts. I'm hazy on the details though. We did that one a while ago. I do remember us talking about the margin drawings that Sergio Arigones did for *MAD* Magazine, and everyone liked the idea that there could be something fun and extra and not necessarily connected to the content featured also happening in the pages.

When the Levi's Dockers people asked you to design a site, did they know what design approach they wanted, or did you propose the humorous golf motif? In other words, how much creative freedom do you have?

That campaign was about reaching guys who were right at the edge of accepting real adult responsibilities, and helping them present an image

There's always plenty of license when we're initially sketching things out.
The clamp down comes after the direction is set and all the parts need to interrelate.
The fact that most corporations want a Web presence is a good thing; it means more
work for us designers!

consistent with business success, having kids and taking on mortgages, etc. Dockers had commissioned their agency to write a book containing lifestyle advice and also set up an endorsement deal with a golf pro. It was thought that golf would be a good fit for this more establishment positioning than the alternatives—people liked Tiger Woods. Golf fashions were situation-flexible and also reinforced the demographic's casual self-image.

We were free to understand all that and then come up with an appropriate and clever visual treatment, animations for sixteen golf tip banners happening over the life of the campaign, and a destination site for

the banners that let you to scan the previously released golf tips. We also worked on another section of the site that featured answers to general lifestyle questions—which wine goes with fish—that type of stuff. I remember it all going very quickly because we subcontracted the job and there wasn't much money.

Do you find that there is more license or less now that most large corporations are doing Web components? Has the bloom fallen from the rose?
There's always plenty of license when we're initially sketching things out. The clamp-down comes after the direction is set and all the parts need

to interrelate. The fact that most corporations want a Web presence is a good thing; it means more work for us designers!

What do you look for when hiring designers for Twenty2? Do you want design experience or software expertise?
My partner, Nori, and I are kind of militant in our desire to remain a two-person shop, and our focus will likely remain motion graphics and visual design for interactive projects. When we look for collaborators, it's almost always for engineering and production work. ■

Starting from a Print Point of View

An Interview with Scott Stowell, principal of OPEN, New York City

You started in print, and still do a healthy part of your business in print. Why the switch to motion?

For me, it's not a switch. As designers we have to deal with different sets of constraints all the time. Motion projects just add their own constraints to the mix, just like editorial or environmental or interactive work does. I do love projects that we don't know how to do, so that's part of it. But I think that we approach every project in a similar way—we think about what the message is and how it's being delivered and to whom.

How difficult was it for you to move off the static page into a time-based medium, where storytelling over time and space is a major component?

I think the page is a time-based medium, where storytelling is a major component, too. And there are a lot of similarities between a book design and a storyboard—both are about constants and variables. In our work, I think we often start from a print point of view, in which each page (or frame) should work as well as the whole. And storytelling is the most important part of any project that we do.

Did you have to learn new tricks—you old dog—to make this transition feasible?

I think the biggest thing I've had to deal with is the constantly changing work process. When we did broadcast projects back at M&Co [an innovative New York design firm in the 1990s], we made storyboards and had type set and went to edit facilities to do the work. Over the years that changed into working with animation companies, and then with freelance animators in house, but now most animators work at home. Now the line between designer and animator is disappearing.

Are there bridges between your print and motion work that are both natural and consistent?

I'm proud of the level of typography that we've been able to bring to our motion work. As someone who considers himself a typographer, I think it's important to retain that rigor in every medium. So the type in our work for the screen is as refined as the type in our print work. And in some cases, I think that we've been able to think about typography in a three- and four-dimensional way as well.

For some, the transition is difficult. Does thinking about type and image on a screen come as second nature to you now?

No. There is something about motion work that's always a little nerve-wracking. With print work, the elements are all set—there is imagery and there is type, and there is the printing itself to deal with. But on-screen there is always something new to think about—besides the design, there is sound and music and live action and editing, and every new technique that comes along.

What has been the most challenging story for you to present on-screen?

For me, the basic requirements for a designer remain pretty much unchanged, even if the list of specific useful skills seems to change and expand on a daily basis.

▲

BRAVO Network Redesign

Client: Bravo

Date: 2004–2005

Designer(s): Susan Barber, Rob Di Ieso, Gary Fogelson, William Morrisey, Scott Stowell, Corinne Vizzacchero

Software: After Effects, Final Cut Pro, Illustrator, InDesign, Photoshop

We've worked on two basic kinds of motion projects: those that exist as a frame for content (i.e., show packaging and network redesigns) and those that are the content (i.e., short films and videos). In the first category, I'd say the *Art: 21* packaging for PBS has been the most rewarding. We had to develop a concept that was both abstract and meaningful, but could evolve—it's had to for eight years so far.

In the second category, it would have to be our videos for the inductees to the Jazz at Lincoln Center Hall of Fame. Our original plan was to make videos for "people that hate jazz," in order to convert them into fans. But in both cases the challenge was to communicate to a specific group of people (art lovers, jazz fans) while also reaching out to a mainstream audience. So everything has to work for insiders and outsiders, too.

Do you now define yourself as a graphic designer, or is there another description you'd apply to your practice?

I usually just say designer, but I'm proud to be a graphic designer. That term has always encompassed new kinds of work in new kinds of media, so why change now?

When seeking out designers and interns, what do you look for? Should they be motion and time-base savvy, or must they just be good designers?

It's great when we can find someone who has experience with motion, just like it's great when someone is also a photographer or can draw well or write well or whatever. But a good designer is a good designer.

What in this digital world is a good designer?

For me, the basic requirements for a designer remain pretty much unchanged, even if the list of specific useful skills seems to change and expand on a daily basis. You have to keep an open mind, know how to communicate your ideas, and have a real attention to detail. And, of course, you have to be ready to deal with surprises at any moment, no matter what. ■

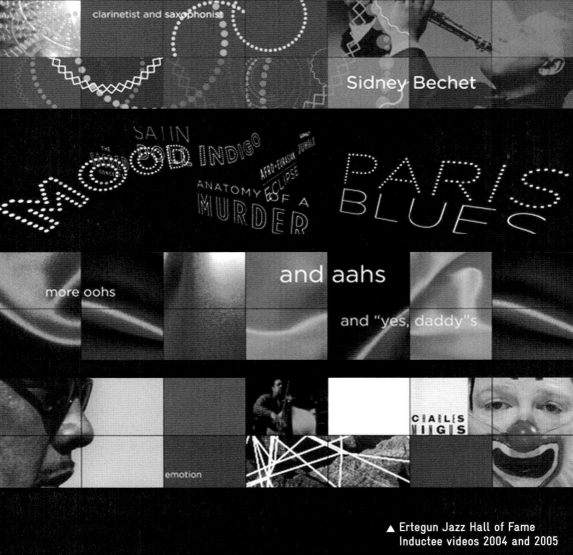

▲ Ertegun Jazz Hall of Fame
Inductee videos 2004 and 2005

Client: Jazz at Lincoln Center

Date: 2004 and 2005

Designer(s): Susan Barber, Cara Brower,
Rob Di Ieso, Gary Fogelson, Scott Stowell

Programs: After Effects, Final Cut Pro,
Illustrator, InDesign, Photoshop

The New Golden Age of Animation

An Interview with Fred Seibert, president of Frederator, New York City

There was a golden age of animation with Ren and Stimpy and Beavis and Butthead back in the 1990s. Are we still in the golden age?

I guess I might refer to a "silver age" of animation we're in; it's hard for me to believe—as good as the creative period we're in—anything could be as good as the years that gave us *Looney Tunes*, *Tom and Jerry*, *Felix*, *Donald Duck*, *Pinocchio*, and all the others. That being said . . .

It's been an amazing fifteen years, and there's no end in sight. Original cartoons are still on the rise. First *The Simpsons*, then *R&S*, *B&B*, and *Rugrats*. *South Park*, *Dexter's Laboratory*, *The Powerpuff Girls*, *Cow and Chicken*, *Johnny Bravo*. And just within the last four years: *The Fairly Oddparents*, *Jimmy Neutron*, and the first megastar of the age, the modern *Bugs Bunny*, *SpongeBob*. In the wings: *My Life*

as a *Teenage Robot*, *ChalkZone*, and *The Grim Adventures of Billy and Mandy*. And many people would think I'm narrow-minded if I ignored features like *Toy Story* and *Finding Nemo*.

The business of television began a seismic change in the eighties, which really became mature in the nineties, and that maturity created the circumstances that allowed for a revival of animation as a powerful commercial art form. In 1983, the average home in America had four channels of television; by 1988 that same home had twenty-seven channels (and many had fifty or more). Competitive pressures to launch mass-appeal programming forced cable networks to create, and then create some more; the traditional broadcast networks were fiddling while their symbolic Rome burned.

Actually, weren't new viewers roaming over to an increased number of more interesting stations?

The broadcasters still had the largest audiences and made the most money, so there was laughter at what they thought were amateur efforts from the upstarts; the loss of audience share the traditional networks were experiencing were considered negligible. Meanwhile, the cables were learning the new craft of show business, saving their money for programming production war chests, and realizing that innovating past the stale network fare was the way to capture the audience attention.

All in all, the ambitions of a creatively pent-up creative community, and the force of new cable-centric

capitalism, met in an explosion of innovation we're still feeling today.

The bar seems to have been pushed higher on TV and film. Kids' fare is much more adventurous. Does this mean that the market for challenging animation is large?

The audience isn't stupid, no matter what executives think. Given the choice between Hanna-Barbera's *The Snorks* and Hanna-Barbera's *Dexter's Laboratory*, they can recognize the superior comedy.

That being said, I'm not so sure the market is actually larger than it was before the cable age; the population is marginally larger and still watching the same amount of TV weekly. But the competitive environment—jeez! An average of more than one hundred channels are trying to get a piece of your viewing time. In the past, a network looked forward to a 30 percent share of the audience for a hit; now it's happy with 5 percent (and 1 percent or 2 percent for cable!). The result is that each program and each channel has to fight harder and harder with every character and every story.

Before 1980, the viewer had no choice; if you wanted to watch cartoons, maybe watching crappy ones was better than nothing. Today the audience must be satisfied, they truly can watch another show, or watch a DVD, or go online and find cartoons there.

You've been in the forefront of new animation. How do you find new talent?

Isn't that the magic question? Ten years ago I didn't need to look far. In the trenches of the animation business were hundreds of classically trained animators who were toiling on the *Yo Yogi!* (the adventures of a teen-aged Yogi Bear, hangin' at the mall) or *Fish Police*. These folks were dying to save the business they had trained their whole lives to join. We would put out the word we were seriously interested in the animator's stories (for forty years the creative people were merely the hands of management's ideas); over five thousand pitches were presented for our first set of forty-eight short films. And dozens of world-class hits were launched.

Today, our net has extended significantly wider because our competition has caught on and also scooped up the most available talent. There are many American and international cities with centers of cartooning that haven't participated in the new hit boom. We're busy setting up development centers all around the world.

©2007, Channel Frederator

How did the artists of the golden age achieve their successes? And does this open the door even wider for students today?

As you might imagine, there are lots of parallels, but plenty of differences between the golden age and today.

In the first half of the twentieth century, it was a dog-eat-dog world in animation, though it had a true innocence. Many artists looked to animation as a career because it employed so many more men (it was primarily men, white men at that) than any other cartooning outlet. But there was no formal training, so he had to find a job at a studio that was willing to train him, teach him the rudiments of a new art form (actually, sometimes he needed to *invent* the steps). He had to figure out how to draw, animate, sure, but also how to tell a story, a funny story, with characters that were better than the competition.

**My Life as a
Teenage Robot**

Created By: Rob Renzetti

Art Direction By: Alex
Kirwan and Rob Renzetti

©2007, Channel Frederator

And until the 1940s there was not even any geographic center; New York and California had the most successful studios, with Chicago and Miami weighing in, too. The employment network was fueled by friendships, often started in childhood or nurtured at the entry-level studios, and often an artist friend dragged in a completely untrained, talented friend and helped him become a story man, or a production manager. Additionally, all aspects of an animated film were made on-site, so there was a lot of room to train as an in-betweener, a model or layout artist, or as an animator before debuting as a director, trying to take a shot at the golden ring.

What's the role of the school today, as opposed to the old apprentice system?

Now there are schools to do the initial training, so few studios use their scarce resources to start talent. And while we do most of the creative production in the studio, layouts and animation are often done off shore, so there are fewer opportunities for artists than in the day. And we expect even entry-level artists to have a minimum standard of skill.

But the market is more open to more kinds of people than ever before. While it's still a white man's

The Fairly Odd Parents
Created and Designed By: Butch Hartman. ©2007, Channel Frederator

world, walk through any major studio and you'll see men and women, African-Americans, Latinos and Latinas, Asians, Africans.

What must a student have in his gut to be a great cartoon creator? Is it enough just to have skill?

You know, then and now, the elements of success are pretty similar in cartoons:

Talent: You've got to have "it." I'll let biologists and psychologists explain what "it" is.

Skill: Animation is an exacting proposition, commercial animation even more so. If you can't draw, you can't play. And if you can't draw, storytelling and directing in cartoons is all that much harder.

Ambition: The most ephemeral, the most ignored, the most misunderstood element of a great creator. The person who wants commercial success brings an extra oomph to his or her films. Trying to appeal to an audience, communicating with their hopes, dreams, and funny bones, is the magic of the modern world. I've always admired the Beatles because they had the desire to create great art that didn't intrude with their craving to amass great fortunes. Great cartoons are motivated by no less.

What does the future hold for kids who are studying cartooning and animation today?

Whatever they want. ■

Game Design

There are a lot of reasons to love games. The digital gaming industry has now surpassed the motion picture industry in terms of revenue[1]. Not only does gaming bring in more cash than the movies, but gaming offers designers a shot at the triple crown: the opportunity to combine motion graphics, interactivity, and product design into one package— and to blow things up while you're doing it!

Despite the fact that game design is bringing home the Benjamins, it's still a relatively young field, and it does seem possible for lowly scrubs (like yourself, perhaps) to become the new stars in this huge industry that is getting huger.

If you want to get a job in the game design industry, you need to know your technology. Specifically, you need to know animation and 3D modeling programs such as Maya and 3DS Max. But, equally important, you must be able to dream up characters and scenarios that other people will want to engage.

So, what makes a game fun? Your ability to answer this question in an interesting way is key to your career. Although there are an infinite number of answers, there are also some principles as to what makes a good game. For example, for a game to be fun, you have to want to win it. There has to be a goal that the player is trying to achieve. In the case of PacMan, that goal is to gobble up the points and not get whacked by a ghost. And, for most games, the primary goal is survival. But what you have to do in order to survive varies greatly. In games like the Sims and Second Life, it's not enough to just get by; the goal is to do it in style by creating a functioning city, or to accumulate wealth and score with hotties. Another principle is that games get harder—otherwise, once players learn the system they lose interest. Video games often have progressive levels. Sometimes, like with Texas Hold 'Em, for example, the game becomes harder, not because the game itself changes but because your opponents improve. The goal is to learn faster than they do how to count the cards.

So, if you're interested in getting into game design, keep a notebook where you write down ideas for games. Then get other people engaged. Nothing will teach you the principles of game design faster than working with real people: You will quickly find out that they seldom behave the way you expect or want them to. But that's part of the game. Here's a challenge for you: If you can create a game that keeps a group of eight-year-olds actively engaged for half an hour, not only will you have done their parents a big favor, you may just have just discovered a career. ◼

Parappa on PSP ▶

Date: 2006

World and Character Design: Rodney Alan Greenblat

Original Game Concept: Masaya Matsuura

Photo: ©2007 Sony Computer Entertainment, ©2007 RG/IP

Designing Whimsy

An Interview with Rodney Alan Greenblat, creator Rodneyfun.com, New York City

You were one of the first designer/artists to create games for computers. And your games were worlds of crazy Greenblat characters and digital funhouses, like Dazzeloids and Parappa the Rapper. I haven't seen much of them lately. What happened?

In 2003, I decided to retire from the character design and digital media business. Near the end of production of Parappa 2, which was the second sequel, I was feeling pangs of yearning to be back in my studio alone, making my creations, whatever they might be.

It was a difficult decision, but I could feel the momentum of Parappa and his friends slowing down. I tried desperately to try to push the powers at Sony and the various companies involved to improve and expand the franchise, but it became impossible. Everything changes, and in the world of pop culture Japan, everything changes very rapidly. I left while I was still famous and beloved by my fans.

With all that is going on the Web since the bubble burst and we're now into Web 2.0, how has the environment changed from when you were pioneering? Is it different from what you expected?

I could have never predicted that the Web would become so huge. PCs are basically sold as Web-viewing appliances these days. I was right that it would become an amazing community of offbeat groups and really kooky people with diverse and specific interests, but I never guessed the gigantic size!

I think the metaphor my comrades and I in the nineties were applying was that the Web would be a kind of combination of books and TV. For me, eBay totally reformatted that notion. I realize now that book/TV content idea is one small packet of what the Web is—but the real power is in the massive user-filled databases like eBay that are indigenous to what the network

As a trailblazer in the art/toy industry, I hope other artists can learn from me,
and surpass my successes if they can.

environment is.

Your recent work seems to be large oils on canvas. Although so many artists are moving to the digital, why have you returned to acrylic on canvas?
I really missed the physicality of art supplies and the studio. The computer is very versatile, but basically it involves sitting in a chair for hours on end. I need to get dirty and dusty and move around. I love woodworking and ceramics, and smearing paint all over the place.

The computer just doesn't offer that kind of fun. There is something incredibly challenging and satisfying about facing a huge blank canvas, or finishing an involved sculpture. Digital media is just not presenting me the kind of physical experience I need in my life these days.

I know that you are not estranged from the Web. You have the site http://www.whimsyload. com/, and it's filled with toys, animations, and artworks. What do you want your audience to get from the site?
Whimsyload.com is a place for

anyone go get acquainted with my work, or to keep up with what I am working on. It also offers a place where people can buy some of my difficult-to-get goods from Japan, and also prints, postcards, and selected original works. I've worked hard on the database of my fine art, and it is very up-to-date. Some of the work from the eighties is not there yet, but I'm working on that, too.

You produce a wonderful assortment of primitive—almost EtchASketch—animations, like Grin Tree. What's the purpose of these things? Is it to entertain? Or keep your finger in the digital pie?
I haven't added to that collection lately, but I still think they are great. The original purpose was to entertain myself and create some original content made exclusively for my Web site. I'd like to make an animation based on my new abstract imagery, but I'm not sure when I will have the time. I like the idea of keeping my finger in a digital pie. It sounds messy.

It's interesting to me that your style of the early and

mid-1990s has been co-opted by the vinyl and plastic toymakers of the 2000s. Would you agree with that assessment?
I do not feel my work has been *co-opted* by younger designers and artists. As a trailblazer in the art/toy industry, I hope other artists can learn from me, and surpass my successes if they can. The more artists and designers that are inspired by my work, the more my karmic energy grows. I think that energy will allow me to go on forever being an innovator, which is what I'd really like to do.

Even if you don't, it seems to me that you influenced the Japanese toy aficionados. Hey, didn't they create a site called Rodneyfun.com, about "everything Rodney"?
Rodneyfun.com was created by the rep agency that promoted my work in Japan. It was a showcase of my goods and characters for my fans in Japan.

Are you familiar with Jim Flora's work? Many of your sweet,

Rodneypod

Date: 2006

Small wooded constructed sculpture that
contains an iPod and battery powered amplifier.
This work will supply original music for an
upcoming exhibition. It will be part of a series
of small metaphysical appliances and shrines.

Photo: ©2006 Rodney Alan Greenblat

▲

Dazzeloids

Date: 1994

Client: Voyager

Designers: Rodney Alan Greenblat, Jenny Horn

Additional Credits: Programming: David Anderson

Software: Director, Freehand, Photoshop, Studio Vision (sound)

©1997 Rodney Alan Greenblat

monstrous creatures remind me of his sharp-edged, goofy illustrations.

Yes. I think his work is great, and it is possible he was inspired by some of my creations, but I don't know that for a fact. If so, it's more filling for my karmic pie.

Do you plan to spend more effort on the nondigital these days, or are you looking for a balance of both?

Although I am focused on painting canvases and building sculptures, I'm planning to add some digital magic to some of the works. I'm working on small, boxlike sculptures that contain an iPod Shuffle inside a secret door, and a battery-operated amp and speakers. The sculptures will play very odd electronic minimalist music that I have been composing and recording. The music contains long and short gaps of silence, and with three or four sculptures all playing at once in shuffle mode, it should create the cartoon-abstract modernist Shinto-shrine atmosphere I am looking for. I'll send you a picture of one of these as soon as it is ready.

I had a show of my paintings and sculptures at Gallery Centella in Tucson Arizona (September 15 to October 21, 2006). I'm also returning to Japan this fall to show limited-edition digital fine-art prints of my new abstract images. The company is called Art Print Japan, and it has galleries all over Japan.

Oh, yeah, where did Thunder Bunny come from?

Thunder Bunny is a cloud bunny who accidentally fell from his nest in a giant egg, then after being adopted by a group of children, was returned to the sky, where he was reunited with his mother. This all happened in a children's book that I wrote and illustrated in 1997. It was published by HarperCollins in the United States, had moderate success, but then became very popular in Japan.

In 1999 I wrote a sequel for the Japanese market, and the translation was written by Ami from the famous J-pop duo PuffyAmiYumi. Sony made many toys and stationery and clothes with the Thunder Bunny characters and logo printed on them. In 2001, Sony and a famous animation company called Avant produced a twenty-minute computer animated film. I wrote the story and some of the music myself, and did the storyboards. The video and DVD were sold in specialty shops with Thunder Bunny character goods. ■

Cultural Game Making

An Interview with Eric Zimmerman, CEO of Gamelab, New York City

▲ Shopmania

Client: Published by iWin

Date: August 2006

Designer: Gamelab

Software: Orbital

©2006, Gamelab

Why did you become an online game designer? Were you a graphic designer prior to this?
Actually, I was trained as an artist before becoming a game designer. First I studied painting as an undergraduate, followed by an MFA in art and technology. But actually, becoming a game designer in some ways returns me to my roots.

As a child I was always creating games—not just playing them, but making them. I created a science project in fifth grade that was a board game where the player was a food particle inside a body. I made themed board games for my family to play on holidays. And I created elaborate rules with my friends for resolving combat between plastic army men.

From physical neighborhood games like Kick the Can to complex imaginative role-playing games with *Star Wars* action figures, the games I played as a kid were often redesigned by myself and other players. This has all had a tremendous impact on my current game design work.

Of course, I also grew up through the early rise of video games. When I was very young, I played Pong on a cousin's TV set. My best friend in fifth grade had an Atari, and I spent junior high school in the early eighties in arcades and playing on my Apple II+.

As a graduating art student in 1991, I looked around at the landscape of art, entertainment, and popular culture, and it seemed to me that video games were a form of culture that was radically reinventing itself on a regular basis—more so than anything else I could find. This was during the rise of *VR* and *Wired* magazines, so there was a lot of technological optimism going around. As an artist, I wanted to create something genuinely new and original that the world had never seen before.

So my decision to go into game design as a career was a combination of my childhood love for game creation, my long-standing study to be a cultural producer, and the modernist belief in the possibility of doing something new.

Your work is exclusively online games. What is the fundamental difference between this and those sold via disk?

◀ Out of Your Mind!

Client: Published by Gamelab

Date: March 2007

Designer: Gamelab

Software: Orbital

©2007, Curious Pictures

Actually, although Gamelab (the company I cofounded with Peter Lee in 2000) focuses on online games, my past and present work with games spans many media. I got started creating PC games on CD-ROM as part of the mainstream game industry. I have also created card games and board games, physical games played in museums, as well as social games played by thousands of people at conferences and events.

Are there differences between online and on-table games?

From the point of view of game design, there aren't fundamental differences between all of these kinds of games. I would argue that there are fundamental similarities. What makes a game a game, what makes game play meaningful to players, and how it is that games are designed, are all more similar than different across different game media. Of course, different media make different kinds of player experiences possible. You can't get the face-to-face interaction of a so-

cial card game in a console game, and you can't get the cinematics of a console game in a card game, but the fundamental design principles remain the same.

How about from a business perspective?

From a business point of view, on the other hand, differences between different game media are very significant. Gamelab has gravitated toward online games because we want to do experimental work, and the small scale of online games lets us do more games that are more interesting to us than the more conservative multimillion-dollar large console and PC games. Everything about online games—who plays them, how people find out about them, how they are purchased, what the customer looks for in a game—is different than console and PC retail games. These factors all impact the game design as well.

How do you decide on what games to create? Is this a collaborative effort?

Generating ideas for games is very much a collaborative and ongoing effort at Gamelab. Sometimes the parameters for a game project are given by the situation.

For example, if we are going to do a game for LEGO, there is usually a set audience (boys aged eight to twelve), and a particular product we need to showcase in the game (such as a new line of LEGO toys). Plus, since it is a LEGO game, we will want the game to reflect LEGO's play philosophy of modular, construction-based, imaginative play. From these parameters, we will work out our initial ideas.

Other times we have a more open-ended opportunity to create new game concepts, such as when a publisher wants us to pitch new ideas. In these cases, we have to generate concepts ourselves. We have an ongoing set of design ideas and areas of interest that we pursue from game to game. Some of our interests have to do with inventing new forms of interactivity. Others have to do with storytelling and games. Others are about

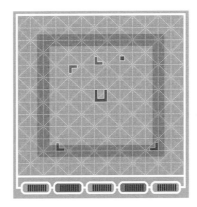

◀ BLiX

Graphics/Code: Peter Lee

Game Design/Process:
Eric Zimmerman

Audio: Michael Sweet/Audiobrain

exploring new audio and visual languages. These little pieces of ideas
fly around during brainstorming
meetings (and during the regular
workday as well), and organically
they turn into full game concepts. I
like to think that the actual games
we produce are just the residue
from our ongoing process, the wake
that Gamelab leaves in the ocean of
culture as we move from project to
project and idea to idea.

How much programming and coding expertise must a game designer have?

None is required, but some experience is helpful. Game designers are
not programmers, and they are not
visual designers. They create the
rules of a game and help shape the

player experience. Think of a board
game: A board game designer
doesn't draw the pictures that end
up on the board, and doesn't physi-
cally manufacture the board, but the
game designer does structure the
layout of the board and determine
all of the rules that tell the players
what to do each turn.

Programming can be a helpful skill, because knowing a little
about programming helps a game
designer understand what a computer can and can't do. But it is
not essential. Actually, because
game designers and programmers
both work on a very structural
level (code for programmers and
rules for game designers), they
usually can communicate very well
together, and studying one of these

two fields can often help with the
other. Many game designers start
out as programmers, and some
people work as both programmer
and game designer. But these days,
with large project teams, people are
more specialized and usually work
as one or the other.

What should one study to enter the game field?

One of the great things about games
is that like film or other complex
media, it takes many people with
very different skill sets to make a
game. You can study programming,
graphic design, animation, music
and audio design, project management, game design, and many other
game-related fields, from journalism
to business.

Is there a good site to visit for games?

The best site for people looking to study games is the International Game Developers Association Web site, www.igda.org. There is an extensive section on "breaking into the game industry, including a list of schools with game-related programs. The site also includes a white paper I helped coauthor with curriculum recommendations for what people might study who want to eventually make games. The game developer community site www.gamasutra.com is also very helpful, with lots of new content added to the site on a regular basis.

What do you look for in a young designer?

The most important thing is someone who loves games and is passionate about making them. People just entering into game development as a career also should have some kind of job skill. People usually get hired as game programmers, visual designers, game play testers, or something quite specific. Many people want to be general game designers, art directors, or creative directors, but these positions are not entry-level.

That said, too many university programs stress practical job skills and knowledge of software over critical thinking and problem-solving skills. Most game development companies are not looking for robots that know how to use a particular piece of software. More important is a refined sensibility in whatever you do, whether it is visual design, interactive design, music composition, etc. I would rather see a potential game designer show me an original and innovative card game than a boring but flashy digital game. Any company can show you how to use software—and software tools are going to change every few years in any case. The most important thing you can demonstrate to a potential employer is your passion and talent for what you do. ■

▲ LOOP

Code: Ranjit Bhatnagar

Graphics/Game Design: Frank Lantz

Graphics: Peter Lee

Game Design/Process: Eric Zimmerman

Audio: Michael Sweet/Audiobrain

Digital Entrepreneurs

According to a recent article in the *Harvard Business Review*, "An arts degree is now perhaps the hottest credential in the world of business."[1] That's the good news. The better news is that designers are being hired for their brains and not just their ability to produce a mean PowerPoint slide presentation. Designers can bring a unique perspective to the world of business.

While MBAs learn what makes something profitable, design MFAs learn what makes something useful—as well as beautiful. They learn how to identify the needs of the end user and shape products and services to meet those needs, whether that need is to move a billion dollars or find a fellow traveler who shares your fascination with muscle cars.

Digital tools have made it increasingly more feasible to create new products on the desktop. Not only to conceive but actually develop and produce the prototypes and even the final objects. Some products are not objects, per se, but Web sites that showcase product ideas (see the School of Visual Arts MFA Designer as Author projects on pages 201–202). Empowered by digital power, designers have options they never dreamed of twenty years ago. Design is still the driving force, but concept is both fuel and engine. Design frames these concepts and organizes the ways by which they reach the world.

Increasingly, digital design is the point of contact between a business and its customers. What you know about a business is what you know about its Web site. Is it efficient? Can you complete your transactions quickly? Is it helpful? Does it give you the information you need to make a decision?

[1] Pink, Daniel. *Harvard Business Review*, "The MFA is the New MBA", February 2004.

. . . .designers are either working for clients—designing Web sites, designing processes, illustrating business concepts—or they are skipping the middleman and reaching out to end users directly with their own products and services.

The same qualities we used to look for in the person standing on the other side of the counter we now look for in the interface that shows up on our screen. And businesses have learned that if we don't like what we see, chances are we won't hang around. After all, while the Web makes it easier for your customers to find you, it makes it just as easy for them to find your competition.

Big companies need designers to work for them, but do designers need big companies to work for? More and more designers are setting up shop straight out of school. These designers are either working for clients—designing Web sites, designing processes, illustrating business concepts—or they are skipping the middleman and reaching out to end users directly with their own products and services. Although this may be a tempting option, just remember that good design is harder than it looks. Also, the marriage of design and business can sometimes be rocky. ■

Making Presentations

The toughest thing for a designer (or any artist), and particularly an entrepreneur, is to sell oneself. While ego is no stranger to art, how to best represent one's work demands a self-critical acuity. Selecting the right work (knowing what to leave out as well) takes a certain discipline that comes only with experience.

Today, so many portfolios can be loaded onto the Internet, and there are various ways of being represented:

1. Take space in a collective or organizational site (i.e., AIGA.org). The benefit of this is the neutrality of the site and the simplicity of presentation.

2. Design a personal Web site, which has the dual benefit of showing off your Web aesthetics while presenting other elements of your work.

3. Create an online studio and show your work in concert with other designers. Possibly, the critical mass will help you get work.

4. Send out e-mail promotions either directing prospective clients or employers to your Web site, or linking to projects you have already done on the Web.

Don't oversaturate clients or employers with e-mail promotions—one every four or five months is enough, and only if you have something totally new to show.

If you design your own Web site, don't make it difficult to load, view, or navigate. The worst thing you can do is become carried away with your own design prowess. Let your finished work speak for itself.

Student Digital Entrepreneurs

It's become a cliché to say the personal computer has brought entrepreneurial worlds that were once too high in the stratosphere down to planet Earth. Well, maybe it hasn't been said exactly in this way, but you get the basic idea. The PC and Mac both come with software that enables many to make books, produce Web sites, edit films, record music, and make radio shows. In fact, one can easily make one's own book on a Web site that includes video or film, contains a musical sound track, and can be uploaded to the Web as a video podcast. What a miracle.

Although most of this miraculous software is meant for the amateur, it is just as easy to get professional tools that enable publishing and broadcast-quality results. The computer age promised, and is now delivering, a wealth of entrepreneurial potentials in so many different areas.

Each year individual students attending the School of Visual Arts' MFA Designer as Author Program must develop a Web-based business, which not only is handsomely (and at times brilliantly) designed, but also is more or less entrepreneurially viable—if not profitable. Designers are traditionally required to frame messages, and Web design is certainly a means of framing (and establishing hierarchies for) messages and ideas.

This class, taught by Chris Capuozzo, the creative director of Funny Garbage, New York, challenges students to develop functional concepts using the digital universe as a platform. Of course, many of these ideas could probably be launched in the real world, but the Web has increasingly become second nature to most consumers and many entrepreneurs for previewing and purchasing goods and wares.

Here are some web-based web site proposals from the MFA design class of 2007 at the School of Visual Arts:

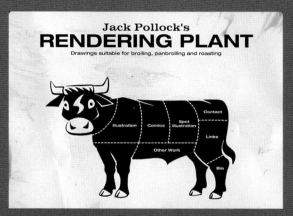

Jack Pollack's Rendering Planet

Design: Bekky Pollack.
A Web site devoted to selling illustrations and drawings

Underthings

Design: Jessica Jackson.
A Web site devoted to historical lingerie and the people who wore it.

Snapshots

Design: Lara McCormick.
A memorial site to Lara's father that highlights his photography.

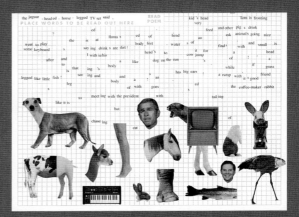

Reconfigure

Design: Maria DeLaguardia.
A Web game that challenges the user to make new words and pictures out of old.

Rest in Piece

Design: Shannon Lowers.
A Web site devoted to burial sites of musicians in the New York metropolitan area.

Dream Factory

Design: Pelin Kirca.
A fantasy where users can make their own surreal tales.

ClearRX:

Design: Massod Amed.
A Web chronicle documenting an exhibition of the Target Clear Rx prescription drug bottle created by Deborah Adler.

5As$Zs91!xTU+dxVbbID

◄ Nokia Nseries Studio

Nokia Nseries Studio

R/GA created the Nokia Nseries studio, a mobile video initiative, to foster online distribution of mobile videos. For the initial launch in April 2006, creative visionaries, including Gary Oldman, were empowered to develop video clips using the new N93 device. Later, the site was opened to everyone. R/GA 2006.

Building Multiplatforms

An Interview with Robert Greenberg, president of R/GA, New York City

Your firm began, in part, by doing film titles and TV commercials. Did you foresee the level of integration between motion and design when you started? And if so, how did this affect your plans for the future? Did you see the future?

R/GA was founded on the principles of motion and design. In fact, our trademark was "Moving Pictures. By Design." The original vision of R/GA was to take great still print/photography and apply motion to it. We were highly specialized at that time. I'm not sure if I "saw the future," but I can say we predated any classification of motion graphics and animation.

Over the years, you've employed print and motion designers. Do you feel it is still important to have a print background? Or have the tenets of print been totally integrated into digital media?

Every creative candidate who comes to R/GA has a basic print background—it's still a good foundation for our industry. However, early on, when looking at candidates, we had to hire people whose portfolio imagery had implied motion within it. Back then, the transition into digital production was tricky. People were not technically savvy, and even the concept of digital graphic animation was new. We had to train people to think and design in new ways.

All the candidates we see now have a strong background in using the software tools of our industry—Photoshop, InDesign, Illustrator, and Apple-based audio and visual editing technologies. Designers today, especially the younger generation, have a natural understanding of computers, so even if they have

Designers now must learn to design flexible templates. They need to develop content that works across the four screens, which we define as mobile phones, laptop/desktop computers, TV, and dynamic/digital signage.

a strictly print background, they can be trained easily in digital media.

Have the definitions (and conventions) of design changed now that other platforms—like cell phones and iPods—are integral new venues?

Designers now must learn to design flexible templates. They need to develop content that works across the four screens, which we define as mobile phones, laptop/desktop computers, TV, and dynamic/digital signage. It's not simply reformatting a design but knowing how the design will look and feel across all four screens.

I like to compare it to the design of music album covers. Historically, a designer was tasked with designing an LP cover; as technology advanced to cassettes and CDs, designers had to learn these new formats. That's how I see advertising. Art directors and designers need to learn how to work in all these formats so they have the skills to execute truly integrated campaigns for their clients.

At R/GA, do your clients now come to you to invent new forms and systems for the new media? Or do they want you to follow the paradigms you've trailblazed?

Many of our clients are highly innovative technology/telecomm companies —Nokia, Verizon, Verizon Wireless, Avaya, and Lucent are all R/GA clients. We're constantly challenged by them to engage and educate their customers in new ways. These brands require that the message and platform be as innovative as the products they create.

At R/GA, you've always been ahead of the curve—wedding technology and aesthetics. What is your most exciting and challenging venture at this time?

Our most exciting challenges now are creating a bidirectional interactive dialogue between our clients' brands and their customers. The way we create these conversations is very different, depending on the needs of the client. As an example, for IBM we built a highly informational Web system that spanned

one hundred countries and contained a total of 4.5 million pages. Contrast that with our Nike work. Those sites are very experiential, heavy with video and audio. IBM's Web sites are designed to provide information to customers; Nike, on the other hand, wants to inspire their customers.

R/GA has hundreds of employees. How do you keep a rein on the quality of work?

The quality is controlled by the new organizational structure of our agency. We work in collaborative teams made of art directors, copywriters, technologists, user-experience experts, and data experts. Each team sits together and is connected by the Internet, extranets, dev sites, our wiki, wireless devices, and a media asset management system. In a sense, each client team operates like a boutique agency, which fosters innovation. The quality is further monitored by a creative producer and account manager overseeing the project. We're 450-plus people on site and roughly forty boutiques.

When you hire new staff,
what is the prerequisite?
Must they have technical
expertise or creative
know-how? Are these skills
found easily in one person?

You definitely need technical
expertise, but today most designers have a certain amount of that.
The qualities we look for are a
great design portfolio, knowledge
of the design tools and software,
great communication skills, passion, and the willingness to do
things that haven't been done
before. It is also a plus if our
creative hires have the ability to
tell a story.

We've built a great design
team—probably the largest—with
about two hundred designers,
and while they are not easily
found, we're fortunate to have
a client roster and environment
that attract and support the best
creative talent. ▪

Nike Rockstar Workout: ▶
'Hip Hop'

Nike wanted to inspire women around
the world to express themselves
through dance. R/GA worked with
Nike to direct and produce a full-
scale, interactive music video for
Rihanna's single, "SOS." Visitors to the
site can choose to watch the video
uninterrupted, click to learn the dance
moves, or choose to shop the video.
R/GA 2006.

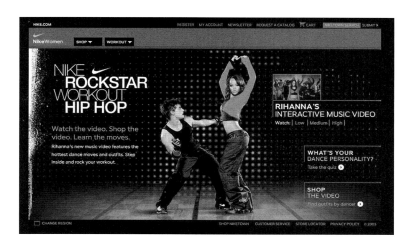

The Good, the Bad, and Technology

An Interview with Clement Mok, principal, Clement Mok, San Francisco

You started as a designer at Apple, leading the way in our digital revolution. What did you take away from that experience that is still valid in your consulting and planning work today?

Perhaps the most important lesson I took away from that experience was about creating and defining standards. Because it's a new medium, the digital medium has its own constraints as well as strengths. The challenge as a designer working in this uncharted territory meant that you have the opportunity as well as the responsibility to define and shape what is and is not best practices. If you are there early enough, you get to create the standards which others are measured by. It's harder to influence and make the kind of impact you want if you are not at the inception stage of a product, a service, or an idea.

Along those lines, how do you feel the field—particularly the technology and creativity rooted in technology—has changed in the past twenty years?

Technology has been and will continue to be a great equalizer—creating good as well as bringing about destructive changes to design, the practice of design, and the design profession. Technology has created many categories and classes of design practitioners. It has enabled designers from all disciplines to collaborate more effectively, as well as enabling them to create some truly hideous disasters. Just because you can does not mean you should!

And where will this lead?

This will lead to better design and a better appreciation of the design solution.

For a long time you were a hands-on designer. Now you are using your accumulated knowledge and experience to consult with companies like Sapient. What shifts in expertise were required to deal with strategies, as opposed (or in addition) to aesthetics?

The ability to decipher and articulate the problems of my client in the language they understand is paramount. Making sure that "we," client, designers, engineers and other stakeholders, agree on solving the same problem is an essential skill to have in this new role. The ability to execute and articulate aesthetic choices is still important, but they are now playing a secondary role.

This means a change in methods, the kinds of deliverables, and collaboration style. Instead of looking at the problem as a project, I am looking at the problem as a system—how each piece depends on another to be effective. The solution has to fit culturally and be economically feasible.

How would you define experience marketing?

Experience marketing is designing, building, and aligning customer experience by harnessing the power of the Internet.

How much is based on design principles versus other business concerns?

It depends on what you consider design principles are. In my world, I am using big "D" design-principles, and it's not a world where one set of concerns is pitted against another. It's about creating a balance where

IBM.com ▶

Design Firm: Studio Archetype, Inc.

Creative Directors: John Grotting, Mark Crumpacker, and Clement Mok

Brand Content Strategists: Judith Hoogenboom, Tom Andrews

Creative Integrator: Donald Chestnut

Art Directors: Bob Skubic, Tom Farrell

Information Architect: Isabell Ancona, Richard Weber

Designers: Philip Kim, Brendan Reynolds

Production: Betsy Gallegher

Programming:
Juan Molinari, Henry Poydar, and a cast of thousands at IBM.

All rights reserved.

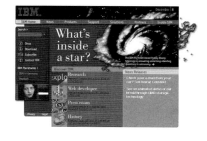

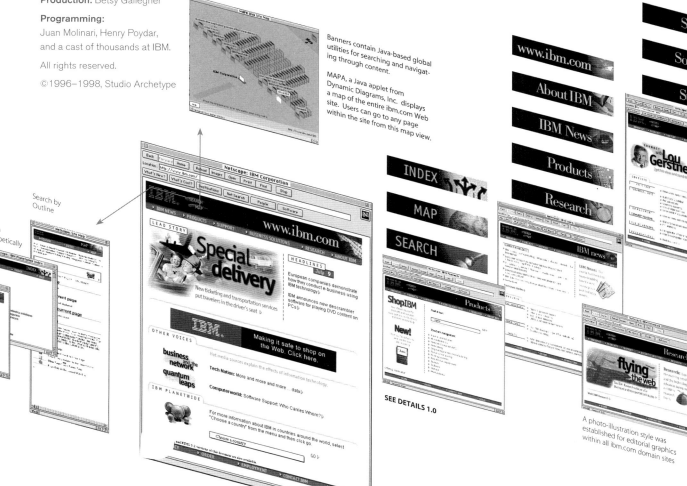

Banners contain Java-based global utilities for searching and navigating through content.

MAPA, a Java applet from Dynamic Diagrams, Inc. displays a map of the entire ibm.com Web site. Users can go to any page within the site from this map view.

Search by Outline

SEE DETAILS 1.0

A photo-illustration style was established for editorial graphics within all ibm.com domain sites

*At this point in time, I do think designers who work with the digital medium
tend to tackle a problem with a users'-need perspective.
The aesthetic component is not the driver.*

social, user, and business concerns are attended to. I am not advocating designing to the lowest common denominator or creating pieces with no soul or point of view. The ability to manufacture and distribute a product effectively is also a problem that requires a design approach.

Would you say that a digital designer starting out needs immersion in how to assess business concerns, or does this come with experience?

At this point in time, I do think designers who work with the digital medium tend to tackle a problem with a users'-need perspective. The aesthetic component is not the driver. It only becomes important when a category is maturing or viewed as a commodity. Technological platforms are constantly changing, with new capabilities looking for applications. Designers will need to assess what kind of technology is being deployed and to what stage of market evolution they are designing for. It's only with this understanding that you are able to make the appropriate calls.

Some critics argue that the Web is becoming a mélange of words and icons, void of design standards. How do you respond to this? Are traditional design concerns still valid today?

The medium is still too young to have design standards. If they don't like what's going on, they need to play and provide meaningful and relevant design solutions. Market forces will eventually define what industry standards are. Traditional design concerns are still valid because there are many things we can learn, borrow, and incorporate into the new medium.

If you were recommending to a client whom to hire to oversee its Web presence, what qualities— and what expertise—would you highlight?

Again this will depend on the kind of business problem the client needs to solve. Here are just a few that are top of mind right now:

1. Does the firm or individual have any experience or knowledge in creating and managing systems?

Will the design scale for future enhancement?
Do they have technological competencies? If not, do they have the ability to collaborate as a team member?

2. The understanding that a Web project is a marketing, business, or technology platform, and not a one-off project.

3. Ability to articulate a process to make decisions.

Do you see your evolution from designing to assessment as a rather typical career arc for today's designer?

I suspect it will be one of many career paths that designers will evolve into as technology democratizes the ability to execute and distribute creative content. The thing that will differentiate a professional and an amateur designer is providing value other than just pure aesthetics. There will still be a place for those who want to practice in the pure aesthetic vein. Unless you are a superstar, your contribution will be marginalized out of ignorance. ■

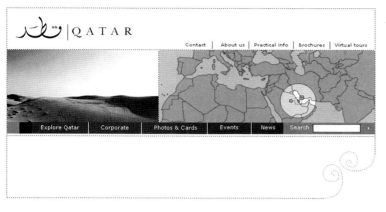

◀ experienceqatar.com

Date: 2004

Client: Ministry of Tourism/Qatar

Designer: Tarek Atrissi

Photographer: Rashed Al Mohannadi

Software: Photoshop, Illustrator, Flash

©Tarek Atrissi Design

Global Outreach

An Interview with Tarek Atrissi, principal of Tarek Atrissi Design, Amsterdam

A decade ago or more it was imperative for a designer to work in the city where his or her clients were located. In the Web world, does this matter? How do you find working with clients all over the globe from your studio in Amsterdam?

I find it actually the best and most efficient way for working—and the Internet became a very easy and convenient way to communicate with clients, particularly for Web-related projects. What makes it very practical is the fact that the end result of any Web-based project will be seen by users on the Web, on their own computer screen, so that is also the best way for the client to view the progress of the project: on his/her own screen. There is no need for glossy printouts or a large projection of the projects.

Is the Web actually a better way of presenting work to clients?

Generally speaking, even for print and identity work, working with distant clients is not an issue anymore. The key is to create your presentations online so that they reflect the process and work, and be able to convince the client with the design work. One can use the Web medium to actually help make the presentations richer and more convincing. Everything is possible now, even short online video footage to start any presentation with.

What are the pitfalls of working like this?

I work with clients over the globe. Only difficulty to deal with is to adjust to different time zones so

that the communication remains smooth. But clients are generally at ease in working with a design studio not closely located, particularly if they initially have learned about your services though the Web. That is positive change in the practice, because on the one hand it opens your business to different markets and cultures. It gives you, on the other hand, the flexibility to continue working even when you travel for business.

You've worked in print. How is working on the Web fundamentally different, both conceptually and aesthetically speaking?

Conceptually, it is a very different approach. In Web, one has to know and understand the medium well to be able to create appropriate

The most important element is to have the information architecture very clear.
As complex as any environment is, users must be able to find their way
quickly and clearly.

ideas and concepts. The technical possibilities are hence very related to the early thinking and conceptual process. Same applies for the visual design. The typographic details are different—legibility and the color usage as well. Web projects appear differently on different screens and different settings, and the visual design must be able to accommodate that. The Web is also highly interactive, and that is probably the main fundamental difference from working in print: You are designing an entire experience and, hence, must take every consideration to communicate best to the user.

You create Web environments for others. What are the most important issues in creating successful interactive experiences?
The most important element is to have the information architecture very clear. As complex as any environment is, users must be able to find their way quickly and clearly. Defining a good structure and usability/navigation is a key step.

Then it is important to think very clearly and ahead of time of the updates and long-term existence of

any interactive/Web-based project. Nowadays, it is almost a must to build a solid content-management system that allows the moderator to easily manage the content without sacrificing the initial design, concept, or interaction design. And, of course, the challenge is to think of all this, have the technical part well developed and still keep room for creativity, fun, and strong, innovative visual design.

In addition to working for clients, you've created sites in an entrepreneurial way—like your Arabic Typography site. What do you do differently for clients as opposed to yourself?
As a "Web design entrepreneur," you have the very clear big picture of a Web design project in all its aspect: You know your goals, your business plan, your target group, your content, your technical abilities, and the appropriate visual graphic and typographic design that you believe would best serve your ambitions. That makes you make faster decisions, and build the online environment quickly and naturally, as a designer allows you to be very free in your visual design approach.

All this makes projects less complex to approach and develop. I think the approach is the same for all projects, but with an own project the fact that you play the double role of the designer and the businessperson allows you to bring the best out of both sides. And this is exactly the case when developing www.arabictypography. com, which made the site quickly achieve its goals. It addressed technical limitations with the Arabic script on the Web—it brought an innovative Arabic design to the Web world and created an online platform and showcase for Arabic type and design.

There seems to be a new piece of software or a novel development in this medium every few months. How do you keep up? And how do you integrate progress into your work?
You can understand clients' and users' expectations when you are yourself active in surfing on the Web and trying any emerging Web-based platform. On the other hand, one has to keep on learning and keeping up with the technology. When educated as a digital designer, it is

arabictypography.com ▶

Date: 2000/2006

Client: Arabictypography.com

Designer: Tarek Atrissi

Calligrapher: Samir Sayegh

Software: Flash

©Tarek Atressi Design

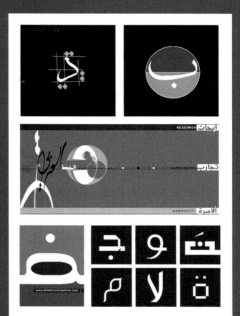

Branding/Digital Design ▶
for the Dutch Muslim TV

Date: 2007

Client: Nederlandse
Islamitische Omroepp

Designer: Tarek Atrissi

Software: After Effects,
Photoshop, Illustrator, Flash

©Tarek Atressi Design

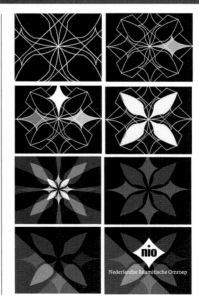

When educated as a digital designer, it is very important that the education teaches you how to teach yourself.

very important that the education teaches you how to teach yourself. I recall in my interactive design education in Holland, the school never provided courses for teaching us the use of software. We had to learn it on our own, and the logic was that the software changes very quickly and we have to have the ability to work with any new software. That applies on the bigger picture on most of the trends, technical issues, and design aspects of Web design.

Speaking of progress, do you feel compelled to work with existing programs, or are you the type that wants to push the envelope with your own discoveries?

You have to be very adventurous and always be willing to push the limits, so I am often looking for new possibilities, and trying to implement any interesting technology or approach I experience in the next project. Because our work in the studio is focused on cross-cultural projects, we often have to work with different languages, and different scripts can often be problematic in complex Web applications. I often find that many programs do not accommodate non-Latin scripts easily, and we often have to develop our own solutions for specific projects—and that is really the spirit any digital designer should have.

What do you feel the technology does not, but should, offer that would make your aesthetic work more satisfying?

Technology is moving rapidly, and many things that a few years back seemed limiting or frustrating are solved now. At this point, my only wish would be if file sizes were not a limit for Web application: I feel a lot of freedom in the design and creative work can be made if I had to worry less about Internet speed and loading time for users. I feel as well that there are some limitations still with small-text typography on-screen.

You work with young people —though you're not so old yourself. What do you look for in an upcoming designer?

I look for a designer who is very multidisciplinary in his/her skills. It is almost a must nowadays to be at ease both with traditional graphic design and Web/interactive design. Solid visual design and visual communication skills and a refined typographic sense are still an ultimate must. But I expect that the designer will have the basic fluent technical knowledge for digital projects, such as working with Flash, basic knowledge of HTML programming, video editing, but also the ability to understand more complex programming in order to communicate it to an advanced technical person—and of course, the ability to learn and explore new techniques. An upcoming digital designer should have a good knowledge of the current trends in the field, and should be able to bring this knowledge as an addition within any project we are working on. ■

The Design Office of the Future

An Interview with Brett Traylor, partner in Thinkso Creative, New York City

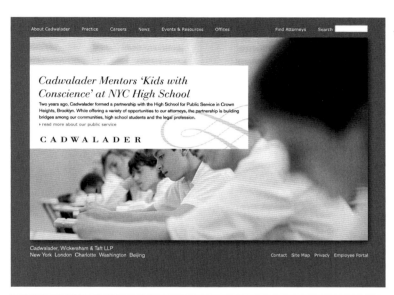

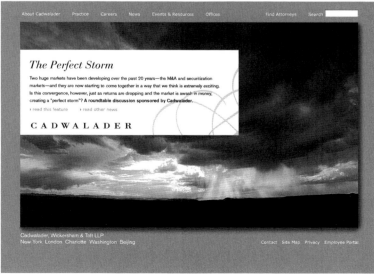

◄ Cadwalader Web Site

Date: July 2006

Client: Cadwalader, Wickersham & Taft LLP

Designers: Brett Traylor and Jedd Flanscha

Software: Adobe Illustrator CS2, Adobe Photoshop CS2

©Thinkso Creative

You are primarily a traditional designer. How much of your work is currently in the digital realm?

We're definitely doing more and more design within the digital realm. It took a while for the mainstream to get completely comfortable with the idea of electronic interaction—be it on the Web, at an airport self-check-in kiosk, or ringing up their own groceries—but these things have now become a way of life. Businesses that got caught up in the Internet boom have also since recovered from the "bust" and now recognize the need to be more purposeful in their approach to the Web.

To answer your question directly, though, of the last five projects to come through the studio, three

At its core, brand identity is about consistently expressing a certain personality—preferably in a seamless way.

have been specifically Web projects and the other two included digital elements as part of the scope. We almost always recommend some sort of electronic component as part of a balanced marketing diet.

Web sites have become major venues for corporate identity. How important is the Web in your strategies?

Webster's added *Google* as a verb to its dictionary this year, so it's no surprise how Web sites have now become the standard corporate calling card. Even the least savvy of our client's customers use the Web as their first resource for researching and interacting with a brand. This is a change in behavior that we as designers and marketers would be fools to ignore. The adaptation of an idea, a campaign, or a brand identity to the Web is always an important consideration for us, especially for clients that don't have a traditional storefront or for those selling intangible goods. In these cases, many times the Web is the venue for their corporate identity.

Do you design (in fact, do you think) differently for the Web compared to print?

When I was a boy I really loved reading the "Choose Your Own Adventure" paperbacks, where, depending on which decision you made, the story would take a different turn and ultimately produce a unique outcome for the character. This is not unlike our approach to designing for the Web. Many of the Web sites we design must address large and diverse audiences, all of whom may need different information at different points along the way. No one can be left out or ignored, and every character must be able to finish their story in an appropriate way. The multitiered ways in which information must be organized, delivered, and consumed by the user is what makes designing for the Web so much different than print.

In your firm of three principals, do you have someone who specializes in digital media? And if so, what competencies do you look for?

One of Thinkso's great strengths is that, in terms of experience, we all come from different creative and marketing backgrounds. My partner Elizabeth is an expert communications strategist and writer. My partner Amanda leads marketing and PR strategies; and as creative director, I look for the big ideas that conceptually and aesthetically tie things together.

So the three of us bring our core competencies to every project, no matter the medium. No single person is necessarily *the* digital media expert. Because we're different people, with distinct interests and points of view, I think our collective take on new trends and best practices is richer and more informed than if we were to rely on one specialist.

Integration is the big word these days. How do you go about integrating media? Must it be seamless, or does each different medium serve a unique function that should be seen as medium-specific?

There's nothing I find more enjoyable than spending the day shoveling media into our brand-new MediaIntegrator 3000. The smell of freshly integrated content, the sound of neatly bundled media packs rolling off the conveyer belt . . . Sorry, you're right, it is quite the buzzword these days. But I'm not so sure that it means all that much. After all,

◀ Promotional microsite developed for Ted, United's low-cost carrier

Date: 2004

Client: United Airlines

Designers: Brett Traylor, David Neswold, JoAnn Leonard, and Tim Rawls

Writer: Brett Traylor

Software: Macromedia Flash

©Thinkso Creative

what's the alternative? Disintegration?

At its core, brand identity is about consistently expressing a certain personality—preferably in a seamless way. But just as a person can behave in different ways at different times, brand personalities should be allowed to as well. If it's justifiable from a strategic standpoint to use a certain initiative as a breakout moment, designers should reserve and exercise the right to do so.

With so many digital media around—from Web to handhelds—do you find that the standards of design are changing? Because of technical limitations, do you lower your aesthetic bar?

In my view, and certainly as it pertains to the work we do in our studio, I don't think that working with digital media requires the lowering of design standards or aesthetics. However, I would agree that perhaps there are different design standards for different design applications. Something that is rendered in smoke by a skywriter will obviously be significantly more limited than something that appears in a beautifully printed catalog, or something seen on a high-definition television.

Within the world of digital media itself there are subsets of these same conditions. Whether they recognize it or not, users understand this as well. They don't expect something to look the same on their cell phone as it does on their flat screen. Designing to meet this expectation means providing the best design solution that the application can support. It's striking the balance between form and function.

Do your clients increasingly want more digital, or is the ratio the same as, say, three years ago?

The clamor for digital and interactive design is directly proportional to our own dependence on the Internet. The more we use it to manage our lives and pursue our passions, the more fluent designers must become in order to satisfy the demand. This fact, combined with a steady refinement of technology and Internet accessibility over the past three years, has easily doubled the amount of digital work I'm doing today. ∎

An Idea Business

An Interview with Marshall Clemens, idiagram, Lincoln, Massachusetts

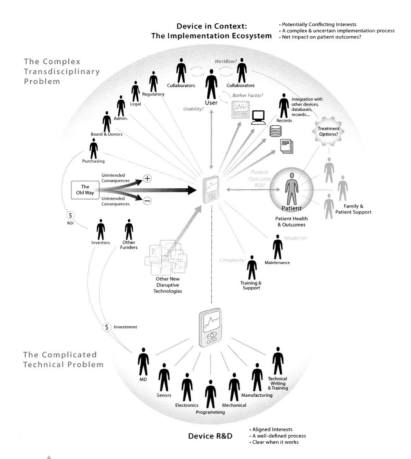

Device in Context:
The Implementation Ecosystem

- Potentially Conflicting Interests
- A complex & uncertain implementation process
- Net impact on patient outcomes?

The Complex Transdisciplinary Problem

Workflow?
Collaborators
Regulatory
Collaborators
Legal
User
Bother Factor?
Admin.
Usability?
Integration with other devices, databases, records...
Board & Donors
Records
Treatment Options?
Purchasing
Unintended Consequences
The Old Way
+
Unintended Consequences
−
Patient Outcome ROI?
Patient
Family & Patient Support
$ ROI
Patient Health & Outcomes
Reliability?
Investors
Other Funders
Complexity?
Maintenance
Other New Disruptive Technologies
Training & Support
$ Investment

The Complicated Technical Problem

MD
Technical Writing & Training
Senors
Manufacturing
Electronics
Mechanical
Programming

Device R&D
- Aligned Interests
- A well-defined process
- Clear when it works

▲

Medical Device Development

Date: 2004

Client: CIMIT—Center for Integration of Medicine and Innovative Technology

Designer: Marshall Clemens

Software: Adobe Illustrator

©Marshall Clemens, 2000–2006

What was your goal in starting your firm, Idiagram?

First, it was an irrational desire—inherited from my father—to be self-employed. I've always been pretty self-directed and autodidactic, so starting my own shop seemed like the natural choice. Second, I had absolutely no education, qualifications, or experience to do what I wanted to do. So there was really no possibility that anyone would hire me. And third, I had this vision of a hybrid discipline, a new application of visual representation, that I didn't see other people doing. So there was nowhere I could go to learn or practice what I had in mind. If I wanted to realize this vague vision I had, it seemed that I would have to figure it out myself.

Has digital media given you abilities to do complex work, well far beyond that of mortal (or conventional) designers?

Absolutely. Despite a being a dedicated doodler for the length of my grade-school career, I have limited hand-drawing skills. If I was confined to pen and brush, if I didn't have the drawing prosthesis that digital tools supply, there is no way I'd have a career in graphic design.

I imagine that digital tools are enabling other people as well, people with good ideas and good graphic sensibilities but who lack artistic skills and/or the patience to acquire them. In regards to complexity, just the basic capabilities of digital media—the infinite editablility, copying/pasting, etc.—make it practical to build the kind of complex visual models we're often called on to create. It might be possible with pen and paper, but the time and frustration of editing/revising would quickly wear down one's patience.

The ability to create libraries of graphic icons, styles, and palettes also permits us to efficiently implement a consistent visual grammar across multiple models. And the ability to layer graphics is also key. It allows one to divide the complexity into manageable slices—keeping the pieces coherently aligned and turning them on and off as needed.

◀ Strong Exploration

Date: 2000

Client: ISCE—Institute for the Study of Coherence and Emergence

Designer/Illustrator: Marshall Clemens

Software: Adobe Illustrator

©Marshall Clemens, 2002—2007

Do you do everything on the computer?

I should note that I do all my initial ideation by hand. Pen and paper are much more immediate—they seem to interfere much less with my thinking process—than keyboard and mouse.

You do something called complexity illustrations that draws from systems science. How do you use these tools, and toward what end?

There's really just one simple trick to my work: It's about drawing out the system of interest—its elements, causal connections, hierarchies, and dynamic behavior. It's taken me ten years of study and practice to get proficient at doing that, but the basic idea is simple.

Part of that proficiency is having the graphics chops; part of it is having a deep understanding of how systems work. Somewhat paradoxically, the more complex the system is that you're trying to illustrate, the more important it is that the graphical elements be as clear and simple as possible. You need to be ruthless about eliminating extraneous bits of visual information. For more simple illustrations, a certain amount stylistic detail is what makes the picture work; for complex illustration superfluous bits of style quickly get overwhelming, obscuring the relationships you're trying to bring out.

In one of your illustrations, you say, "Management is knowing what to apply and when." I've got to ask, are all these complex graphic means of illustrating

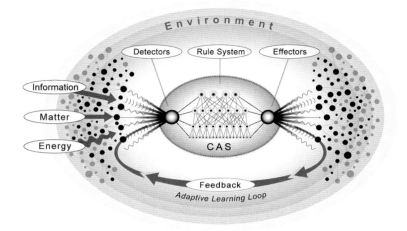

◄ Complex Adaptive Systems

Date: 2000

Client: Macroinnovation Associates

Designer: Marshall Clemens

Software: Adobe Illustrator

©Marshall Clemens, 2002—2007

managerial schema on the level? Some clients make it clear that they will not entertain any critique or suggestions regarding their content. They just want someone to represent their ideas as given, regardless of any helpful insight you might have. All the clients I've encountered honestly believe that their ideas make sense, although I don't always share their opinion. In management theory, there is certainly no shortage of faddish nonsense floating around. But for certain clients—it's usually pretty obvious which ones—"the client is always right."

So, these complexity illustrations are really trying to help clients visualize their underlying concepts?

The process of illustrating their ideas involves helping them make sense instead of nonsense. It's a difficult processes to describe, and a difficult value proposition to sell, but most clients remark that in the process of visualizing their ideas they've actually revised and improved their ideas, and come to a deeper, clearer, better understanding of their content. This intangible clarity and insight gained through the visual modeling process is often as valuable as the illustration itself.

I presume you are well aware of Otto Neurath, the founder of the ISOTYPE sign systems. Do you believe that using icons to guide and tell stories is the most efficient of graphic methods?

Neurath was an important pioneer of information design, but I think his conception of iconic visual language was somewhat limited. More recently, Robert Horn has greatly expanded the idea of visual language, but in my opinion it is still missing some key insights into how we "think with pictures," and what such thinking is useful for. There is a string of cognitive science research, starting with J.J. Gibson's ecological perception and running through Stephen Kosslyn's work on visual perception and Lackoff and Johnson's work on embodied metaphor, that points the way to a more sophisticated and efficient visual language design. Although I'll be the first to admit that I'm still trying to figure out just what exactly it is . . .

Do you consider yourself a designer, an illustrator, information architect, or some other kind of communications hybrid?

Definitely some other kind of hybrid. There are two important ways in which what I'm trying to do—complex conceptual knowledge visualization—diverges from illustration and information design. First, instead of focusing on the visual representation of quantitative information or physical things (e.g., the Tuftian Display of Quantitative Information), I'm after the representation of more abstract conceptual knowledge. Second—this is the complexity part—I'm not interested in just rendering single simple concepts—which good illustrators do much better than I—but in capturing a complex systemic network of concepts. I'm trying to get at the web of knowledge from which to make sense and make decisions.

In my practice, the graphics are just tools to help people solve problems, make decisions, and communicate clearly in complex situations. It's a hybrid discipline that combines graphical know-how with a suite of other knowledge and skills around building accurate systemic models and facilitating group knowledge sharing.

So, it's fundamentally graphic design . . .

Good graphic design skills are important, but without the other stuff—the modeling and facilitation know-how—it's all too easy to create illustrations of nonsense instead of sense-making illustrations.

What skills do you have that are the most invaluable in accomplishing what you do?

Primarily, it's the ability to see systems—to extract the essential ideas and mechanisms that are hiding beneath all the verbiage. It's something that can only be acquired through a certain amount of study and practice. Second, it's the ability to constantly self-correct—to continually question and critique one's own work and the work of one's colleagues. It's important to constantly be asking, "Is this the best, most clear, most accurate, most compelling, most helpful way to represent this?" It can be a bit crazy-making, but good work evolves from this constant questioning and striving for improvement.

What skills do you look for in others who work with you?

Beyond the particular knowledge or technical skills that might be required, I try to work with people who possess a basic intellectual curiosity and humility—people who are interested in getting the right answer, not just their answer. The best people to work with are those who will argue enthusiastically for their point of view and then entertain other opinions and change their mind as soon as a better idea is offered. ∎

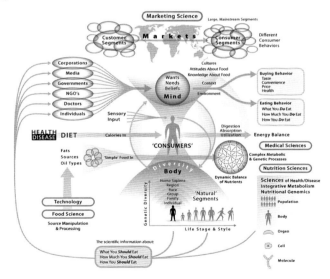

▲ Lipid Nutrition Landscape

Date: 2004

Client: Bunge Limited

Designer: Marshall Clemens

Software: Adobe Illustrator

©Marshall Clemens, 2000–2006

Follow the Money

An Interview with Michael Roberts, client experience executive, JPMorgan Chase, Trasury Services*

Let's talk money. Tell us about what you do.

I work in Treasury Services, which is all about helping companies—small, large, and huge—manage their cash.

So, what's your role?

My title is client experience executive. My group is responsible for the interface design, prototyping, and usability of our Web-based products. I also review any screen or editorial content that will go in front of a client and do what we call *client experience planning*, which involves looking at the interactions clients have with our business—every step of the way—and trying to improve that experience. I oversee many aspects of client communications and am the sponsor of the business's client research programs.

When you're dealing with that volume of money, is it difficult to make changes to the system?

Well, yes. Even minor changes are hugely significant. Nothing can go live unless it's perfect. We have huge test-ing cycles. We do quality-assurance testing—which is basically making sure that what we asked for is what was actually built—and user-acceptance testing and change-readiness management—which is making sure that everything that needs to be done to support the change is in place.

For example, do the call centers know how to explain the change? Does the help copy describe what to do? Does the sales team know about it?

There are tremendous lead times for these projects. We're also starting to do more user testing. My team is now working on things that will go live in nine months, and we're planning changes that will go live two to three years from now. Part of this complexity is due to the scale of the systems. On a big project, there can be hundreds of people involved.

OK. So how do you convince your boss that a change is actually necessary?

Well, you can't just say, "It will look better." We have to quantify every-thing. I've had discussions with very senior executives, even the CEO of the bank, about usability. The way I framed it was this: If products are not usable, they drive up call-center volume. Every call costs us X dollars. Clients keep asking a certain question, and I can show that making a change in the interface would reduce the number of times they call with that question.

It also takes less time to train people to use well-designed products, and less time to train staff to support well-designed products—so that's a savings I can calculate, too. When I sit across from senior executives and say, "We can save X dollars a year if we do Y," they listen.

We don't talk about design. We talk about business. Excellent usability, the quality of the products, and the end-to-end client experience are fundamental to the success of our business. I've trained my team to talk in terms of claims we can substantiate from a top- and bottom-line standpoint.

*The opinions expressed herein do not necessarily reflect those of JPMorgan Chase.

Tell us about your background as a designer.

I have an undergraduate degree in visual communications and graphic design from the University of Delaware, and a master's degree in design planning and management from the Institute of Design at the Illinois Institute of Technology. I got out of grad school and worked at the Doblin Group in Chicago, which did a lot of strategy work. That was a great learning experience. I learned how to help clients really understand what their needs were. Then I worked at the Web-consulting firms Sapient and Scient.

When I started at JPMorgan Chase, I was working on things like the ATM usage and issues such as how you encourage a client base that is largely older to use online banking. When I came to Treasury Services, I got to build a group. Now I'm on the management team of that business.

It doesn't sound like your group does a lot of design now.

Actually, we do a lot of design—*and* a lot of analysis and testing.

What do you look for when you're hiring designers?

My team works with everyone, across the entire project life cycle. So I hire people that are good at relationships, are good at negotiating, and are eager to solve really big problems. Design and usability are new things here, and we need to be able to explain it in ways that our colleagues and partners will understand.

I won't even call someone for an interview unless they have significant experience with large corporate clients. They need to understand the atmosphere and environment and how decisions get made. They need to know what they're getting themselves into—I don't want them to be disappointed when they get here.

I also need them to be well-spoken and credible so that they go head-to-head with other people in the organization. Basically, no *flaky* designers. You have to understand that this is a business, and design, in this setting, is a business function. And you also have to be able to think strategically, and not just about the design but about relationships.

Can you give me an example of this kind of strategy?

Negotiation involves give and take. Right now, for example, we're work-ing on a project that was started be-fore my group was fully in place, and there's some disagreement about whether or not to make certain usability improvements. We have a list of about ten changes that we'd like to make—but changes take time, and the product is supposed to launch soon. So, rather than just digging in our heels and holding up the project, we say, "OK, we want make ten changes, but these two are really important. Make them now; we'll address the others in a later release."

What kind of designer does well in this setting?

The people who do well on my team are very dedicated to dig-ging in and seeing something evolve over several years. We are involved end-to-end. And it's a very rare opportunity to learn how to sit at a table and be taken seriously when making business decisions. I mean, we are determining not just how changes get made, but what changes to make in the first place. We have a seat at the table. And actually, we have very low turnover. The people I hire tend to stay. ■

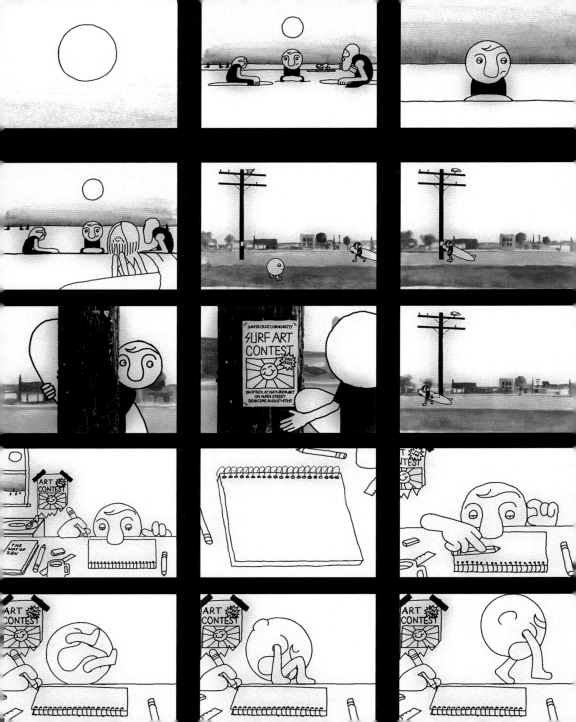

◀ The Sprout Trip

Date: 2005

Directed by: Thomas Campbell

Distributed by: Woodshed Films

Directed and Designed by: Geoff McFetridge

Animation: Geoff McFetridge, Johannes Gamble, Brian Covalt

Music: Mike Andrews

©Geoff McFetridge–Champion Graphics

Personal Business, Personal Journey

An Interview with Geoff McFetridge, proprietor of Champion Graphics, Los Angeles

You've built a practice that transcends traditional graphic design definitions. You work with graphics, print, film, video, and even toys. What inspired you to be so multimediaed?

I feel like the root of it all is that I have always looked pretty critically at the world around me. Anything conventional has always made me uncomfortable.

When I started to learn about making graphics, there was such a thing as commercial artists. My undergraduate program was called visual communications. You had to draw and learn about type, and a lot of felt-pen stuff. By the time I graduated, we had a Mac lab, and they had changed the name of the school to the Alberta College of Art and Design. We were always pushed to choose between being an illustrator or a designer, but the logical choice was neither. It always seemed short-sighted to think that way.

So where did you veer off?

I grew up—from high school until now—making art for skate-boarding and snowboarding. So while instructors around me were telling me to choose, I was just do-ing it. I was drawing and designing stores, doing clothing lines and posters, designing entire lines of snowboards. It became clear to me that the people around me had great knowledge of craft, but were operating from an archaic view of what being a designer was.

Then I went to Cal Arts for graduate school, a place where there was no craft going on, but, rather, an amazing critical and con-ceptual take on design. At Cal Arts they really supported the belief in the designer as author, which seemed radical at the time. My essay to get into Cal Arts talked about applying these ideas to the youth culture world, instead of the high design world.

There is a McFetridge style, but you also defy getting mired in constricting styles. Still, one of the most characteristic traits is a love of decorative elements. How would you define your graphic sensibility?

An analogy: In surfing, longboard-ing in particular, there is a thing called trim; the point on the wave, and on your board, where the wave is propelling you forward, but the board is braking enough to keep you there, so you do not move too forward on the wave and over the shoulder. Invention must be countered by consistency, complexity with simplicity, decora-tion with purpose. That is where the energy that propels forward motion comes from: purposeless reductivism, shape-based poetry, drawing with clichés, minimalist psychedelica, familiar inventive-ness, clichés you have not heard before . . .

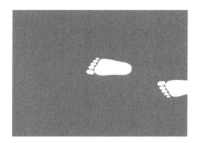 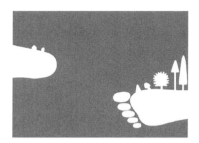 

I also think that the narrow themes that I find throughout my work help to give me some leeway in the styles I am able to work in. Most of the work tries to find a sort of clarity, which in itself is an endless quest. Exploring visual language is endless. Finding simple and universal images and retasking them to talk about familiar ideas, often it seems like an endless game of chess or checkers—you don't add pieces, you just move them around. When all the pieces are gone, its over.

Hopefully when you look at my work it really reveals itself for what it is. That is sort of the point. A lot of the work seems familiar, but new. Some of it looks very simple, and other times it has a labored stream-of-consciousness, sort of doodled feel. I like the work to be clear, not tricky or pretending to be something that it is not. If I was a magician I would do tricks and then immediately reveal how they were done. I want people

to look at the work and say, "I could do that" but then also feel like, "I wish I thought of that!"

How important are the digital media to the form and content of what you do?
It is pretty important to getting everything done, but I more often hide the digital-ness of what I do.

In your mind, do you isolate your animated and filmed work from your print and textile work?
No, I go back and forth. Right now I have a lot of the film and animation work on hold because I was not feeling inspired. Now a year's worth of graphic work I have done is starting to bring about some film and animation ideas.

You speak a lot about personal work for a mass audience. Are you trying to change minds, move mountains, or merely emote feelings?

If you can affect someone in some way, if you make someone cry with a plastic cup, you are changing the way they perceive things. If people were more critical of what was going on around them, I would be happy. We all are prisoners to our perceptions. Personally, I am always trying get to a clearer view of my world. My work is doing the same.

The billboard you produced that looks like the bulletin board in your studio was a wonderful public-space piece. But I wonder, was it art or design? Does it matter?
Can I call it all design, but then call myself an artist? In reality, I call myself a designer. I have always done so, but then call the things I make art. So I "designed" an art piece? So much of what I do plays with delivering art as design. It is back to playing with perception, people's relationship with the thing. We let a lot more design into our house than we

  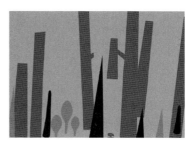

©Geoff McFetridge–Champion Graphics

do art. Our closets are full of it. I did many pieces based on the bulletin board idea. Each piece is part of a collage, and subconsciously we assume that one person has put up all these different pieces. The randomness starts to imply a personality, the "someone" behind it all. In the case of the billboard: a giant.

Quantity. And everything. I couldn't have done anything I have done without it. There were many people doing what I was doing before me, but I was part of the early days of designers to work solely on the computer. I know that the snowboards I did 1989 to 1990 were some of the very first ever to be delivered as digital files. Then when I went on to do motion graphics, I watched the same revolution happen. The benefit of this has been to work and know a lot of the old ways, as well as the new ways, learning from the optical printers and camera operators while everything started to go digital.

Now a lot of opportunity and responsibility have been put up to the designer, so now there is a bit of a scramble as to what to do with it. Maybe we are all authors now, but what are we going to write about? I hear a lot from frustrated designers who want to be self-sufficient, not to have jobs. But they are also finding that the world does not need another T-shirt company.

I believe that these young designers will wrestle design from the greedy hands of corporations. There is no reason for graphic design to be solely a tool of marketing. I think the kids are starting to figure that out. My coup was to work independently in a corporate economy; the next generation will have a completely independent economy of its own.

Think broadly, and when the time is right, work to your strengths. If your strengths are broadly spread, pursue them. If you are going to work in many disciplines, it means you have to be really efficient and focused. I do many different things, but do it in a pretty systematic way. Being multifaceted is only worthwhile if it helps to propel you forward; it is not interesting in itself. Michele Gondry *used* to play in a band, *used* to draw comic books. ■

Keep Loose
Clothing
Away From
Machinery

Safety First

**Do Not
Drink
Gasoline**

✚ **Safety First**

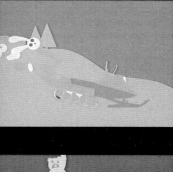

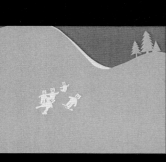

✚ **Safety First**

**Never Ski
With
Scissors**

Inventing Entertainments

An Interview with David Vogler, vice president, creative director, NBC Universal Digital Media, New York City

You began as a print designer. What was the process of becoming digital?

It's a mildly amusing story, so please indulge me. My transformation from print design to interactive design was the result of a happy accident. Years ago, when I was first working at Nickelodeon, I was put in charge of designing products that were "off the air." This included print, consumer products, marketing materials, promotions, etc. At the same time, I was fascinated with the early incarnations of the online medium. Although I was a print art director by day, I was a passionate online geek by night.

Okay, I'm waiting for the amusing part . . .

Tinkering with this new thing called "the Internet" was simply a nerdy hobby of mine. At the risk of dating myself, this was the real early days, when three players dominated the burgeoning online medium: Prodigy, CompuServe, and a scrappy little start-up called America Online. And of course, these offerings weren't really the Internet, but rather crude closed systems using their own proprietary dial-up software.

In early 1994, my parent company, Viacom, had the foresight to dip its big toe into the online waters by deciding to place Nickelodeon, Nick at Nite, MTV, and VH1 onto AOL. The folks who ran Viacom considered the Internet to be unfamiliar territory, and they looked upon "the Web" (and digital design) with skepticism. And they had good reason. It wasn't clear how any big brand could monetize the experience and justify the expense of devoting resources to an unproven medium. Still, the pundits were predicting big things, and the prebubble Internet buzz of the mid-1990s was born.

So, when did the transformation happen, and was it a joyous event in your life?

So here's how I got hoodwinked into changing my discipline from print to digital: One day I was in the MTV Networks cafeteria, and by pure accident bumped into Dan Sullivan, a pal of mine who ran Nickelodeon's magazine group. Dan confided in me that he was recently charged with launching a new division called "Nick Online." (As you all remember, back then the world of magazine publishing was considered the closest business model for "publishing" on the Web. As a result, many entertainment conglomerates were turning to seasoned magazine people to find the answers.)

Dan said he needed a creative director to help him figure it all out. Since he knew I was already passionate about interactive design, I jokingly suggested I could be an asset to him. The very next day, the company's top brass hunted me down and essentially made me an offer I couldn't refuse. They formally asked me to transition from the established world of print products and devote all my time to making digital products.

A year later, working with Dan and a shoestring budget, we launched the Nickelodeon brand into what they used to call cyberspace. (God, that's an embarrassing term when you look back on it.) The punch line here? It's a curious thing when your hobby becomes your full-time job! So thanks to Dan and pure serendipity, I've been digital ever since. I'm still not sure if I should be thanking him or cursing him.

Much of what you do is create products and environments for entertainment. How do you go about conceiving a viable digital idea?

As with any good consumer product, you start with the consumer. I'd say that the genesis for the ideas I've been creating online is pretty darn similar to what I'd do with any traditional medium. By knowing your audience and what they're hungry for, you can best serve their needs. I think putting the consumer first is not only good for design, but good for business—regardless of the medium.

Naturally, the sorts of experiences we create are tied to the intrinsically unique properties of the Web. The best solutions are not just repurposing entertainment or design from other mediums, but rather leveraging all the qualities of multiuser

▲ Nick.com

Date: 2001

Client: Nickelodeon Online

Designers: David Vogler, Michael Redding, Jason Arena

Software: Adobe Photoshop, Illustrator, Flash

In a world of infinite content created by both pros and amateurs, the great differentiator is quality. The destinations with the best content design and execution will be the ones that win.

and participatory communication. Unlike print, which is fundamentally a monologue, digital design is more of a dialog. It's not a one-way visual conversation of the designer communicating a message to the reader. It's orchestrating the means for multiple users and multiple voices to interact with each other. Creative concepts built on this foundation are usually the ones that resonate best with the end user. They're not only more viable, but heck, they're just plain more fun!

In addition to conceptual concerns, what must you know about your medium to make your ideas come alive?

At NBC-Universal, the yardstick we use to judge this is known as "The Three Cs." The leader of our division, Beth Comstock, described this in her recent keynote address at the annual Television Bureau of Advertising. It's safe to say, in the digital age, it's all about context, community, and content. Allow me to paraphrase this.

Successful design solutions depend on the context of the experience. The interface and digital products you'd design for accessing entertainment in the living room are naturally going to be different from what you see on an iPod. I doubt there's many folks who'd curl up on the sofa and have friends over to watch the Super Bowl on a two-inch cell phone. But as a commuter taking the MetroNorth train into Manhattan each day, I can honestly tell you that the same two-inch screen is perfect to watch news bits and short segments. So in the right context, the design solution fills a niche.

Where does community come into play?

Possibly the most inherent aspect is the power of community. Depending on who you talk to, you'll get a different definition of this. For some users, community is best exemplified by the experiences you have on sites like MySpace.com.

For others, it's things like chat rooms, instant messaging, peer-to-

peer file sharing, or basic bulletin boards. The common bond here is that community is all about gathering people with shared interests and giving them a place to interact with each other. A printed page can't do that. I'd say that any creative concept that harnesses the power of community is a perfect fit for the digital medium. And this applies to all competencies, whether you're on the content side or the advertising side or something in between.

For example, here's a cool marketing idea my former Modem Media colleagues Tom Beeby and Mark Galley cooked up for Heineken a few years back. It was a stunt called "The Heineken Hoax." In a nutshell, the idea was to enable users to pull pranks on friends by giving them the tools to create a faux Web site filled with customized gag headlines. It was an experience that could only be deployed on the Web and really leveraged the community's viral qualities. I won't explain it all here, but trust me on this one, it's pretty friggin' funny. Put this book down right now and do a Google search on "Heineken headlines." Go ahead. Send a hoax and scam a friend today!

And the third "C?"

Lastly, the third "C" is, of course, content. In a world of infinite content created by both pros and amateurs, the great differentiator is quality. The destinations with the best content design and execution will be the ones that win.

So, the notion of the "Three Cs" is devilishly simple, but often overlooked. I believe using it as your guide when inventing creative concepts is a solid approach and is relevant to all digital designers.

You've worked with Nickelodeon, Disney, and other entertainment concerns, and you were around from the beginning of the digital revolution. What has changed over the years?

I've had the opportunity to work with some of the biggest brands and the most popular content franchises. Most all of them have been born into television families, and they faced the same awkward challenge of developing from a linear medium into a nonlinear, interactive one. But the basic building blocks of good

▲ AOL Video Interface System

Date: January 2006

Client: America Online

Designers: Brent Pruner, Paulo Melchiori, David Vogler

Information Architecture: Terence Nelan, Curt Knox

Software: Adobe Creative Suite

storytelling are timeless, and that stayed consistent. Good content is good content.

The biggest instigator of change is obviously the advancement of two things: technology and bandwidth. In the beginning of the digital revolution, our experiences were always dictated by the limits of speed and resolution. The limitations of the user's viewing environment often snuck into the creative process and killed a lot of beauty.

The way designers optimized their work for a 28.8 baud world was

incredibly neutered. The lack of speed certainly affected the way we practiced our craft. There were a lot of big ideas, but the technological infrastructure just wasn't there to support the creativity. We all knew the promise of true "interactive television" would arrive only when the masses had fat pipes into their homes.

That day is almost here. A DVD that you can download today in an hour would have taken almost three years in 1985! In the next decade, that same volume of data will take just five minutes. Right now, about 60 percent of the country has broadband access, and it's growing every quarter. The faster the bandwidth, the richer the experience. These advancements will naturally change the way digital designers problem-solve.

What is the most challenging product you've developed for NBC-Universal, and why?

As we speak, NBC-Universal is in negotiations to acquire iVillage, the successful and wildly popular Web site for women. Once that deal is complete, we'll all join forces to supercharge the site and integrate some of NBC's best brands into the iVillage experience. I'm sure the integration process will be a challenging project but also an incredibly rewarding one, as well. It's an exciting time for the authors and designers of content in the Internet's history.

Celebrity Rants ▶

Date: 2005

Client: Questrel Inc.

Designers: David Vogler, Mark Pagano

Writer: David Vogler

Audio and F/X Editing: David Vogler

Technology: Art Holland, Chris Cole

Programs: Flash

Would you ever go back to print?

I don't feel like I ever left. Despite all my rambling about interactivity and my pontificating about digital design nonsense, I still work off-line occasionally. I love print—specifically, magazine and book design—and it's where I got my start after graduating from Pratt Institute.

What do you look for when you hire digital personnel?

First and foremost, a sense of humor, flexibility, and curiosity. Anyone devoting him or herself to design in the fragmented, volatile world of the Internet has to be open-minded enough to break the rules and try new things. I certainly can't predict the future. And over the years, I've found that folks in this industry who claim to know the answers usually haven't a clue. I think there's some sort of nutty Zen proverb that says, "The wise man knows that he knows nothing." Well, that's probably true for anyone working in the Internet business. A great digital designer should embrace the future, but also honor the past. ■

VERY SHORT LIST ▶

Date: Fall 2006

Client: VERY SHORT LIST

Art Directors: Emily Oberman,
Bonnie Siegler,

Designers: Holly Gressley, Chelsea
Cardinal, Alison Matheny

Programs: Adobe Creative Suite

©2007 Number 17

CASE STUDY:

Very Short List

Bonnie Siegler, partner in Very Short List and Number 17, New York City

From designing print and TV graphics, you've moved into Web design—but not just design, developing content. How does this differ from your other design work?

Very Short List is different from other projects we work on because we were part of its invention. That said, we believe that part of doing our job as graphic designers involves bringing content, in varying degrees, to the project, whatever it may be. On Web site design, we have found that contribution tends to be even greater because, in some ways, on Web sites, graphic designers are the equivalent of the movie director. We determine the mood, tell the viewer where to look and what to pay attention to, and, through the site map, dictate the story.

For the entrepreneurs reading this book, why did you decide to do this service? Did you feel a void that needed to be filled, or was there another motivation?

We really believed in the idea because we are definitely the audience for this service. We craved something like this. And it's always an extra special treat to design for yourself and your peers.

How did you become a partner in Very Short List to begin with?

A friend had an idea for a new business, which we helped develop, and then that eventually became Very Short List.

There is always a lot to communicate, and never enough space.
And this is especially true on the Web. You just have to pay extra special
attention to having room to breathe on every page.

And was it because you are a designer, or because you are a content provider?
Both. All of the five partners bring something unique to the project.

What exactly does it mean to be a partner in a Web venture? How much control do you retain? How much more profit do you accrue?
We partnered with Barry Diller's InterActive Corporation (IAC) to help bring this project to life. We retain a great deal of control as the creators. It is way too early for us to know how much profit, if any, there will be.

From a technical standpoint, what do you need to know that you didn't know as both a print and motion designer?
We have designed Web sites before, but creating a Web business is a whole other ball game. We don't need to know the technical side of programming, but we do need to know enough to ask the right questions and make good decisions.

Do you experience a different kind of design? By that I mean you have a certain style of typography and image preference. In the Web world, do these things change?
Not really. There are different restrictions and different possibilities, but our sensibility remains the same.

Many people complain that Web design, with all its layers of information and typography, is pretty ugly. How do you avoid clutter and ugliness in a site that must carry so much information?
This is the big challenge in designing anything, really. There is always a lot to communicate, and never enough space. And this is especially true on the Web. You just have to pay extra special attention to having room to breathe, on every page.

Do you have to test your design with focus groups to determine what's working and what's not?
Sometimes we do, but we didn't do that with Very Short List. Once we got to the place where all the partners loved it, we just went with it.

In gearing up for a Web business, do you look for additional skills or talents in the people you hire? If so, what?
We always look for people who have good ideas and can communicate them in a beautiful and original way. If they can do that in one medium, they can do it in another.

If this site becomes successful, will the Web be your new frontier?
We have really enjoyed the work we have done so far on the Web. Since TV and the Web will be together on your desktop in about a minute, we really think of our move to the Web as more of a dissolve. ■

VERY SHORT LIST

OCTOBER 4, 2006

This fall's best new singer-songwriter
(watch his music video)

MUSIC VIDEO: Chris Garneau's "Relief"

Starting early next month, when Chris Garneau performs at the CMJ Music Marathon in New York — the cool-music record industry convention where artists ranging from R.E.M. to Eminem got some of their earliest exposure — watch for a ripple effect: As usual, music journalists will be descending on the conference looking to anoint the best new talents, and Garneau will be one of them.

Actually, he already has serious momentum: He's signed with an A-list indie label called Kosher Records, where his poignant, spare, orchestral songs about love and loss fit right in. His patron and producer is hot-again performer and composer Duncan Sheik. And Garneau's delicate crooning connects nicely with the ongoing male singer-songwriter Renaissance that began in the '90s with Jeff Buckley and Elliott Smith and is currently embodied by chamber-pop star Sufjan Stevens — i.e., sensitive boys not afraid of sounding real pretty.

But most helpfully, Garneau's first single, "Relief," teetering on the edge of melancholy and hopefulness ("I love the way you dance / We can work it all out"), has an equally lovely music video.

▶ VIEW the music video for Chris Garneau's "Relief," directed by Dori Oskowitz and Daniel Stessen // alternate link HERE

▶ LISTEN to four songs, as free streaming audio, from Garneau's upcoming debut CD, *Music for Tourists*. (Absolutely Kosher Records, employing the sort of pent-up-demand limited-edition marketing approach that's worked so well lately for the likes of TV On the Radio, is doing a limited release later this month of Garneau's Music exclusively through its website, absolutelykosher.com. National retail and digital release is set for January.)

▶ MORE VSL 'Music' picks

Blogs

Want to know what it's like to be a designer at Google? Check out Kevin Fox's blog, Fury, and find out about the trends in search as well as his thoughts on Yahoo! What about working at the *New York Times*? Digital design director Khoi Vinh holds court on his blog, Subtraction. Because most blogs are written from a first-person perspective, they offer the opportunity not only to learn about issues in the industry, but also to see the world through the eyes of an expert. What are game designers interested in? What irritates an animator?

The folks behind Core77 were industrial design students who decided that they needed an online forum where like minds could gather, debate, and share resources. They started Core77 in 1995 right out of school and have succeeded in building one of the leading design Web sites from the ground up. They had no funding beyond a small grant from the university, but they did have enthusiasm. Over time, what at first seemed like an obstacle—the fact that they didn't have the backing of an organization or company—has turned out to be a benefit. They've been able to develop a unique and independent voice while still managing to make a living.

If you're considering starting a blog of your own, be warned: Doing it well takes up far more time than you might think. But blogging does have its benefits, both intellectual and financial. Not only does starting your own blog give you a chance to flex your design muscles, but it also provides you the space to capture your thoughts and forces you to articulate them clearly. Being able to write convincingly is probably the second-most-important skill a digital designer needs to succeed. Clients who don't know how to evaluate your talent as a designer will be able to appreciate your writing skills. Blogs also give potential employers and clients a way to get some insight into your personality and interests and to get comfortable. Keep in mind that blogs are public documents, so you may want to find another outlet for your treatise on midget bowling.

Before you start your own blog, you should consider contributing to others. Posting comments is an easy way to start, but many prestigious blogs such as Core77 also accept article submissions. If you have an idea or perspective that you think others might be interested in, write it up. Because blog budgets are tiny or nonexistent, they are always looking for free content. ■

Designing Podcasts

Since the introduction of the iPod—that sublime instrument of media communication that has revolutionized how we receive sound and picture—every media establishment, cultural institution, and business has offered podcasts. In fact, these ersatz radio and television shows are so popular that they've become regular information and entertainment fare for hundreds of thousands of people who simply download their favorite shows and listen to or watch them on their way to school or work.

At this formative stage, designers are increasingly becoming involved in the production of podcasts—not simply in a purely visual capacity (i.e., designing titles or graphics for video applications), but as content providers (i.e., scripting, directing, and even announcing). The range of podcast themes is vast, and many are about design.

It is, therefore, incumbent on the designer to understand, if not also be proficient in, the overall production of podcasts. Although it has not yet become a specific genre of digital design, it is a component of Web creation, and is associated with broader motion and even magazine design. As traditional print media integrates with new media, the podcast (at least for the foreseeable future) will be used to supplement the current diet of streaming media.

How does a designer become podcast savvy? Although there are a few technical courses that impart the fundamentals, most skills are acquired by doing. Trial and error is the road to proficiency. The basic podcast is as simple as recording a voice on a digital recorder; more ambitiously designed versions require typographic and other animations. The methods for doing this are the same as any motion design process. To make a podcast ready for broadcast, however, certain compression software is necessary. But once the basic technologies are mastered, the podcast is a tabula rasa, as complex or not as the designer wants to make it.

Crap Detector

An Interview with Kate Bingaman-Burt, assistant professor of graphic design, Mississippi State University

You are a twenty-nine-year-old assistant professor of graphic design at Mississippi State University. How and why did you become a designer?
I thought I wanted to be a journalist until someone told me that they liked my hand lettering and hired me to do a packaging project when I was twenty. My English major was finished, so I thought I would pick up a Graphic design major as well. I realized halfway into my Graphic Design One class that this was the field for me.

It was like journalism in that I was communicating and able to investigate a variety of topics, but I liked having a variety of tools at my disposal to achieve that, rather than just Microsoft Word.

You were born into the digital world. But what inspired you to turn to blogging as both expression and teaching tool?
I started my Web site Obsessive Consumption in 2002, and I didn't even realize I was blogging when I wrote about my daily purchases. Toward the end of my twenty-eighth month of purchase documentation, the term blogging was being used more, and that was when I realized that I was doing it. When I started teaching in 2004, it was obvious that this was the way that I should communicate with my students.

Your primary blog is Obsessive Consumption. The term is self-evident, but not the motivation. What triggered this site?
The site happened in stages. The first stage was triggered by wanting to know the history of objects, why people buy what they buy, how they interact with their personal belongings, and just the general emotions that go along with personal consumption. I decided to document my personal consumption for twenty-eight months and create work about consuming.

The second stage involved exploring debt and the shame that goes along with overspending, along with exploring the mundane aspects of spending. This is when I started drawing all of my credit card statements.

The third stage is really when I made the conscious decision to blog. I wanted my site to have more dynamic content rather than just being a portfolio site that acted as a static monument. So with this last redesign, I continued to draw my credit card statements and continued to make work about personal consumerism, but I also started drawing something that I purchased every single day and blogged about it.

I am happing about the melding of a portfolio site and one that is dynamically driven. This version feels the best to me, but I am excited to see what version four holds.

Blogging is communication, and design is communication. It is just another way to dispense information effectively.

As a designer, you are well aware of the limitations of the Web for, let's call it, good design in the traditional sense. How do you (or do you?) overcome the handicaps to make a Web product as good as a print one?

One of my pet peeves is looking at a site that functions like a printed brochure. Static content does not belong on the Internet anymore. Walled gardens are no longer relevant. Print can evoke emotions that are not possible online, but a dynamic Web site can evolve with you.

I expect different things from each one. I realize that a Web site can't be a tangible object. When I approach my sites I make sure that they achieve something print can't. Good sites evolve with the viewer. They convey emotion; they interact with the audience, more so than a printed piece.

You use a lot of hand drawing and collages on your lively site. What are you saying through this style or manner?

I am insistent that I make all Obsessive Consumption products myself. I screen-print the T-shirts, I sew the dollar-sign dolls, I make the buttons, I stitch the samplers, and I draw the credit card statements and daily purchase drawings with my trusty Pilot v5™ black ink pen. The drawings are shaky and scrawled. In no way could any of my products be mistaken as being created by a machine and mass-produced.

In your view, is blogging related to design? If not, what is it, beyond a pleasant distraction?

Blogging is communication, and design is communication. It is just another way to dispense information effectively. That may be an overly simplistic way to look at it, but yes, I believe it is related to design. There is good, effective design and bad, ineffective design. There are good, effective blogs and bad, ineffective blogs.

You have also started a student blog called Crap Detector. What does this add to the students' experience?

I have used blogs since I started teaching in 2004. Crap Detector is what happened when I combined all of my classes into one big, bad blog. I decided to combine the blogs when I realized that students from my ad class were checking the type class blog, and the kids from type class were checking the graphic design blog. My primary audience is my students, but I love it that people outside of the design department at Mississippi State are enjoying it as well. My students like it that they have a place where they can find all of their assignments, due dates, and many relevant links to their specific assignments.

You teach Graphic Design One, Typography One, and Advertising One—all introductory courses—how much digital media do you inject into the neophyte student's entry to design?

I emphasize the importance of hand skills and critical-thinking skills over technical skills. We do several projects that continue to develop their hand skills, but computer usability (especially how to use the Internet effectively for research) is a large part of their critical development as designers.

A lot of students are really intimidated by the computer, especially girls, and I try to take away the mystique of it by telling them that it is okay to push that button or to click all over the place in a program. To just explore. I remember being very overwhelmed by the computer when I first started. It is a scary machine at first for some people. I also let them know that it is way more difficult to come up with excellent concepts than it is to run a computer. They can always read a manual to learn a program. You can't read a manual to find an original idea.

Would you recommend that students jump right into the digital world, or build out from traditional media?

A combination of both. I find that the two are becoming pretty seamless. I don't really believe that there are too many divisions anymore. Students are very tech savvy, but they also should value the importance of traditional skills. Sometimes I am surprised at their interest in tradition; sometimes I am concerned by their lack of interest. I have my students approach an assignment on paper first, flesh out the idea, and then move to the computer and use it as a tool to actualize their concept. I don't like for students to use technology as a crutch. ∎

crapdetector.com ▶
Date: 2006
Client: crapdetector.com
Designer: Kate Bingaman-Burt
Program: Typepad

From Blog to Business (or Vice Versa)

An interview with Jim Coudal, principal of Coudal Partners, Chicago

Your Web site/Weblog is one of the most respected in the design field. How and why did you choose this method as a means of promoting yourself?

To be honest, when we started coudal.com in 1999, we did it in order to have a sandbox in which we could play with tools and technologies and an assortment of oddball ideas about Web design and publishing. One thing led to another, and it has grown in many ways, but that's still what we're doing today. Just a lot more people are watching.

As far as using it as a promotional tool for our design consultancy, it works pretty well. We get lots of inquiries from the site every month. We have a beautiful portfolio of work and we're happy to show it to prospective clients, but that's not what our site is about.

As somebody here said once, "If you're chatting up a girl in a bar, the first thing you don't talk about is all the other girls you've dated." The site gives an honest look at who we are as people, what we're passionate about, how we work. If someone gets that from the site, more often than not we have the basis for a relationship. If they don't get it at all, we're probably not going to go home with them.

How much of your current work is digital (and particularly Web-based) versus traditional? Do you foresee traditional being nudged out?

It's about half and half now. We love the practical crafts of print and traditional design, and we love the practical crafts of Web and interactive design. Each feeds the other, and we make a fair amount of films, too. The more stuff we learn, the better off we are.

Are the films a result of your digital expertise, or did you have to learn the language of film?

A bit of each. We've produced dozens of television commercials and long-format industrial films for clients over the years so, like adapting traditional print skills to the Web, we were well positioned to use crafts developed on work-for-hire jobs to the new medium. We tend to choose projects that fit our interests and the skills of our staff at the time. Currently our main writer, Steve Delahoyde, also happens to be an accomplished filmmaker and editor, so we tend to think in terms of film and video more when we're looking for solutions.

Did you come to design practice with any predigested methods, mannerisms, or -ologies, and if so, how has working in the digital realm changed your attitudes toward design?

Our basic approach to any assignment, whether it's naming a restaurant chain or editing a film or designing a site or an identity, is pretty consistent. We get together and talk and argue, then we go mess around individually, then we get back together and throw things away until we're done.

We're about getting rid of things that keep us from seeing the essence of something else. Susan Everett (our design director) and I don't always agree on details, but we always agree on that.

What is the attribute or value you hold most dear concerning design in the digital realm (i.e., simplicity or complexity)?

Human conversation is key. We believe that everyone can learn a lesson about communication simply by understanding the ways in which regular people speak to each other. That, and trying to avoid the flavor of the month and empty marketing-speak.

Do you feel you have a distinctive style? And is style important today?

I'm not sure if it's important, but we tend toward orthodox grid-based systems in layout, simple geometric forms in design, the classicvs in typography, and shorter sentences and active voice in our writing.

You employ a number of people. What are the key positions, and what do you look for?

Quite frankly, it seems like the only way to get a job here is to start of as an intern or work freelance with us first. We jealously guard the easygoing, collaborative culture of the studio, and it takes us forever to decide on someone new. If you're working with us already, it's easier for us to decide if we love you.

Is design talent more important than technological skill?

It goes without saying that an understanding of the basic craft of design is essential: typography, layout, process, writing clean code, etc. You wouldn't hire a cabinet-maker who couldn't drive a nail. We're constantly surprised by the lack of these skills in the work we see from students and prospective employees. A poorly kerned headline is the end.

That being said, we're not too interested in technical skill, or even talent. What we look for above all else is taste. What someone loves is as important as what they do. Someone who can make a subjective judgment about the relative merits of two things and defend it intelligently is someone we'd be interested in.

Also, we have another simple rule. If two people are equally qualified for a position in every way except that one of them can write, we'll hire her every time. Clear, conversational writing is the sign of an organized mind, and is a vastly underrated skill in the design world.

▲ www.coudal.com
©Coudal Partners, Inc.

What do you believe neophytes should know most when coming to sell themselves to you? Should they specialize or generalize?

Restraint is a designer's greatest tool. Show me a small amount of great, refined work rather than a basketfull of good work. Take some time to get to know what we do before you tell us you'd like to do it, too. Send us something unusual and, for God's sake, spell our names correctly in the cover letter. ■

The Blog as Worldview

An interview with Nick Currie (Momus) musician, performer, blogger, London

You are a musician, performer, writer, and Webmaster: Would you also describe yourself as a designer?

No. But I have always been interested in design. I've recognized in it a culture rather than a practice. I think my mother was a big influence on me, and she was interested in design as a class signifier, a mark of bourgeois respectability.

Do you consider music a form of design—indeed, graphic design?

Not really. But I've noticed that there is almost a genre of music you could see as a branch of graphic design. I suppose electronics of a certain type qualifies: music, which seems to be about style rather than substance, to celebrate surface for its own sake. Often, the people who make this kind of music are very attuned to graphic design, have great sleeves,

and treat what they do very much like designers.

These days, being defined as a designer or a musician can be a matter of choosing between one program on a laptop and another. I'm not convinced there's a great vocational difference between loading up Ableton Live and loading up Illustrator. And of course there's sound design—all the plug-ins and filters you can run a sound through. But in the end I think music is more soulful, somehow.

I think the context, the social meaning of music, is very different from the context of design. Music always connects us to the sacred, or the taboo. Design tends to be more complicit, more practical. It's a relatively new discipline, an offshoot of industrialization. And the career structures of the two disciplines are different: Music tends to be something you do for yourself, following

inner impulses toward self-expression. Design tends to be something you do for a client, addressing a specific problem, and suppressing self. There may be convergence, but I think these distinctions will remain.

How do you interact with digital media?

I tend to do everything via the blog Click Opera these days (imomus. livejournal.com). That, too, has some design input from me, but basically works within the LiveJournal shell. With the Web site, I took more care with the look of the thing. In the nineties, I changed it all the time, experimenting with radical skins, flashing graphics, huge drawings.

Basically, though, the HTML was very simple, just text and graphics. I do things very much by eye. I think I'm quite a good intuitive designer and photographer. I have a recognizable aesthetic, but I lack preci-

imomus.livejournal.com ▶

Date: 2002—2006

Design: Momus

Software: Photoshop and
Microsoft Word

sion, knowledge, and discipline. The look I favor is one using hot colors (orange, pink, red). There might be a certain communist or third-world look to it. It combines puritan restraint with a certain flamboyance and sensuality. There are postmodern jokes, but basically it's rather sincere. There's an interest in beauty, although cheapness is not absent.

How much of your creative life is invested and involved in the digital environment?
Well, I'm currently appearing in the Whitney Biennial as an unreliable tour guide, so I'm telling stories in the real world, to real people, through a bullhorn. (Is a bullhorn electric or electronic? I guess electric.) If I'm recording music, I'm in the digital world, but that hasn't always been the case. That, too, went from electric to electronic, although

it was always a mixture of the two during my lifetime.

Blogging is obviously digital. In the end, I don't really pay much attention to the technologies of creation or dissemination. It's all storytelling, as far as I'm concerned. Making stuff up.

If technology can allow us to do anything anywhere, what is the value of being from someplace?
That's a central question for me. It gets widened to the question of necessity versus will, or restraint versus self-construction, or universality versus flavor, or the global versus the local. Is it better to make a human (or a computer character, or a synthesizer, for that matter) rounded, or to leave him flat? Do I want my synth to sound like anything in the world, or like a synth? Well, the simple answer is, "I want my synth to sound like anything, including a synth."

And the parallel in terms of global/local would be I want to be glocal: I want to come from somewhere, but be able to visit everywhere. But we have to ask ourselves whether this is possible.

Flavor is not just about coming from somewhere; it's about staying there. It's very difficult to have freedom and also have flavor. People often doubt that I'm a Scot, and I doubt it myself. Being hybrid is great, sure, but in terms of flavor, it's a bit like being a cocktail. There's a confusion, a muddiness about it.

Do you believe, as you seem to be practicing, that traditional boundaries of design and designer have changed?
I'm in favor of hard and fast boundaries coming down, especially when that's because thematic issues predominate. For instance, last night I attended a reading and

*. . . I feel that no thinking is as good as the thinking you do when no one's paying
you to think. It's that freewheeling which makes the paid work
worth paying for.*

talk by Vito Acconci at a bookstore in Williamsburg. Now, Vito has had an amazing career. He started as a poet, then became a performance artist, then an architect. And yet there's an incredible consistency in what he's done in these disparate areas. His buildings are semantic, textual fictions. His performances and installations in galleries involved both poetry and architecture. And always this theme of blurring the boundary between the private and the public is apparent.

I love it when a personal obsession like that can become the motivation for original work in several different disciplines. I'm all in favor of amateurism, especially when the "love" part of that word comes to the fore. And yes, computers are permitting this renaissance making you talk about, but I'd add that by computers we can also mean all sorts of self-consciously noncomputer or postcomputer activities. The digitization of everything creates an interest in those materials, forms, and activities that don't lend themselves to easy digitization. If

the renaissance is partly based on everyone converging toward the computer, it's also based on some people diverging away from it, too.

Is there something you lack as an artist that you wish you had learned—or feel you must learn now to stay current?

I employ designers (like James Goggin or Florian Perret) to do my record sleeves, although I could cook up some sort of sleeve myself, and have done on occasion. But I employ them because they have skills and sensibilities that go way beyond mine. I employ them precisely because they aren't amateurs! My consciousness of my own lacks and failings as a designer is what leads me to call in professional designers. They keep me current. I tend to work with people who find my ideas stimulating to their work, though. So it's a two-way process. It's worth saying that dabbling and amateurism give one just enough understanding of a field to realize how great some of the pros are at what they do!

Where do you see yourself headed in the digital realm?

I just hope the Internet remains as open, cheap, and accessible as it currently is. I don't want it to centralize, professionalize, turn into television, go two-speed. I want to see more people on there, from more countries. I'd like to see Web translation improve (although I also like its current inadequacy—a lot of my lyrics come from bad Web translations these days).

As for me, well, my blogging has led to a column in *Wired*, but I'm being careful not to let my paid gigs eclipse the pleasure I get every morning just waking up and wondering, "What will I write about today?" I think that problem-finding activity is very important, and I feel that no thinking is as good as the thinking you do when no one's paying you to think. It's that freewheeling which makes the paid work worth paying for. That's the laboratory, the R&D. So my plan is to keep spending a few hours in the lab every morning! ■

Core 77

Stuart Constantine, cofounder of Core 77, New York City

Core77 has attracted a fanatical following among young designers. To what do you attribute the feeling of goodwill that seems to be at the core of Core77?

Core77 started out as, and still very much remains, a labor of love. Everyone involved in the operation has a keen interest in design, the Internet, communities, events, and supporting design and design discourse. The site reflects our own genuine points of view, and this resonates with the audience; people can tell when you're faking it. We also have a pretty broad definition of what we feel is pertinent and important to designers, and our readers appreciate that. It often makes it more difficult to work with sponsors and advertisers, as they tend to want overt connections between their products and the editorial side, but I suppose this is nothing new.

What was it like to start Core77? How long did it take before you could actually afford to work on the site full-time? When did you realize that this thing might actually have legs?

For the first ten years of our existence, we did design work for clients as the primary source of revenue for the company; 2006 was the first year that we stopped all client work and devoted all our time and energies to the Web sites. Turns out that client work is a much easier way to earn a living! But we do love what we do. In fact, in the office we remind ourselves that we're some of the few people we know who don't hate their jobs.

With other forms of design, digital technology has brought the cost of tools and production way down and allowed young designers to set up on their own. Is this also true of industrial design? Or is ID still ruled by the big shops that can afford the fancy equipment?

This is definitely true for ID. It's not just digital technology, but also communications and transportation play a role, too. It's globalization. Many small shops can now do their 3D work on standard desktop machines, and have prototypes manufactured in China and shipped via FedEx. The exposure that the Internet provides lets new designers get more publicity and awareness faster and less expensively than ever before.

It seems to me that, with devices like the iPhone, form and interface are being increasingly inseparable. Right? So, what does this mean for the future?

We had an event last year titled "Products and Their Ecosystems" on just this topic. On the surface, this means that every object will become more powerful and sophisticated. (The Internet refrigerator is the standard, if sometimes ridiculed, example.) But at the same time, there is a big move toward simplicity. Maybe everything doesn't need to be connected to everything else? But you'll certainly see more and more ways to connect devices. And more importantly, there will be increased opportunities to connect the people that use those devices—which will ultimately have a bigger impact on how people use them.

So what's the difference between industrial design and product design? Is it just that saying industrial design makes it sound like you might have cigarettes rolled up in your sleeve?

There's definitely a bit of that. If you tell someone that you are an industrial designer, you'll often get a blank stare. Then you say, "you know, product design," and there will be a glimmer of awareness. Maybe product design is more consumer-oriented and industrial design is for the B2B crowd?

So, right now graphic design, industrial design, and architecture are all thought of as separate fields—but they're all using digital tools, and many of these tools are similar, if not the same. Do you see these areas merging eventually?

I can't see that happening. Just because someone can lay out a page doesn't mean they can build a building. Since these disciplines all share an understanding of aesthetics, relationships, space, hierarchies, and such, then all these people can speak with one another. And they can all have an appreciation of the challenges each other works with. But would you hire an architect to design a magazine? Each discipline is highly specialized, and while there might be some crossover in their personal activities, I can't imagine them merging into some sort of über-designer that can do it all.

You also run a very popular job board. Do you have any sense of what employers in industrial design are looking for in a candidate? Any specific tech skills or programs? Any general tips for job getting?

On the entry-level side, employers are looking for people who can hit the ground running. That means they should have an arsenal of skills and technologies at their fingertips. And the ability to sketch is still of utmost importance. Add to these skills a clearly defined and demonstrated thought process, and you've got a strong candidate.

Being able to communicate your intent and having original ideas with strong concepts behind them are also essential. On a senior level, employers are looking for people who can work across many fields and with many different types of people. IDEO, for example, looks for people who are T-shaped, possessing a broad knowledge and skills across many areas, and deep expertise in one. People like that are great to have on teams, and we all know that design is a team sport. ■

www.core77.com

Site Design and Development: Core77

Beyond the Screen

Years from now you'll be able to tell your children that, back in the day, computers were boxes that sat on a desk.

They might not believe you. Digital design is literally leaping off the screen—covering buildings with an interactive skin, or shrinking to the size of a cell phone. Technology is evolving so rapidly that just listing the new applications of digital design would take up several pages—and it doesn't show any signs of slowing down.

With these new opportunities come new challenges. In the interview with Adam Greenfield, we talk about design that doesn't have an interface—that is invisible but, at the same time, everywhere. Cavan Huang, who works at the Time Warner Center, has the opposite problem. He's designing for interfaces that cover huge walls and even follow you into the elevator. Mikon van Gastel is working on the outside of buildings. His media facade spans an entire city block in Times Square and responds dynamically to global and local market fluctuations, the time of day, and events around the world. It is being viewed by someone twenty-four hours a day, 365 days a year. How do you modify a display that is always being watched?

One of the most exciting things about digital design is that no one knows the answers. The best you can say is, "So far, so good." It may be that, in the future, designers will specialize in these new screens and networks that we don't even have names for today. You will be able to take classes in "invisible information design," "building-sized interface design," and "really tiny screen design." But then you have to ask yourself: How long before these new technologies go the way of the desktop computer (whose obsolescence I am imagining even as I type on one)?

One thing seems certain: Digital design has gone beyond the screen, and you can't stuff it back in. Approached with the right frame of mind, the opportunities are endless. But it's important to realize that we're at the beginning, rather than the end, of a revolution. So be careful when choosing sides. ■

Ubiquitous Computing

An interview with Adam Greenfield, author of *Everywhere: The Dawning Age of Ubiquitous Computing*

You work in a field that is often called ubiquitous computing. First of all, can you define that for us?

The phrase ubiquitous computing was coined by the late Mark Weiser, in work at Xerox PARC that dates back to the late 1980s. He saw ubicomp as the next logical step in our relationship with the digital tools we use, an inevitable consequence of the historic shift from many users sharing one machine to many devices serving one user. As Weiser described it, ubiquitous computing is information processing that has left the desktop behind, and been distributed throughout the built environment: "invisible, but in the woodwork everywhere." Our notion of information technology as being confined to these boxes we call computers is changing. Ordinary objects are being reimagined as places where facts about the world are gathered, considered, and acted upon.

Can you give an example of a ubiquitous system in action?

Well I just got back from Korea, where they are working on a system called T-Money, which is a touchless payment system that contains a Radio Frequency Identification (RFID)—equipped smart card. It allows you to purchase anything from a bus ride to a book to lunch just by waving this little wand. We also went to look at a "model house" that was equipped with ubiquitous systems. The primary interface was a wireless wall-mounted panel that served as a telephone; a stereo; a calendar; it would tell you if there was mail waiting in your mailbox; it would alert you if you forgot to put the recycling out. It allowed you to control your appliances and your lights.

This kind of centralization is all possible with existing technology. OK. Now imagine this scenario without the central console. Imagine that all these systems are communicating with each other and adjusting themselves automatically based on the activities of the user. See what I mean?

If we have the technology, why aren't we using it?

The short answer is that we're starting to—especially in Asia. It's really a question of coordination. In Korea, a few huge companies control most of the manufacturing—it's much easier to get these companies to work together to adopt technology than it would be in the United States. And the thing is that for the console to work, each of the components has to work. Everything has to work together, and, so far, there just aren't that many designers who are able to create this kind of system.

So design in this case is not about creating images or objects; it's about coordinating interactions?

Right. How do you design an interactive experience that may not be centralized on a screen, or even a series of screens, but that consists of invisible interactions the user may not even be aware of? The most basic fact of ubiquitous computing is

What we're going to see is this huge explosion of technological creativity, and the question is, will we be ready for it? Will designers be ready for it? Can designers make sense of it and turn it into something beautiful and useful?

that it takes place out in the world, in a much more volatile, complicated, and unpredictable environment than that presented by the relatively bounded arena of the Web. Over what is now a full decade of experience with the Web, designers have become accustomed to a more or less standard array of deliverables used in site development, from mood boards through to wireframes and technical-use cases. But ubiquitous systems require the designer to accommodate the needs of multiple users, each free to move in both three-dimensional space and time, as they deal with multiple interactive systems. An entirely new type of map is necessary.

What are the documents you use?

It's rough. Ubiquity doesn't arise from the object itself but from the interaction with other distributed systems in the environment. So far the design vocabulary doesn't even exist, and the deliverables don't exist. We don't even have agreement on what kind of design documents we would need to collectively discuss the challenges at hand. In short, we're making it up as we go along and looking to other disciplines for help: everything from architectural blueprints to dance choreography to biological models.

What does this new technology mean for design and designers?

What we're going to see is this huge explosion of technological creativity, and the question is, will we be ready for it? Will designers be ready for it? Can designers make sense of it and turn it into something beautiful and useful?

We're talking about technology that will affect your everyday life to an extent that has not been seen before—everything from how you operate your home to how you pay for your food. Everything. A system that is not well designed could really be a disaster. We'll need designers more than ever.

How can digital designers prepare for these new opportunities?

Well, it won't be enough just to know Photoshop. Designers will have to understand complex systems, and, at least for the time being, the best place to look is at other disciplines. Urban planning is a good place to start. How do cities work? Why do we live in them? Why do traffic lights work the way that they do? But, from a visual design perspective, the devil will be in the details. For example, when I was in Korea I saw a laptop that had a sleep indicator—and it was just a blinking light. On-off. On-off. Compare that to the sleep indicator on my Mac, which was designed by Jonathan Ives's team at Apple. The majestic inhalations as light illuminates and dims. My Mac actually looks like it's sleeping. Now, both computers convey the same information. But only one does it beautifully. As technology becomes more and more prevalent and inescapable, these small, subtle touches of beauty will make all the difference. ■

Grow
A world of development opport

Be Well
benefits and services for you and your

▲

"Grow, Be Well, Enjoy"

Date: 2006

Client: Time Warner Corporate Responsibility

Design/Production: Cavan Huang

Format: Broadcast across a network on 50" and 65" Plasma Displays (1280 x 768), 17" LCD Monitors (1024 x 76),15" CRT Elevator Monitors (720x480)

Technology: Adobe Illustrator, Adobe Photoshop, Adobe After Effects, Apple QuickTime, Apple DVD Studio Pro, Windows Media Encoder, Inscriber

◀ Animated Identity for Digital Signage

Date: March 2006

Client: Time Warner Corporate Real Estate

Design/Production: Cavan Huang

Photography: Adrian Wilson

Software: Adobe Illustrator, Photoshop, After Effects, Apple QuickTime, Apple DVD Studio Pro, Windows Media Encoder, Inscriber Infocaster.

Making Buildings Digital

An interview with Cavan Huang, digital designer for Time Warner Center, New York City

Describe your role at the Time Warner Center.

I'm the distributed media designer. I design, produce, and manage creative content for Time Warner's distributed media system. The distributed media system is an internal network of advanced projection, plasma screens, media walls, and lighting systems integrated throughout the company's headquarters at Columbus Circle, which includes a nine-foot-high and sixty-foot-wide media wall that greets visitors in the lobby, as well as fifty-inch plasmas on both sides of the reception areas for each floor, fifteen-inch screens in each elevator car, and a state-of-the-art screening room that features eight high-end Christie digital projectors.

What kind of content do you create?

At the moment, most of the content is digital signage that can be as simple as an animated logo promoting a sponsor or as complex as a short motion-graphics–based narrative announcing an event. One of the things we try to do with the signage is to create a visual texture that is consistent with the architectural elements, interior themes, and reflects the storytelling media produced by Time Warner.

How does the content on the media wall in the entrance relate to the content in the elevators?

At the moment, it doesn't really. We're just beginning to develop that level of cohesion. Eventually, though, the media wall will act as a welcoming canvas directing visitors for an event (say a film conference) to the elevator banks. The elevators will continue the experience, by playing a short narrative that features elements from the media wall but adds another dimension. The benefit of the elevators is that you have people's undivided attention—they have nowhere to go. In addition, there is audio, which also adds to the experience. Ideas for the future include a more dynamic interactive element. Both media wall and elevator can feature content that is updated on the fly (for example, through RSS feeds from the Internet, live broadcast shots from CNN or Columbus Circle outside, weather reports etc.).

Designers have always had to keep up with changing technologies. This does not lessen the value of traditional media. Rather, it means our design palette is expanding.

Who do you work with at the center to make these projects happen?

In house, I work with the IT department, AV department, real estate, and corporate communications. There are also many third-party vendors—Pentagram is one of the key partners in the identity system. Initially, I was working directly with Lisa Strausfeld.

On the technical side, I work with Technomedia Solutions—the company that installed the media wall and network; and Broadstreet Productions, an AV house that has been producing the high-definition loops that currently play on the media wall. To a lesser extent, I deal with Mancini Duffy, the interior architects of the conference center.

Tell me about your background.

Art and design were hobbies I pursued as early as high school, but it never occurred to me that it would become my profession. I was also interested in history and urban planning. However, one of the first projects I worked on was our high school interactive CD-ROM, for which I composed and performed the soundtrack. In university, I designed short animated PowerPoint presentations for debating tournaments. I also developed publications and Web sites for the student society and various organizations.

After I graduated, I worked as a Web and interactive designer. It became clear to me that I enjoyed the narrative aspect of design. There were limitations as to how Web sites and CD interfaces were created back in 2000, so I decided to get my master's degree at RISD, where I did everything from form studies and typography to semiotics and narrative. The three years I spent enriched my work and process as a designer. And then I got this job as soon as I graduated.

I don't know many other designers who are doing this kind of thing. Who do you look to for inspiration and ideas?

It is a very unique job, and I consider myself very fortunate. Because of the multidisciplinary nature of the work, I look to many different types of sources. I look at poster designers and collage artists (especially the futurists), modern architecture (European contemporaries), films (film noir, animated, science fiction), music videos (Michel Gondry), motion graphic firms (Imaginary Forces). Every week or so I make a pilgrimage to the Chelsea galleries or MoMA to see what other artists are making.

What do you think your job says about the way design is evolving generally?

Digital signage and motion graphic design are clearly becoming a preferred format for conveying information. There are advantages to having large digital canvases that can be instantly updated. The digital medium is just more compelling. For instance, when you juxtapose a large plasma screen featuring an animated poster next to a static poster, the plasma screen will get more attention. Designers have always had to keep up with changing technologies. This does not lessen the value of traditional media. Rather, it means our design palette is expanding. ■

Architecture and Technology

An interview with Lisa Strausfield, partner in Pentagram, New York City

After you received your master's in architecture, you got a master's in media arts and sciences. At the time, those fields must have seemed to many people to be almost completely disconnected. Since then, however, you've been involved in many projects that use digital technology to transform the physical environment. Can you talk a little bit about the evolving relationship between cyberspace and physical space?

I was always aware of the synergy between architecture and digital technology, and felt that my structural design thinking was very much informed by my undergraduate training in computer science. (My major was art history, but I had a minor in computer science.) I'm having trouble with the last part of this question because I'm currently quite disillusioned with the excess of media displays in the environment. I need to think a bit more about this . . .

Whenever a new medium becomes affordable (and/or hip) it turns up everywhere. These days, Times Square is not the only venue for high-tech kinetic media. Should there be a cooling-off period (if such were possible) before the world is saturated? Should there be a point where someone says, "We need standards"?

Recently, I learned that a very well-regarded European steel mesh manufacturer has a new offering with embedded digitally controlled LEDs. The effect is disturbingly attractive. This means that entire buildings can now be wrapped with transparent video displays using an off-the-shelf product. We are at a point now where every physical surface of our environment can become a digital display. I don't think this is a fad, and I look forward to getting to the other side of the infatuation with this type of technology.

For the past five years or more, the installation of large digital displays by corporations and institutions was motivated by a desire to project an image of being technology-forward. There was little if no consideration of the content and message of what was being displayed. Well, everyone is wired now, and it's no longer a differentiator. My hope is that we can focus on identity, information, and overall message first, and then determine the best medium or media through which to express it.

This book is called *Becoming a Digital Designer*, and we've wrestled with what the digital in the title actually means. Does digital define a set of tools or an output method or an approach to projects? Or, since everything is done on computers, has it become a meaningless modifier? In the context of design, do you think digital still has any meaning?

Digital as a modifier is becoming meaningless, on the one hand, because younger designers have no other experience of design. On the

Environmental graphics and dynamic information displays ▶
for Bloomberg L.P. Corporate Headquarters

Launch Date: April 2005

Client: Bloomberg L.P.

Art Director: Lisa Strausfeld

Designers: Lisa Strausfeld, Jiae Kim

Signage and Wayfinding: Paula Scher

Design Firm: Pentagram Design, New York

Project Photography: Peter Mauss/Esto

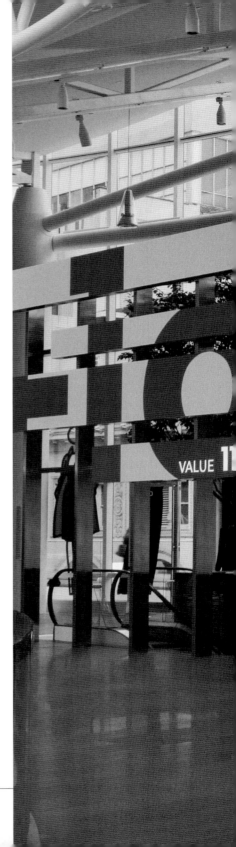

other hand, digital tools and digital thinking have completely and permanently transformed the way we practice and think about design. And as long as technology continues its inevitable state of evolution, design will continue to transform. For example, design practice has transitioned from its exclusive focus on designing artifacts to include the design of systems that generate artifacts.

What kind of projects do you think you'll be working on in ten years? Do you think they will be Web sites? Buildings? Something else?

I would like to be my own client in ten years, creating information products. These are products that leverage the vast resources of information online and improve the quality of our lives.

Do you think it's important for designers to also be programmers?

No. I do think, however, that it's important for designers to be aware of and intimate with digital thinking and culture. It's contemporary culture.

Some argue that design standards have fallen since the digital revolution and that digital design (especially on the Web) is generally uglier than nondigital. Do you agree? Why or why not?

There's a lot of bad design out there, on the Web, in print, and in the environment. All of it could use improvement, frankly.

But specifically related to digital media (and returning somewhat to the question above): Is there a surfeit of bad Web and kinetic signs and other digital stuff because most designers are being asked (and taught) to play with bells and whistles?

Yes, again, I think that clients and designers are enchanted by the image of digital technology. These gratuitous signifiers are being used as poor substitutes for the identity or branding of institutions that want to convey a sense of being future-focused.

◄ Interactive architectural model
for the Wall Street Rising
Downtown Information Center

Launch Date: December 2006

Client: Wall Street Rising

Art Directors: Lisa Strausfeld,
Nina Boesch

Designers: Lisa Strausfeld, Jiae Kim

Design Firm: Pentagram Design,
New York

Project Photography: Peter Mauss/Esto

Software: Macromedia Flash, Adobe
Photoshop, Adobe Illustrator, Jugglor

It may be unfair, but how would you self-analyze your digital screens for the Bloomberg Building? There is something wonderful about cutting the LED in sections so that you can show layers of information but also fragmented imagery. What was your thinking behind this—was it simply to avoid the cliché of the big screen?

Paula Scher likes to explain the slices in that LED display as a response to budget cuts. In reality, our approach is always to integrate any kind of digital display into the architecture as much as possible. In this particular site (the sixth-floor common space), our only option was to compose a freestanding element. We wanted to avoid creating a big billboard and had a need for some transparency. We started slicing vertically, first, and then settled on horizontal bands that wrap around the space. The configuration of the display also worked nicely with the way we choreographed the (literal) information flow.

With regard to the last question, what do you say to yourself when faced with an environmental project that allows you to make something different?

Every project I've ever done is different in the sense that I have never done anything like it before.

In hiring designers and collaborators, what are the key virtues (and skills) you look for?

In addition to intelligence and excellent aesthetic judgment, I look for people who are fanatically interested and passionate about visualizing information.

Do you think that designers should be multiplatform oriented, rather than singular specialists?

I have observed, through teaching, that younger designers seem to be more media agnostic in that they consider the selection of medium (e.g., print, Web, 3D) to be one of their design decisions. I view this trend as a very positive thing, both for the design profession and for the consumer. I believe that mastery is still very important, but is no longer necessarily attached to media. ∎

Managing Interaction

An interview with Masamichi Udagawa, principal of Antenna Design, New York City

Can you define interaction design for me?
Interaction design is a form of intervention. It involves trying to change someone's behavior by inserting new stimulus—carefully, I hope. In order to get someone to do something, they first have to understand what it is you want from them. This understanding is the product of new stimuli reacting with what is already in their head. So it is not just a question of what is new; it is a question of what is next. What is the next step from what is currently in their head to what you want them to be doing or thinking? If the intervention is too radical, then it will not create a connection.

Your work combines physical objects and screen-based interfaces. What is the difference between designing these two elements?
We generally view the physical and digital elements as inseparable. With the check-in system we designed for JetBlue Airlines, for example, people need to be able to recognize the purpose of the machine from a distance of about twenty meters. The closer they get, the more infor-

mation the physical form conveys. This process of layering information continues through the touch screen. It is all part of the same program. The hardware and software are integral.

What are some of the core concepts for designing interactions?
Purposefulness is the most important thing. There has to be a clear purpose. It is surprising to me how often people fail to ask the most basic question: Why should this system exist?

Have you ever done a project with more than one purpose?
There can be a main purpose and then smaller steps along the way. But only one focus at a time.

Can you talk about the Power Flowers—a series of neon flowers in the window of Bloomingdale's—that lit up as people walked past?
The purpose of the Power Flowers was delight. We knew very clearly what we wanted people to do. We wanted them to notice a pattern and realize that they were causing it.

▲
MTA/NYCT Help Point Intercom

Date: 2006

Client: MTA/NYCT

Designers: Masamichi Udagawa and Sigi Moeslinger

Photo: Antenna Design

Photographer: Ryuzo Masunaga

Do clients generally have a purpose in mind when they bring you in?

Generally, clients have a purpose in mind when they bring us in. Of course, charging clients helps them decide if something is really necessary. When the goal is ambiguous, it is difficult to create a business relationship. But generally, the activities of corporations are purposeful. Everything has to be justified.

What are some of the things that students tend to forget when designing interactive systems?

Well, an object—whether it is furniture or a ticket machine or whatever—needs to generate an interaction. Once it is produced it sits somewhere and doesn't do anything unless it has a way to announce its purpose. Users may be attracted by its shape or it may be animated in some way. But the big hurdle is to get the user to understand what this thing does and want to engage with it. Causing this first action is very difficult, and that is always true. Appearance as well as placement, or context, makes a kind of promise to the user. This promise is also called affordance.

For instance, at the moment we are working with McDonald's to automate the process of ordering. The interface looks like a menu, and because of that it generates

certain expectations. For one thing, you have to open the menu to see inside. Naturally, at first a lot of information will be concealed. If you show everything at once, then people get overwhelmed. There needs to be a single entry point and then a decision tree—one decision leading to the next. At each level, more information is revealed. This is also called progressive disclosure. A menu is a very simple example, another example is the iPod. An iPod doesn't look like music because music doesn't naturally have a physical form. The progressive disclosure for the iPod is complex. It is not only how it looks but how it feels, how much it weighs, and how the navigation works. There are hidden messages that are not immediately obvious. Form is a mechanism for communication.

Where's the surprise in all this?

Sometimes looks can be deceiving. A sense of surprise can be a good thing, but not when you're trying to order a hamburger. Not when you're buying a ticket. What may be surprising in this context is that the system is easy to use. People have pretty low expectations with machine interfaces. There are not too many really nicely done machine interfaces out there. So ease of use can be a nice surprise.

23/6 Ulta Mobile PC ▶

Date: 2005

Client: Fujitsu

Designers: Masamichi Udagawa and Sigi Moeslinger

Photographer: Ryuzo Masunaga

What's an example of a badly designed interface that people may have used?

Well, Chase Bank is in the process of redesigning its ATMs. Currently, the interface is modeled on a Web site: It has tabbed navigation and allows people to engage in all kinds of complex transactions—but nobody actually uses these options. It is the wrong metaphor and wrong context. You don't want to access this kind of information when there are other people waiting in line behind you, and so more options means there is more to read and consider, and this slows the whole transaction down considerably.

Another simple thing designers often get wrong is that they forget that on a touch screen there is no rollover state. A touch is actually a click so there is no in-between. Or they make a touch screen interface that requires people to drag something—it just doesn't work.

You mention that having more options on the ATM slows things down—can you explain that a little bit?

Some designers think that having fewer screens automatically means that transactions are more efficient—that is totally not true. Faster transactions are generated by having less text and fewer options on one screen. If you have everything on one screen then the user has too much to consider. Careful layering of options and information is the key.

But is the goal always speed?

It is important to remember purpose. People are interacting with the system for a reason—because they want to get something out of it. Faster transactions are almost always a good thing with digital interfaces. The exception is that the system's purpose is to cause people to reflect—to somehow think about themselves. But, I don't know, for some reason digital interfaces do not tend to inspire reflection. They are good for action.

Some companies have the idea that if customers spend more time on a Web site that they are soaking up the brand or something, which is completely untrue. They are just getting confused and angry at the logo that is whatever, maybe dancing around the screen, while they are trying to do something. Just spending time in front of the screen is no guarantee for anything. As time passes people have less and less patience with digital devices. They demand quicker transactions. Digital transactions are moving from being reflective to being reflex.

I think we are also beginning to see a counterbalancing trend toward slowness in other areas of life—food, for example, and cooking.

What advice would you give digital designers who are just starting out?

If you go into a project thinking you know how things are, then you might not be able to see how they really are. You have to start with a hypothesis, a guess, but then you have to test it. Even simple interactions can be complex, and understanding these hidden complexities can mean the difference between success and failure. If you start with an incorrect hypothesis, then no matter how good the execution is, the project will not work. I am always telling clients, "I don't know." This makes a space so that I can then find out. ■

Designing for the Handheld Experience

An interview with Kim Mingo, freelance user-experience designer, New York City

From a background in graphic design, how and why did you move into interface design?

My move from traditional graphic design to interface design happened a little bit by chance. I took a job with the Sony Design Center when they were developing their online presence. I was working on some print and on some of the early Web designs during the time that Sony began to build a group dedicated to improving the interaction for their consumer products and services. The increased functionality and complexity of the systems Sony was creating meant that there was a need to simplify the user experience. For me, the challenge was an interesting one, although it often meant a greater constraint in the visual design than I was accustomed to.

Are there similarities between what you do now as an interface designer for small handheld devices and what you did as a graphic designer?

There are similarities. Timing and presentation of information are very important in both graphic design and interface design. A graphic designer considers the way in which the viewer sees the information when looking at a poster, or controls the momentum and timing of a book or a magazine, for example. A digital, interactive medium is similar, perhaps a little less predictable, as the interaction is dynamic and not a linear experience. When a user is interacting with a product and trying to accomplish a task, it is important that the information is presented very clearly so that the user understands the steps that need to be taken in order to accomplish that task successfully. There are many graphic qualities of the screen design, such as placement, color, font, that help by giving the user visual cues.

What did you have to learn (and/or teach yourself) that distinguishes design in this digital realm from previous practice?

One thing that I learned very quickly was to be flexible with control of the design. With print, there is more opportunity for control over the finished product. A graphic designer often has the ability to be involved in every step of the design process from ideation to production. Whereas, with digital interfaces, even if the designer is involved from start to finish, the final product is often viewed across multiple platforms—meaning the presentation of the design may be susceptible to changes that the designer cannot always control.

What is the most important consideration when designing interfaces? Are you designing for you, or for a targeted audience?

The interfaces that I have worked on for Sony and Motorola are for mass-market products. These products need to be usable for a wide variety of people. That means it is very important to always keep the target audience in mind when designing. But this does not mean that there is no room for innovation and invention; still, it is crucial to understand the impact of this innovation on consumers who will use the products. We incorporate usability testing into our design process, which means that we are constantly checking our designs against the expectations of the audience and the ease with which users can interact with them.

What are the most difficult aspects of designing for such a small space?
The size of the screen and the limited input (of a keypad) introduce a number of challenges. I think that constraint remains one of the most difficult aspects of designing for such devices.

In designing for Motorola handheld devices, does the company demand certain prerequisites, or are you free to invent?
When designing for Motorola handsets, we as designers are often working on an iterative design of a platform, where there is a paradigm already in place. It's like designing an upgrade for the Mac or Windows operating system. Each time a new version is released, it is an enhancement to a previous version. The design of the new features should follow the existing paradigm so that they are well integrated and easily learnable based on the "rules" of the system.

However, there is a time when a new product calls for a paradigm shift and a designer is able to rethink the design problem from the ground up. (Again, with the example of the Mac in mind, this would be like a design shift from OS9 to OSX.) When designing a new platform, there are prerequisites as well; this includes competitive products and technology limitations, and industrywide design standards that occur naturally.

How collaborative is this medium? Whom else must you work with to ensure that your work is perfect?
This is very collaborative medium. I work very closely with software engineers, usability researchers, marketing, and other designers (both visual designers and other UI designers). All of these people have a very important role in the design process.

Years ago I tried to avoid working with software engineers, as I was sure their purpose was to limit the design. Over time I realized that I could not do my work without them and they could not work without me.

I have since learned that working with engineers can be very rewarding; their knowledge and perspective can help make you aware of ideas that you would never have considered without their expertise.

What do you need from collaborators that you cannot do yourself?
I absolutely cannot program. Without software engineers, my designs are nothing more than pictures.

What is the future of handheld design as you see it?
Functionality of handheld devices continues to increase, sometimes at the expense of usability. Products often suffer from feature creep (too many features creeping into a product), and the challenge of the designer is to continue to make these feature-packed products relevant, compelling, and usable. Right now, I think that there is a reaction to this feature overload, and the response to this could be a move back to simplicity—back to products that do a few things very well rather than products that do many things (but not so well). ■

Client: Morgan Stanley

Art Director: Mikon van Gastel

Designer: Matt Checkowski

Architect: KPF with Kevin Kennon

Software: After Effects, Discreet Flame, Vizrt

Date: November 2004

CASE STUDY:

745 7th Avenue

Mikon van Gastel, principal of averysmalloffice.com, New York City

Whose idea was it to make the facade of 745 7th Avenue a kinetic front?

The idea was born out of necessity. Times Square zoning requirements forced the client to add signage to its building facade. The amount, location output, and movement were, literally, shaped by signage guidelines. However, in collaboration with the architect, Kevin Kennon at KPF, we placed two demands on the sign: the creation of architectural and technological integration and a cinematic rather than an overtly commercial experience.

Architectural interfaces have a long analog history. What was the precedent for this kind of digital display? And how does this differ?

Historic precedent for architectural signage includes mechanically animating billboards, neon signs, news zippers, stock market tickers, and JumboTron video screens. The technological limitations of such signs forced the media to be a layer added onto architecture rather than integrated into the architecture. With the further development of LED technology the structural demands for the integration of LED structurally continue to diminish. The technology is becoming thinner, smaller,

lightweight, and more versatile. It can be folded, used in curves, draped like a transparent curtain, and wrapped around a building like skin. It is engineered to be modularized.

This allowed us to think about LED as an architectural material. Structurally integrated, its presence can be heightened to become a performative display or lessened to become an ambient interface.

What were the aesthetic and technological challenges about such a huge—and changeable—public canvas?

Aesthetically, the focus was on creating an experience that was more akin to film and video art than advertising and television. I looked at artists like Bill Viola and Gary Hill, where simple moments in time are stretched out to become an event on a monumental scale. I had an interest in slowing time down to intensify movement and gesture rather than creating a mirror to the kinetic environment that is Times Square. When working on such a dramatic scale, less is definitely more. In a way, it's better to try to hold on to the mysterious. In an environment like Times Square where everything seems to shout at you,

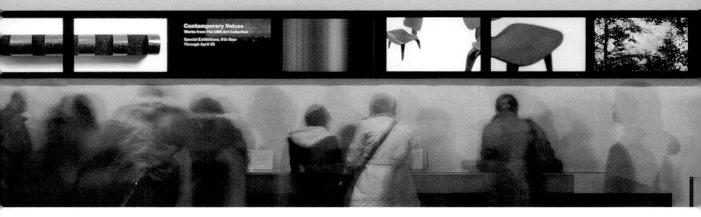

sometimes you stand out by leaving things unanswered. Also, the client was not interested in displaying any form of overt branding, corporate slogans, or flying logos. This allowed us to be more atmospheric.

The media facade on 745 7th Avenue spans a full city block in New York, with nonlinear content on display seven days a week, 365 days a year. Technically, it means time is stretched past the point of linearity and control, and it forces the designer to think in terms of nonlinear, database-driven content. Therefore, information is staged and displayed dynamically in real time, producing a complex, continuous flow in which content is interrelated and changes over time, depending on internal and external variables.

With such a prominent display, what relationship did you develop with the public?

A sense of humor, the amplified scale, gestures, and subtle but powerful choreography of the imagery, created the antithesis to the rest of TimesSquare. It's hard for me to judge the relationship we built with our audience, since the events of 9/11 forced the client to sell the building before they fully occupied it. Judging the effects on people on the streets can only be based on the audience's reaction during the months of testing. I simply figured if we could make fast-paced New Yorkers

stop for a moment to enjoy the sign, we had accomplished something. And they did.

You use the term dematerializing the corporate facade. Please explain.

It refers to the idea that physical transparency can be translated into a culture of corporate transparency. I wanted to create a response to the banal mirrored corporate building facades where corporations can see us, but we can't look in. If media are looked at as a material, it allows for the content to create transparency; it becomes a lens, a window into the company. It enhances the porosity between the organizations inside and the people outside.

In the case of 745 7th Avenue, we worked with the company to translate activity inside the building to content on the outside of the building. People entering the building, working inside the building, or leaving the building all became characters on the screens. Seven Fouty Five represents a new paradigm in which media, technology, and architecture are programmed to perform stories and live events, giving the company a face to the outside world and giving the people that occupied the building a sense of pride. In a sense we tried to use the screens as an internal and external catalyst for behavioral change.

◀ MoMa Fingerprint: Interior Signage

Client: Museum of Modern Art

Art Director: Mikon van Gastel

Designer: Tali Krakowski, Alex Hanowski

Design Studio: Imaginery Forces

Programming: Kurt Ralske with Slinc.Realtime

Software: After Effects, Max/Msp, and Jitter

What training did you have that allowed you to create design on such a grand scale?

It's less about the actual training itself than personal interest and professional curiosity. During my academic career, I was interested in questioning the possibilities of design practice by studying the related fields of architecture, filmmaking, sculpture, and video art. From live concert performances, installation art, to digital architecture, I became obsessed with any form of performance regardless of its medium or field. Escaping the boundaries of traditional graphic design training in Holland, in favor of my graduate studies at Cranbrook Academy of Art, allowed me to create my own parameters of study. Once you've become accustomed to constantly pushing your creative abilities beyond your comfort zone as a designer, the idea of "grand" scale becomes much less daunting.

How much of this site is content versus aesthetics?

I'm no longer interested in issues of content versus aesthetics, form versus content, style versus meaning, design versus un-design. The interesting part of the future of design will be about designers expanding the context in which the profession performs and influences culture. This isn't necessarily a new idea, since designers are constantly pushing the boundaries, but it will help create a space of autonomy for graphic designers.

How many different iterations did you have to create to keep the sign fresh?

The content for the screen is nonlinear database-driven. Various themes are developed in multiple layers of complexity. Video layers are linear, although constantly shuffling, depending on the variables set by the designer. Graphic and typographic layers are constantly changing based on internal and external parameters such as global and local market fluctuations, the time of day, and events around the world.

For someone who wants to work on this grand scale, what must they learn, and how should they train?

The drive in architecture and design to create new forms of spatial experiences requires the participation of more than one distinct contributor. The complexity of many of these projects requires unexpected forms of collaboration and an openness to new forms of practice. Think co-option instead of competition. Since so much of this is driven by motion and interactivity, it's important to allow yourself to have an improvisational attitude, develop animated design processes fueled by innovative use of digital tools, as dynamic generators of ideas. ∎

Ellis Island

Angela Greene, Edwin Schlossberg Design, New York City

This project is about involving visitors to Ellis Island in the development of content. How does design play a role in this process?

The project is based on a text database of the 22 million passenger arrival records to Ellis Island between 1892 and 1924. The database was transcribed from scans of the original handwritten entries in large manifests—each name entered when the passengers disembarked. They are beautiful but difficult to decipher, and not necessarily compelling in and of themselves. We designed the activities to initially give visitors a feel for the immigration experience, and then continue to step them through the necessary questions to find the entry for the passenger they are seeking. There are visual payoffs along the way: the actual manifest when it is found, and the ship on which their ancestor arrived. The visitors are using digital tools, but it doesn't feel like an Internet search. The intent is to simulate handling the original documents.

How did you make this a kinetic experience that holds the visitors' interest?

The on-island visit is a two-part experience. The first part of the visit—the passenger search stations—we included videos of what arrival at Ellis Island was like, and short documentaries of people searching for relatives in various countries to frame genealogy as a personal quest. During the search visitors can add their own documents and link them to the official records (a parallel database), or view past visitors' additions. They may also take away a document depicting the manifest page, and a photo of the ship on which their ancestor traveled.

In an optional second part of the visit people move to enclosed recording booths where they create oral histories and scan photos to add to personal family scrapbooks—the visitors play an active and personal role in the documentation of their families' history.

Was the hard- and software in place for this project to progress, or did you have to have it invented for this purpose?

The database of passenger names is the core of the program. The original ship manifests were microfiched in the 1950s and then destroyed for pulp. Over 3.5 million graphic files were created by scanning the microfiche from the National Archives. The manifests were then transcribed twice by the Church of Latter Day Saints using different volunteers. Discrepancies between transcriptions were then filtered out and resolved by genealogical experts.

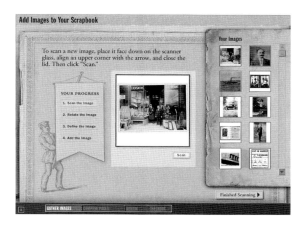

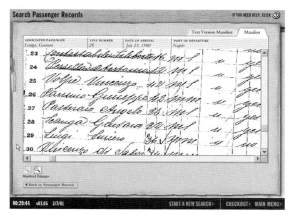

▲

American Family Immigration History Center

Date: Opened in 2001

Client: Statue of Liberty Ellis Island

Interacitve Systems Designers: Edwin Schlossberg, Mark Corral, Gideon D'Arcangelo, Angela Greene, Clay Gish

© ESI Design, 2007

To increase the likelihood of finding a match when searching, a "spelled-like" algorithm was developed with the aid of a computational linguist based on the orthographic patterns of the languages from the regions where the most immigrants came from between 1892 and 1924—Italy and Eastern Europe.

Describe the brainstorming that occurred.

We designed the experience in a long series of meetings using scenarios of different types of visitors and their possible search results—from large groups gathered together to go to the island to seek ancestors together to single online visitors who might not find a specific relative in the database. We created branching paths to allow access to stories, artifacts, user-created annotations and scrapbooks, so that even if the visitor did not find the specific relative in the database they have a rich experience nonetheless. We also designed the search tools to succeed based on successive approximation and alternate name spellings.

What are the parameters of design in this project—what can and can't you do?

Since the site is a national monument, we tread lightly on the interior. The physical design uses wood, glass, and translucent scrims artistically depicting artifacts from the island—ship posters, manifests, stamped documents, and the expressive faces of the immigrants themselves. The technology also has minimal visual impact.

The site is reached primarily by ferry, so the visitor flow was designed to accommodate waves of people. There are booths for both large and small gatherings with generous placement for sound control. We created a previsit online reservation system to control the flow and avoid disappointment, and also to let the visitors prepare materials to bring with them if they want to create a scrapbook. The experience was also designed to be able to continue online—a permanent family archive that can be continually built upon and shared.

Is this a completed project, or as technology advances does this grow too?

It was a closed-ended project from a contract standpoint. Unfortunately, I can't say if they have updated the technology. ■

Illustration

Illustration is drawing, painting, collaging, and otherwise making marks, signs, and images on paper, screen, or any other resilient surface. Illustration in the digital age is no different, although the tools are quite different. Illustrators use pen and ink, brush and paint, clay and wood.

Digital illustrators use all these things but in the virtual sense, using programs, filters, and all manner of digital ersatz material. But the fundamental definition of an illustrator—an artist who illuminates a text or idea, interpreting it through metaphor, symbolism, or allegory, either in a realistic or abstract manner, remains constant.

To be an illustrator in the digital age is no different than in any other age. For many, the look and style of the art is the same—in large part because software is such that it can reproduce the simplicity of a line or the complexity of a brush. Although there are various clichés associated with digital image making (i.e., a tendency among those who use Photoshop to add shadows has been something of a recurring bugaboo), the vast majority of illustrations done on computer are indistinguishable from those produced in traditional media. In fact, many illustrators begin traditionally—drawing, sketching, painting—and then scan their work, using the computer as a finishing tool.

But don't be misled. Digital illustration also has its own integrity, and the computer has triggered new styles that help define the age. Building on the digital language, some illustrators exploit their pixels for the retro camp and ersatz futuristic veneer that's offered. Others use the computer like an airbrush to get the slick and shining approaches that come only from mechanical techniques. Still others produce work that involves many layers, as only the digital media can provide. Illustrators must, of course, determine what functions best in framing their ideas—because conceptual, "idea" illustration is still the most common and ubiquitous of the art forms—and select methods that allow for optimum expression.

Some say illustration is dead. The proliferation of Photoshop "illustrations" done by designers may give credence to the falsehood, but actually, the field has migrated from say, editorial and advertising to other venues. Although editorial illustration may not be as booming as it once was, it is definitely not dead—just look at the magazines that use it. And while advertising may rely more on studio photography, illustration is used in some campaigns as a way to distinguish them from the commonplace. In addition, books, video, and Web-based media all engage with illustrators to produce static and kinetic images. Moreover, with digital options the opportunities for greater experimentation abounds.

The digital illustrator is also a key to creative collaborations endemic to the new media. Whether producing images to further a narrative or brand an idea, or working in a cross-platform manner as pictorial storyteller, letterer, animator, and so on, the growth opportunities for illustration in the digital world have breathed new life into the venerable field. ∎

Date: May 2005
Client: *Men's Journal*
Designer: David Matt
Illustrator: Viktor Koen
Software: Adobe Photoshop

Conceptual Digitalization

An interview with Viktor Koen, illustrator, New York City

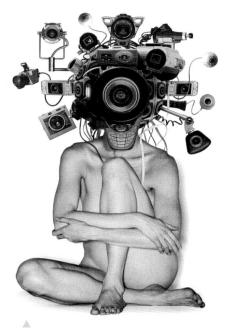

Date: May 2006

Client: The *Village Voice*

Designer: Ted Keller

Illustrator: Viktor Koen

Software: Adobe Photoshop

You were educated at Bezalel Academy of Arts & Design in Jerusalem and received an MFA in illustration as visual essay at the School of Visual Arts in New York City. Now you illustrate for *New York Times Book Review, Time, Newsweek,* and *Esquire,* among others. While you started as a traditional painter, now you are exclusively digital. Why and how?

I was introduced to the computer in my third year of art school in Israel in 1989. I mostly did typography and layout on it, and it took a few years until I used Photoshop. I was painting with acrylics on acetate at the time, and I had formulated a multilayered technique that I thought matched my ideas. It was complicated and cumbersome.

Eventually, photographic elements became important to my work, providing me not only with reference, but with components that were incorporated into my images and gave them a surreal feel that I needed. While in the beginning I was manually montaging compositions from photographs and draw-ings, then we progressed to digital, benefiting greatly from the flexibility, effects, and manipulation potentials of the medium.

How was the transition from one to the other?

The transition was smooth and ex-citing, especially when I introduced color to my digital work. My painting followed the reverse direction and faded, as I found myself getting dirt-ier with pixels than acrylic pigments. There was only a mental barrier left to be crossed in order for me to feel comfortable in my new technique, and a deciding factor was the fact that I started photographing digitally, so I felt a total freedom of choice in the collection of the raw materials for my compositions.

Did this happen overnight?

The transition from painting to digi-tal was long, slow, and seamless. Every step came to better the one before, and my technique evolved by replacing traditional elements of my process with ones that take place on-screen. I think most im-portantly, I was able to gradually replace expressive or accidental or even magic occurrences that take place and shape the final outcome of an image (no matter its use or purpose) with digital equivalents, so to me the computer never was a cold, mathematically based tool, but a platform that brought together all the disciplines and resources I have.

What is your most challenging digital work?

For the last year I have been work-ing on a series of prints titled *Dark*

Peculiar Toys (four prints will be part of the Siggraph Gallery in Boston in July and the series will premiere at the Strychnin Gallery in Berlin at the end of November), so a toy-related alphabet made perfect sense, not only because of the abundance of materials I had in my hands (I collected and photographed hundreds of vintage toy parts), but because I was interested in exploring the combination of these otherwise unrelated shapes while braiding them into something as structured and functional as type.

The letters don't represent a toy molded into a letter form, but the fusion of elements that connect with each other only by their common theme, and a homogenous aesthetic lexicon that characterizes this typeface and my work in general. On the other hand, the Zodiac Initial letters series was aiming to express specific interpretations for every sign. In this case, the long history and cultural references on this classic theme functioned as inspiration but also as a limitation, as I always attempted to present each sign from a fresh angle.

Where do you reference your materials?

I photograph extensively, mostly without knowing why. I listen to my visual instincts and collect parts and details, colors and textures. I love museums, and I visit them every time I take a trip. I get obsessed with objects, usually industrial parts of engines or weapons or tools, and I shoot them from different angles until I run out of memory. I organize the raw images in categories and hope I remember what the hell I named them when I need them. I also use royalty-free stock photography and old photos from flea markets I visit—through my travels but mostly here in New York. I use an analytical approach to these photos, since I break them down to their essential elements and then mold them into something new. It's sort of a renaissance or a second life, especially for the people (now gone and forgotten) posing in the yellowed prints.

Much of your work has a sci-fi veneer. Where did this come from? And has working in digital media made this more prevalent?

I don't believe the digital medium has anything to do with the techno-

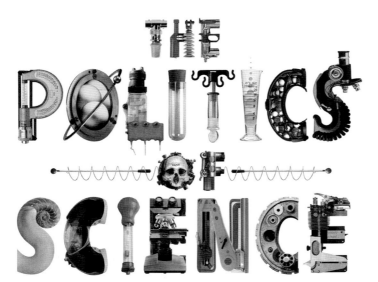

◁ **Date:** April 2005
Client: The *New York Times Book Review*
Illustrator: Viktor Koen
Art Director: Steven Heller

fiction-dark-surreal-futuristic aspect of my work. It was there even when I was painting my images. I am visually addicted to industrial surfaces, machines, and rust, so these are the environments where my creatures and characters feel comfortable.

My work is more environmentally pessimistic than anything else; an early obsession with gas masks has a lot to do with my bleak view about the future. All of the above infiltrate most of my commercial assignments, as well through the color palette I use, my reverse sense of visual humor, and the way I like to create new techno-concoctions out of bits and pieces of things I have photographed and never knew what I would do with.

With all the Photoshop illustration being done today, how do you keep a personality? What makes your work different from the clichéd work?

Being different or having a signature way of making pictures in a plethora of digital creators is simple. My traditional image-making process (digital or not), combined with my thought process and visual obsessions, make my pictures mine.

I also know that people appreciate the fact that I work long and hard and trust my instincts. I am not in love with the computer; I just think it's the best tool I ever used so I can concentrate on the idea behind every image and then resolve its delivery without counting on the beauty of digital effects but the strength of the message. Composition, shape perfection, positive and negative space are important to me, and this is where it's easy to fail if you haven't done your drawing homework. Studying academic painting and drawing in Greece and Israel comes in handy every time I click my mouse. I usually don't think of other people's work until I am faced with it. When it's good I hate them, get jealous, curse in Greek, and run home to work harder. When it's bad, I hate them more. ∎

Date: April 2002
Client: Attic Child Press
Designer: Viktor Koen
Illustrator: Viktor Koen
Software: Adobe Photoshop

Digitally Surreal

An interview with Ray Bartkus, illustrator, New York City

Your artwork has long been a very realistic (if not surrealistic) painting method. When and why did you switch to digital media?

Well, this is the methodology for my painted illustrations revealed:

Upon receiving the assignment, I would slide onto a sofa with a pencil and a paper and would start sketching rough ideas. If an assignment happened to be especially tricky, and I received my fair share of these (e.g., racial, religious, philosophical issues), I would slip into a daydream, and there, between sleep and reality, usually some great ideas would pop out.

Upon deciding which idea would suit the best, I would collect the necessary visual references. Ten years ago I would go to a bookstore. Nowadays, thanks to Google, I can just pull out the necessary files from the Internet. Also, I would do a lot of Polaroid pictures as reference material for different poses, light, draperies, portraits, etc. (Many of my illustrations are inhabited by the characters resembling me, my wife, or my son, because these were the people always available to pose.)

After collecting all this visual data to create a realistic, convincing image, I would proceed to painting, using and adjusting the photo material to better suit the compositional requirements of the idea. When you think of this, there is not much difference in this methodology when using digital media instead of painting. I am eliminating one step in the process: the need to copy the photographic images on paper with paints and brushes. I am using a digital camera now, and I am altering the photos directly with a computer, abandoning the more subjective hand stroke in favor of a more impartial view through the camera lenses. I always aimed for the easiest and most direct way to get the idea across to the viewer.

Conceptually, I always aspired to the impact of signs, like "Sale, 50% off" or "DANGER—HIGH VOLTAGE." These are instantly recognizable messages. Visually, though, I always was amused by the beauty of the realistic details with which you can occupy your eyes for hours: forms, light, shadows, and textures. Digital photography breathes life into a bare-bones idea, as a painting would, but photographic images are getting across the idea in a more direct and objective way, because in the eyes of the viewer a photographic image is associated with the documentary and the impartial. Digital media is less me and more what I want to say. I think the idea becomes more pure in its digital form.

What was your learning curve? It seemed that one day you were painting and the next day you were using Photoshop.

That's the story of my life! The first illustration assignment I received from you was my first illustration ever. When newspapers turned to color I bought a watercolor set and started to use color in my work, even though I had neither, at the beginning, any passion for color pieces, nor any knowledge of color

theory. For some strange reason, clients were paying double for a color illustration, and I started to enjoy it.

Then came a fascination with the new possibilities created by computers. I initially found computer-generated images a bit artificial and stiff, until I bought my first digital camera and was able with ease to incorporate photography to produce more realistic images. I have pretty good visual imagination; hence I can see in my mind well how the finished object—be it a drawing, a sculpture,

or an interior design—should look, when finished.

Medium is just a road to get there, although I am always open to and often employ all kinds of un-expected visual trickery I encounter from the medium along the way. Every medium dictates the rules specific to itself, and I try to be very open to the limitations and advan-tages of each, though at the end I am just trying to re-create the image that is already in my mind.

Of course, the first digital pieces took so much more time to create,

▲

Dollhouse

Client: The *New York Times*

Date: 2006

Illustrator: Ray Bartkus

Art Director: Steven Heller

Software: Adobe Photoshop

◄ Barack Obama Inc.

Client: *Harper's* magazine

Date: 2006

Illustrator: Ray Bartkus

Art Director: Stacey Clarkson

because I didn't know the ropes with the software, but the end results were not necessarily inferior to the pieces I make now, which take me less time to produce because of all the experience I have gathered up to today.

Next year in The Hague, Netherlands, I will be playing a guitar in a band with three more guitar players, though none have any musical experience nor any formal musical training. As far as I am concerned, it's just another medium for expressing myself. Hopefully someday I'll be asked the question: It seems you were doing the illustrations one day, and suddenly the next day you are a guitar player?

While your keen ability to conceive great concepts remained constant, your style changed considerably. Was this counterintuitive?

The style to me is just a limitation: I look at it with a deep suspicion. Maybe it's just a form of attention deficit disorder, but I am always ready to try a different approach. It's hard for me to relate to the artists who are painting the same painting again and again through all their life. Even if they will be achieving a perfection by endless repetition, I'd rather choose to be unfinished and wondering. It's hard for me to accept and adopt one point of view, which is necessary to develop the style. Because of my upbringing in the single-mindedness of a communist state, I treasure too much the possibility and the freedom to choose.

On the other hand, I feel that the illustrator is a bit like an actor. You have to live the life of so many different characters, you have to look into the world through so many writers' eyes, that, as a good actor, you are trying to channel the vibes of your character, not of yourself. It's hard for me to stick to a particular style and to try to stretch all the various ideas and points of view I have to illustrate on one particular pattern. Of course, with this approach I am running into many problems with many art directors, who expect a certain style from me and are getting freaked out when I am delivering something quite unexpected to them, though my best intentions always are to express the idea in the most convincing way.

If I have to adopt some new style to achieve that, I would do it without much hesitation. As one *Wall Street Journal* art director put it: "When I see interesting illustration in our pages, but I don't know who did it, I think that might be you." That was the biggest compliment.

I do not miss much, especially because there are magazines and art directors who do not allow digital images in their pages, which allows me to continue to practice the traditional medium as well. I use pencils and watercolor in my own projects, and I am also finishing ten large-scale oil paintings. I definitely would not appreciate the idea of limiting myself to just digital images, and for now I am enjoying various mediums, with each one enriching my work in the others.

The real challenges in transition did not come from mastering the software. The really hard part was to break the stereotypes some art directors had about my work. Like, "Ray, what is this, you should be drawing, not using a computer! I did not expect that from you." I understand their problem: In such a competitive and compartmentalized field, art directors are able to choose among thousands of artists to find exactly the medium and the style they are envisioning for their pages. Under pressure from the editors and the tight deadlines that they work under, they are trying to eliminate any surprise, pleasant or not.

Therefore an artist's image and style makes perfect business sense in the overpopulated field, and any kind of transition becomes potentially risky. From my perspective, though, I feel that my strength lies in my ability to generate many interesting ideas under tight deadlines. Therefore, upon receiving the assignment, I would like to enjoy the freedom to choose whichever particular medium or style expresses the particular idea best.

About seven years ago during a Japanese street fair in NYC I observed a guy who had this huge wooden press to pleat the handmade paper for traditional dolls' clothing. As he proudly explained, there were just ten or fifteen living persons in the whole world who had mastered this art of pleated paper. I was fascinated by the guy's passion to keep the tradition alive, by the beauty of pleated paper; but I also felt the irrelevance of his occupation and uselessness of these outfits in the midst of the bustling modern street scene of New York. I feel the same about the traditional drawing or painting. Yes, I am sure it's a dying art form.

There will be many beautiful pieces of art created using traditional methods for many years to come, but I do not think that it will ever again be relevant to the evolution of thought and aesthetics in mankind, as it was just a hundred years ago, and will become more of an oddity for some closed circle of connoisseurs to enjoy.

I certainly don't think that such curious minds as da Vinci would be painting oil paintings today: Maybe they would be writing the software for video games, making videos, or working on the Human Genome Project. Regarding the artistic survival, I am sure that you have to do only what you are enjoying doing very much, and you will survive somehow. And if you are not sure what you want to do, just move into the opposite direction from where everybody else is going and you should be fine.

I sincerely hope I'll be shifting my media at least three more times in my lifetime. ■

What would you say was your
most ambitious digital piece?
And why?

It would be hard for me to pick one illustration, because I can execute technically complicated works considerably easily; it's just a matter of how much time I am given by the art director. Therefore, if I had to choose one, it would have to be one of the covers for *Book Review* that I did just before you left the art director's chair there.

I am choosing these not because they were technically complicated pieces, though they were, but because I had to create the final product without submitting the sketches for approval. That was the scariest and most rewarding challenge I have had through my career. From conceiving the idea to the *New York Times* cover without any interference, that's ambitious!

Let me point to the illustration I did for the Claire Messud book *The Emperor's Children*. I had to come up with an idea that would present the young professionals trying to realize their dreams in NYC around the same time the September Eleventh events unfolded. I had to reconcile in that one piece the tremendous weight of the tragedy with the POPiness of these greenhouse flowers. I decided to re-create the morning of September Eleventh.

I did many pictures of the downtown's skyline in the same hours as when the first plane struck, to have the same lighting as on the original day, to which I added an original Twin Towers photo. To show the formulaic mind-set of the characters in the story, I used Barbie dolls, which I dressed up with real clothes with the help of Photoshop. The challenge I was facing was to combine so many different parts into one organic sum: my photos of downtown, historical references (WTC, plane pictures), various proportions (dolls in the real interior), different lighting, etc. The dollness of the characters, combined with the realness of the plane about to strike the WTC, revealed the story line quite successfully.

Finally, how do you feel about
not having an original any
longer? Do you feel that your illustration is just that much more
ephemeral in the digital form?

The space under my bed was getting really tight for all the originals I kept piling there. Digital format came as a blessing, a space saver to protect my square feet in NYC's real estate. Now I can store hundreds of illustrations in a small hard drive.

Illustrations are ephemeral by design; their life span lasts until the paper ends up in a recycle bin.

▲ Egg

Client: The New York Times

Date: 2004

Illustrator: Ray Bartkus

Art Director: Steven Heller

Software: Photoshop

Some very good illustrations are to be judged only within the context of the text it was created to illustrate, but the better ones can endure as a piece of art in their own right. Fortunately, from time to time I have the possibility to show my illustrations in the exhibitions. The interesting thing about the digital format is that it is so much more amorphous: long after the file was created, it's very easy and inviting to change the dimensions, colors, proportions, eliminate one layer, add another, enhancing one or another aspect of the original idea, and presenting it as a digital print. The painted originals are so much more set and dead. ▪

Method Before Style

An interview with Mirko Ilic, principal of Mirko Ilic Corp., New York City

◄

Cyberhate

Date: 1996

Illustrator:
Mirko Ilic

Art Director:
Wayne Fitzpatrick

You were something of a pioneer in editorial illustration using digital tools. When did you switch from pen and ink (and scratchboard) to digital, and what did you use?

In Europe, I was both a designer and an illustrator. Partly because of my poor English and partly because it was easier to be an illustrator, when I arrived in the United States, I worked predominantly with illustration. From my variety of illustrative styles, art directors tended to choose my black-and-white scratchboard technique, and I immediately became typecast as a scratchboard artist.

In 1990 I purchased my first Mac. First of all, I did this because I like playing with new media and new possibilities. Secondly, I figured out that that this was a way of getting back to background in design. The computer allowed me to be a one-man studio without needing multiple people doing mechanical work (typesetting, pasteup, etc.). Additionally, the computer medium introduced something new and colorful to illustration.

Your work is highly conceptual. Did the new tool allow you to make images that you could never have made any other way?

First, I was bored and fed-up with doing scratchboard illustration. I wanted illustration to excite me again. With classical/traditional techniques, ideas get lost in handwriting. Through computers, one can be much more realistic and cold—detached, in other words. At the same time, there is the risk of losing the individuality and uniqueness of illustration through the electronic medium.

What is style for you?

I am much more interested in the way of thinking as a style, and because of that, the computer suited me well.

Were you ever worried that these effects would look too stylish or dated, given that others eventually moved into your territory?

Of course that's always a possibility if your idea or concept relies on the latest program or Photoshop filter, but if your work is conceptually driven, everything else becomes a side dish.

Technically speaking, were you able to master the software, or did you use other masters to do your bidding?

As I stated earlier, my English is quite poor, especially when it comes to "computer English," which is how I refer to the language that appears in computer manuals. However, I know that if I don't throw the computer or program out the window, after a few days, everything will work itself out.

And your first attempt?

My first attempt at Photoshop resulted in a cover for *Time* magazine, and my first attempt at Illustrator ended up as an illustration in one of the pages of *Time* magazine. In the process of doing these works, I "mastered" the software, with the exception of Maya—that's something I do with my coworker Lauren DaNapoli. She has been working for me for six to seven years, and she knows my way of thinking and my aesthetic. I'm familiar with the technical capabilities of 3D programs, so we are able to work together very well.

Even though you are working on the computer, do you still draw?

In my case, every piece of design, every logo, every illustration, and every layout is first sketched on paper. That way, it's faster and more direct. Especially in the case of illustration, it is important to have a sketch for the client's approval. It's much easier to have a hand-drawn sketch rather than one done on the computer.

How important is drawing? And given these technologies, is drawing the same as it's always been, or is there a new definition?

The Renaissance achieved one of the greatest advances in Western art by bringing everything down to human scale through drawing. How can you do things at a human scale/proportion if you can't draw? Drawing is extremely important, regardless of whether you're a graphic designer, an industrial designer, and so forth.

Of course, with the appearance of the computer, the need for drawing has been reduced in favor of photography, or illustrations that look like those in the emergency exit cards provided in airplanes (vector style). At the same time, many illustrators went in the opposite direction by adopting a style I refer to as, "Look Mom, I can't draw anymore." I believe the solution lies somewhere between these two opposing ends.

What's the most successful or satisfying image or images you ever produced in this manner?

This would probably have to be my series of illustrations entitled "Sex & Lies," because it would be very difficult to create something close to it through traditional methods of illustration.

Do you have go back to the more traditional methods, or have you left that behind forever? What's next (for you)?

No, again, I'm a little bit typecast in doing computer 3D illustration. I'm feeling that soon, for my personal amusement, I should start doing something different. Perhaps this will be returning to more traditional methods. ■

▼ Liberty Kiss

Client: *Village Voice*

"I'd Leave the Country, but My Wife Won't Let Me"

Illustrator:
Mirko Ilic

Art Director:
Minh Uong

Saint of the Month Club ▶

Client: Self

Date: 2000—2007

Designer: Josh Gosfield

Software: PhotoShop, Illustrator, QuickTime, Flash, Ecto, Soundtrac

CASE STUDY:

Saint of the Month Club

Josh Gosfield, principal of Mighty House of Pictures, New York City

You started out as a painter, illustrator, and collagist. Why did you become a digital designer?

I'm an insatiable autodidact with an addictive personality—I want to do everything. I've also made films, been a music video production designer, a window designer, a carpenter, a cartoonist, and even lived on farms. It's like art-form alcoholism—so, when the pixel world opened up with computers and software powerful enough to make something more than EtchASketch–y art, I got a Wacom pad and taught myself Photoshop.

Your Saint of the Month Club is built on original photography that you manipulate into satiric vignettes. Could this have been done without the benefit of digital media?

Impossible. First of all, because the Internet allows you to send images and files out into cyberspace without seeking the approval of gallerists, art directors, editors, or producers, this project never involved an unsuccessful pitch to some higher power—I just did it.

And although the early saints I sent were static images (JPEG files that had to be downloaded), as they evolved I began to add animation and sound in flash or QuickTime files. Doing that in analog media and getting more than twelve people and my mother to see them would have been a feat.

Your Web site is a veritable orgy of color, form, and symbol. What do you want your audience to take away from the site?

"In visual art, *horror vacui* (a fear of empty spaces) is the filling of the entire surface of an artwork with ornamental details, figures, shapes, lines and anything else the artist might envision." Wikipedia. I just throw it all out there and hope it sticks somewhere, somehow, with someone.

Do you see Saint of the Month as a means to make income, art, or both?

Well, it has brought me a job or two, but the Saint of the Month Club is mostly a labor of love. I devote myself to

February 12, 2007

Saint Angie of Pontani

The Saint of the Month Club is honored to have the beatified beauty, **Saint Angie of Pontani** gracing our digital portfolio this Valentine's Day. Worship her and a big hunk of love is likely to come your way. Need more Angie or need to meet the other Pontani Sisters? Go here.

Comments (2) | TrackBack (0)

January 26, 2007

al-Cuties

The most politically incorrect saints of all time: **al-Cuties**. A co-creation with the fabulously brilliant multi-media artist, Alex Sherwin.

Technorati Tags: al-cuties

October 25, 2006

Saint Roxie (again)

Although **Saint Roxie** is no elder states(wo)man - she's still got something to say about leading your life.

▲

Saint of the Month Club

Client: Self

Date: 2000—2007

Designer: Josh Gosfield and Alex Sherwin

Software: PhotoShop, Illustrator, QuickTime, Flash, ProTools

my saints, and if they see fit to warp the psychic energy of the universe so that a few extra shekels come my way, I'll just have to pray harder to them in the future.

How long do you spend on making the content for your site? Is this a profession or an avocation?

I spend *way* too much time. Some of the saints take as long as a week. It is great to have the enforced discipline of an art project with a monthly deadline, but it is sometimes a burden, bleeding away my days. Definitely more of an avocation than a profession.

Has the technology changed since you began? And if so, how has it affected what you do?

Not a huge change—mostly a question of speed—browsers and computers can process larger files, so I can add more sound and animation. There is always an issue of keeping files small—for those who have older computers or the few who still have dial-up connections—so there have been times when I've had to scale back my ambitions for a particular saint.

What have you been unable to accomplish because of the limits of technology?

Like oil paint or charcoal, I think of digital media as if it was a material. The limitations and strengths of the medium contribute to the qualities of the finished projects. For instance, images that are few and jerky will make smaller files than multiple or smoothly animated images. Ditto for short sound loops versus lengthy sound files.

Is this design or art or something else?

It is beatification!

It's been a few years; do you foresee taking Saint of the Month into the twenty-second century?

Hmmmm . . . Got to make my way into the twenty-first century before I make too many plans for the next one, but I will keep you posted, say, when we get into the 2180s. ■

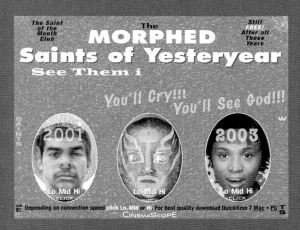

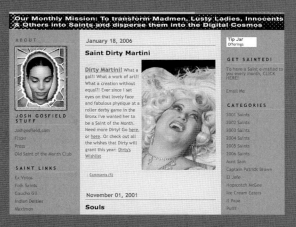

Typography and Graphic Design

For hundreds of years, the technology of type was left unchanged while the world sped into the future. Actual letterforms may have become more sophisticated—indeed, more outrageous, too—but the fundamental means of making typefaces in wood and metal remained constant.

Then in the 1950s photo typesetting reared its head in various ways. Different brand-name processes, including Magnetype, Typositor, and Adressograph, allowed for letters to be reproduced one letter at a time to form headlines on film strips, which were then pasted on boards with glue or wax. Body copy was also set in crisp columns as well. Phototypography was, however, merely a blip in the continuum of progress. It wasn't much longer before the digital, which already had taken the recording industry by storm, was poised to enter the precincts of type design and typesetting.

As high-resolution printers came on the market, digital foundries—such as Emigre Fonts and T-26, among many—started producing, and encouraging, radical new typefaces (some grungy, in keeping with the styles of the times, and others classical for basic everyday use). Where previously type design was the exclusive domain of skilled craftspersons, in this new digital era anyone with Fontographer and other type-designing software could produce viable—if often eccentric—alphabets. Eventually, the old methods were obsolete. Like the doomed eight-track tape player, phototypesetting was rejected entirely. Hot-metal typesetting continues, but only as an anachronism, practiced by passionate purists.

But even in the beginning type was still set by typesetters until Apple introduced systems that made everyone a typesetter. The idea that such specialized jargon as font entered the common vernacular still has some old-timers scratching their heads, but the computer decidedly democratized typography, just as the old Gutenberg printing press helped bring democracy—and literacy—to the world. Everyone can work (or play) with type on their desktop, and some neophytes do it well. Yet the professional

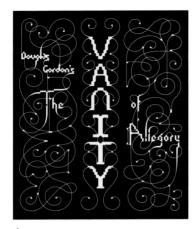

▲

AIGA Tape Banner

Date: October 2005

Client: Stefan Sagmeister/Deutsche Guggenheim

Art Directors: Stefan Sagmeister, Matthias Ernstenberger

Designer: Marian Bantjes

Software: Adobe Illustrator

designer is still the master of this medium. Knowing the history and understanding the aesthetics of type is essential in making a professional practice.

Today the average computer is loaded with hundreds of typefaces, but that does not mean that one need use them all. In fact, the abundance of faces is counterproductive. A designer must learn how best to use type as a vessel of meaning, as well as a tool of style. In the digital realm, on the Web and handheld devices, type is still in its adolescence. The user often has more control of typefaces than the designer. But that does not absolve the designer of typographic responsibilities. In fact, the digital designer must anticipate the various ways that type will be used and viewed in these new environments.

Not every digital designer will be a type designer—this still requires a great deal of skill and talent—but typography is an essential art for anyone who answers to the title *designer*. With the plethora of faces available, it is necessary for designers to be acquainted with a range of functional forms, but also to be aware of the newbies coming on the market. Since type can be a sign of the times (as well as time-honored form), designers must understand the difference between new and novelty. Still, being a typographer and graphic designer in the digital environment is no different than it was back in the days of hot metal or phototype, only the options are greater now than before. ■

AIGA Tape Banner ▶

Date: December 2006

Client: AIGANY

Designer: Marian Bantjes

Software: Adobe Illustrator

Wonderland ▶

Date: September 2006

Client: De.Mo

Art Director: Giorgio Baravalle

Designer: Marian Bantjes

Software: Adobe Illustrator

Vector Artist

An interview with Marian Bantjes, type and lettering designer, Vancouver, Canada

Your work is so handcrafted; how did you reconcile working with digital tools?

I'm not sure there is reconciliation; it's just an extension. There were certain things I couldn't do by hand—or not without a great deal of effort—so I ended up digital. It started with patterns. There is nothing more tedious than drawing the same thing over and over again, so it's logical to take that into an environment where you don't have to. It was also the obvious tool for perfecting tiling units.

Your work is also very calligraphic, which is unusual for a digital designer.

When it comes to lettering, it's very important to understand that I'm not a calligrapher. I actually have a really crappy hand. A calligrapher takes a pen or brush and makes a really beautiful line. I take a pencil and draw the line, erasing and adjusting. Then I rely on the computer to help me with the perfection of the curve and the smoothness of line. I can't draw a line like that, especially at any decent size, so I do it in vector art. So there wasn't any "switch" for me, like I do this thing by hand and now I have to relearn or try to emulate it on the computer. If anything, it was the other way around. I had some stuff I wanted to do, I had good skills with vectors, but how was I to get there? Start by drawing.

Why is your work so elaborate?

My work is elaborate because it makes me happy. I like things that are complex—that you want to look and look at, or figure out, or have things that reveal themselves over time. When I work, I really need to get into it and concentrate on it for a long time. I don't multitask. I can't skim along the surface; it's boring, and boredom makes me unhappy.

Can you be simple?

I can be simple. Sort of. But simple is deceptive, isn't it? There's a lot of complexity in simple. A lot of planning, a lot of structure. I have a great affinity for that formal, modernist Swiss design (e.g., of the 1950s to 1970s): I'm a fanatic for grids and alignment and sense and order. I can be simple, provided it's actually complex. It has to take all my attention. There have to be fiddly details even if those fiddly details are only straight lines.

Drawing appears to be so important in your elaborately decorative lettering. Has the digital made this easier? Or instead, has it made you think of lettering anew?

To me, the computer is just a finishing tool. I can't think on the computer. Sometimes I try to take a shortcut, go straight to the computer, and at some point I'll be struggling and I'll realize that the computer is limiting me. I don't know why or how this is; I just can't think or plan or even draw properly until I have that pencil in my hand and a piece of paper. What the digital makes easier is the endless minor adjustments in search of the perfect line, repetition and reflection (flipping the art); and I love that crisp line, along with the fact that it's infinitely scalable. But there is a look that comes with digital, and this does affect how I imagine the final work.

How much technology must you know to get along?

You know, it's hard to know how much technology one knows until you try to explain it to someone who doesn't know it. I have a lot of technological knowledge that I'm not even aware of, but having said that, in terms of the software I'm using and how I'm using it, "Not very much." I use Illustrator a lot—a very common

program—and I use it at a very low level (not that it's doing all that I need it to—far from it). That is, of all that it can do, I'm using maybe five percent? Of Photoshop, I use maybe ten percent? I need to learn more about FontLab; I probably know about 1 percent of what it can do. InDesign is another story—I use it to maybe eighty percent of its capacity, but that's a different part of my life.

Where do you draw the line between technology and art?

Well, I guess the answer for me goes back to your previous question. The planning, thinking, and drawing are the art part. The finishing, when I use the computer, is the technology. I could conceivably hire someone to do that part for me—a trained monkey, maybe (albeit a very well trained monkey). But it wouldn't be much fun for me, and we might fight over the bananas.

Do you like the monkey part?

I actually do enjoy the production work: just getting it right. I would have been a great production artist. I used to typeset for [the veteran typographer and author] Robert Bringhurst: He was the art, and I was the technology. And I thoroughly enjoyed it: He had meticulous markup, and I just loved getting it right.

Is there anything you cannot do on the computer in terms of your lettering?

Yes, lots. If I'm doing something with lots of little unique, itty-bitty parts, that I'll do by hand. I can draw little squiggles or hairy lines for hours, but on the computer? Ugh. Boring. Tedious. Almost impossible.

And then there's texture. Texture of line, of color, and of material. When I draw in ink on paper, it bleeds a little. Sometimes that's annoying, but sometimes I really like it. I can't get that in digital. And again, my wobbly, imperfect line: If I want that, it has to be done by hand. When you see the work I do by hand you want to touch it. It has incredible depth; it's warm, it has humanity. My digital work is cold. Cold isn't bad; it's just a little distant.

Color is also a big one, and sometimes a problem for me. I'll do flat colors and a little gradient sometimes, but in general I don't like digital color very much—again, because it lacks texture. Yeah, you can fake it, but then it's fake, so why would you? So for color I really love inks, and ballpoint pen—especially for shading. There's no way I can do proper shading on the computer. Maybe someone can, but not me.

A lot of your work is very dimensional. The digital must be a boon to that?

Actually, you know what's really funny? I can't do 3D on the computer. I'm really into spacial ideas, but I can only draw them on paper. Sometimes I think I should learn a 3D program, but I'm too busy and too lazy and too old. But also, I'm not crazy about the way computer 3D looks (except wire frames, which are wonderful).

It's getting better, but there's just no way I have the time to learn those skills at the level that I'd be satisfied with. Maybe someday some hotshot studio will ask me to collaborate with them on something, and they'll have some young 3D genius and we'll all have piles of fun, make something really interesting, and all live happily ever after.

Would you say you are a purist, or do you relish mistakes?

A little of both. I would never describe myself as a perfectionist. In fact, I've often said I'm an imperfectionist. Though I go a certain distance down that road, I'm perfectly capable of leaving something at good enough. But I'm pretty snobby about purity in line—especially digital line—and I hate mistakes. Hate, hate, *hate*! They torture me, they ruin my life, they make me so unhappy. It's one thing to say something's good enough and be satisfied with its slightly imperfect state. It's

another altogether to suddenly see something—after it's done—that's not good enough. Oh, the horror.

Could you work efficiently today without this tool?

No, I would have to give up a whole chunk of the work I do. Maybe even everything. I would be devastated without it. Sure, I could just draw and work on paper, but it wouldn't be the same, because even though I can't think on the computer, it still affects how I think. It's like you have a box of crayons and you use all the colors; sometimes you make only blue-green drawings, and sometimes you make only red-yellow drawings, and sometimes you make both. Then one day, someone takes away all your blue-green crayons? That would suck.

You teach graphic design. Do you also teach typography of the kind you practice?

No. I teach a very basic crash course in typography. I'm very traditional and very strict. I learned typography by being a book typesetter for ten years, and I believe in it: I believe in the rules and the structure and that there's a right way and a wrong way—even though I break those rules myself all the time.

To me it's like writing: You have to learn your ABCs; you have to learn

how to write according to the rules. Then write like James Joyce or e.e. cummings, or whoever. So I teach them all this stuff, and then at the end of the course I blow their minds by showing them my work.

I do, however, teach little workshops when I visit schools, and then I have an exercise I do that gives them a little hint into the way I think, and one of the ways I sometimes view type. It's fun; it gets great results, and I'm pretty sure the students enjoy it and learn something useful.

Do you insist that your students draw, or do you accept that digital is their métier?

Well, I'm teaching typography, not type design, so there's very little drawing to do. I do get them to do some. But the bigger part of this question is about accepting digital as other people's métier. My answer to that is yes, I definitely do.

Younger people have grown up on computers, and I'm perfectly willing to accept that they probably can think in the digital realm in a way that I can't. I would encourage students to try drawing, because it's how I would best be able to teach them, but if they said, "I can't think this way" (and it has happened in a workshop), then fine.

On the other hand, if they were working on the computer and having trouble, I think I would be able to recognize by the kind of trouble they were getting into if it was the computer that was doing it—then I'd say, "Take this pencil; you might find it easier."

Your work has an old-world flavor, but done with new-world methods. Do you see any irony, paradox, or paraironydox in that? Not at all. Everybody, all the time, is stealing from the past. I'm just one of those thieves who's re-imagining,

remixing, remaking, using the tools of my time. If I'm very, very lucky, maybe in the future someone will springboard off my stuff with the latest Hyperconfabulatronicum and make something within my graphic lineage. ■

ESPN Magazine ▶

Date: 2005

Art Director: Jason Lancaster

Designer: Marian Bantjes

Software: Adobe Illustrator

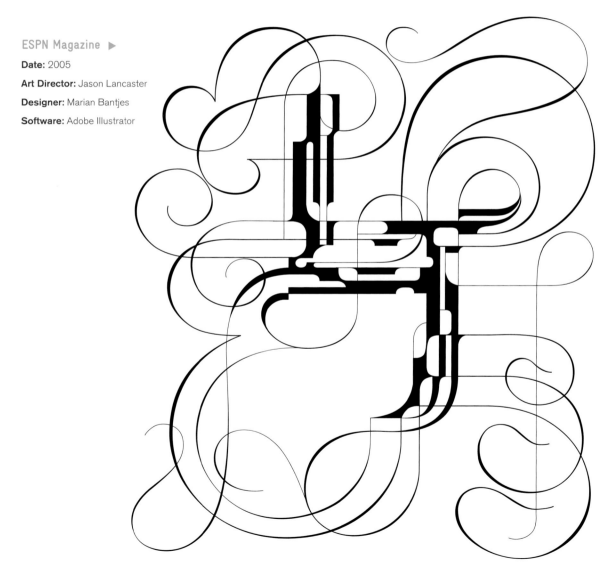

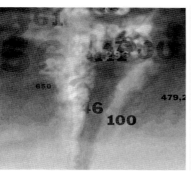

Modernism Goes Digital

An interview with Richard Turtletaub, Richard Turtletaub Design and Illustration, San Francisco

You began as a print designer/ illustrator of single images. What made you transition into sequential work?

I've been interested in film and animation as long as I can remember. When I was a teen I used to make super-8 films that were very much an imitation of Terry Gilliam's animations for *Monty Python's Flying Circus*. The interest in the more experimental side of film/motion graphics developed more gradually. I've always wanted to do more motion-related work; I guess I just got caught up in the illustration and still graphics and never made a full-fledged effort at promoting that interest professionally, at least until recently.

Your style has a certain retro quality. You are influenced and inspired by classic modernists. How does working with digital tools underscore this reinvention of the predigital era?

It's true that the style does have a certain retro quality, although I'm trying to bring it more into the present. While I am clearly influenced by the classic modernists, I think there's a lot of exciting things happening now in the design world in general, and am trying to look more to that in my search for inspiration. In my new pieces, my goal is to look more contemporary, to point more toward the future.

Are you referring to animation/ motion graphics? Working with

digital tools definitely makes things easy. It's mind-boggling to me what one can do in the program AfterEffects.

What are the different, and contrasting, characteristics between your motion and static work?

The motion work takes a lot longer! Seriously, most of the motion pieces seem like a series of different illustrations set up as separate scenes, which some object enters and interacts with in a certain sequence. These illustration scenes will usually undergo movement or change in addition to the overlying object that is interacting. Often, the motion pieces begin with one illustration as a basis.

▲ Plastic Bird

Designer: Richard Turtletaub

Associate Designer: Dana Smith

Software: Adobe After Effects and Photoshop

©2007, Richard Turtletaub

Are you content to work with the tools available, or have you had to create custom programs to suit your needs?

I wish I had the vision to be creating work that expanded beyond the capabilities of the current programs, but it seems so far that everything I could think of doing (plus a whole lot more) has long been a part of the programs I use.

You've created animation projects for Wolfgang Hastert/ZDF-Arte films (Germany) and macys.com. What was your role in these?

Wolfgang Hastert has been making short films for German television. For Wolfgang I did some titles for films, as well as an animated trailer. The titles for him were mostly still-image, while the trailer was an animated piece.

I did some freelance design for macys.com and had an opportunity to do an animated short for a denim promotion for their home page, which they changed weekly. For this short I established the look, did the storyboard, produced the altered figures and backgrounds. I had the fortune to have a team to work with in this case, including a photographer and someone to do the actual Flash programming for me, in addition to the creative director who knew of my interest in motion graphics and provided the opportunity for me.

But now you are working on your more self-directed projects—what is your goal? Are you pushing the digital limits, or happily working within them?

I'm working on a series of small motion pieces, ideally showing a range of styles that I'm interested in. I'm always in the process of redoing my reel. I would very much like to push beyond (starting with) my own limits and explore new territory. I don't intend to always be a one-man band. There are many interesting firms out there that interest me that are producing exciting work. I guess my goal is to be producing stuff that I think is exciting, whether it's solo or a collaborative situation.

Do you feel it is necessary for the continuance of your career to shift from conventional illustration and design to the digitally kinetic world?

It seems to be more potentially lucrative than illustration, but I would say I'm doing it out of interest in exploring motion graphics, not out of having to do it in order to survive.

How far will, and can, you go with this new media?

I suppose until I'm bored with it, but I can't imagine that happening. ∎

Coding the World

An interview with Jonathan Puckey, Amersterdam

How did you get started designing digital tools for print publications?

I started out as an interaction designer, and a number of years ago decided to move away from the Web and went to the Gerrit Rietveld Academy in Amsterdam to study graphic design. Because of my background in scripting, it was a natural step to start to experiment with dynamic principles for print-based media.

What, specifically, do you think is interesting about making your own tools?

A tool doesn't have to be something as simple as a fill bucket. It can also be a very personal and precisely defined thing that only a couple of designers will ever be interested in using. So something that before was reserved for the programmers of Adobe is now open to everyone.

Could you describe your working process? Do you usually have a specific effect in mind that you are trying to create? Or do you start playing around with the code to see what happens visually?

Scripting is like speaking a language. As long as I can describe in words what I want to accomplish, I can also put those ideas into code. Before I start developing a tool, I first look for a good question that needs to be asked. Although, while I'm coding a tool, often I'll end up with a much better question than the one I had in the first place.

When I'm creating a new tool, I try to keep its possibilities as open as possible so the outcome rests mainly on the hands and ideas of the designer using it. In a lot of programmed design the results can become rather stiff and generic because the creativity happens mainly in the code and the computer executes it perfectly. I think it's important to emphasize the handcrafted quality of the design and not the outcome of a machine. Actually, I think the battle between these two—automatization and intuition—is what fascinates me.

Usually when I finish a tool, I feel overwhelmed by its possibilities and have to spend quite a lot of time learning how to work with it. A good tool doesn't automatically create interesting work.

Can you talk about how the tools you've developed reveal your particular interests?

At the moment, one of my big interests is finding ways of using the hand as an important element in my design. In a way, I want to perform my work; I want the process of my design to be an intuitive and fluent thing.

I try not to look for a certain aesthetic; instead I want my aesthetics to be a logical outcome of the way I work.

My tile tool, for example, is partly a product of a fascination with constructed typography and design created out of tiles. I have produced constructed typography in the past, and the process was so complicated and boring. There were no accidents left in the work.

It felt like working with one hand tied behind my back. I created a tool that allows you to design tiles and draw with them. By drawing, I mean that the tiles are placed by moving the mouse. The tool knows when to use a tile for a top right corner and when it should use a horizontal tile. Since the act of placing a tile doesn't consist of five steps anymore, it frees you up to work in another way.

This tool is actually very open to all kinds of design, since graphically it's almost completely dependent on the design of the tiles and how you draw. But on the other hand, it's a very specific way of working, and it can only be performed well with enthusiasm. You can't use it for everything, and that doesn't matter. I think tools should be more like fonts. We should be able to pick and choose or create our own from scratch.

Software companies have now started adding on their own very specific tools into the standard tool set of their applications, and I don't understand it. Were we really all looking for a tool that creates twirls? Make it optional, and all at once it doesn't matter anymore how specific you get. Make it possible for anyone to create their own tools, and it becomes very powerful.

You mention that before you start developing a tool you first look for a good question that needs to be asked. Can you give me an example of a good question? Or a question that has been good for you?

The questions are usually very simple: "What if pixels had corners?" "What if I could link the gradual boldness of a font to meaning?" "Why is it difficult to make typography not go straight; shouldn't it be the other way around?"

I talk about questions because in my work I try to find things that people can look at and understand the problems I was dealing with while designing it. A problem can be a system with a set of logical limitations or limitations based on a technique I came up with.

I remember a lecture by Karel Martens. He was talking about how much his work is based on the limitations of printing techniques such as letterpress and litho. I felt very jealous, because with my computer I seemingly had next to none.

Being able to produce anything feels like a heavy weight on my shoulders. Every single decision becomes so full of meaning, because I could have done it in another way. Tools are able to create a little world of logic that breaks up all these little decisions into larger pieces. You've already solved a number of problems by creating the tool and now you're left to spend more attention on performing a design.

I also don't want my work to emulate styles while the technology I'm using has no relation to the original limitations that were necessary to produce them. There are so many new possibilities with the coming of computers, and I feel that only redoing the visual layer of the way it was done before isn't enough. We should come up with our own limitations—and, of course, in a certain way, we already have.

What's the point of designing your own software? Doesn't the current design software offer enough opportunities—and limitations?

We all use the same software and agree with the options the software companies provide us. But I feel that these applications force us into working in a very specific way. All the options are there in a very split-up fashion, and we have to string them up after each other, and (I, at least) end up questioning every step.

For me, programming tools are a way to bring back limitations that I can work with(in). By having more control over software, I can give away control over my work on my own terms.

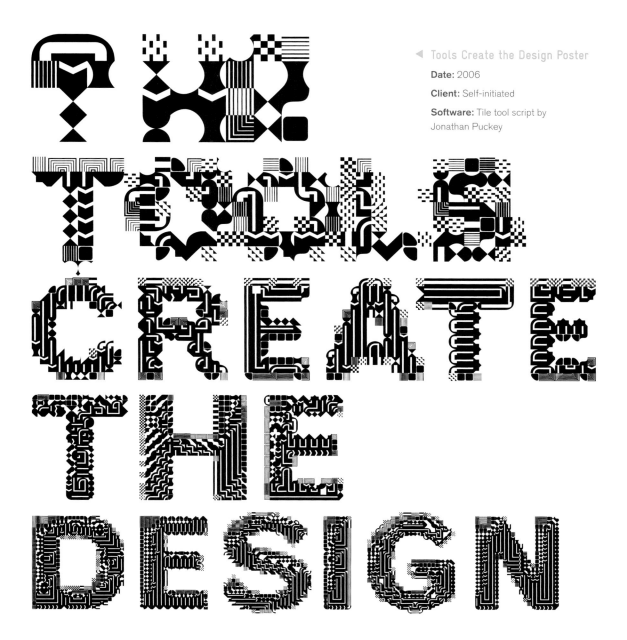

THE TOOLS CREATE THE DESIGN

◀ Tools Create the Design Poster

Date: 2006

Client: Self-initiated

Software: Tile tool script by Jonathan Puckey

Before you know how to use the tool, how do you know if it is good or not?

It's quite difficult to predict, actually. I developed a tool a while ago with the idea of having text point to certain magnetic areas on the page, creating a kind of chaotic logic in a page filled with typography. I really liked the idea, but I wasn't able to produce good work with it. Perhaps the work I was making just didn't fit in with the possibilities of the tool; maybe another designer will create amazing things with it. ■

Mixing Media and Jazz

An interview with Bobby Martin, design director, Jazz at Lincoln Center, New York City

▲

Jazz at Lincoln Center Home Page
www.jalc.org

Art Direction: Bobby C. Martin Jr.

Designer: Daryl Long

Animation: Johnathan Swafford

You began in magazines. How much did digital design tools play a role in your practice?

I view digital design as developing and organizing content to communicate an idea for screen. Digital design is more than design for the Internet, television, and other multimedia applications. It is also the creation of imagery using digital programs.

My first job out of college was as an associate art director for a magazine. Even though it was at the height of the dot-com era, we didn't even have online access at work. All of our photography was analog. However, we often had photographers shoot chromes because it was the quickest turn around time. The prepress department created match prints out of film, which was a slow process, but it helped me to understand the printing process. I worked with the art director to lay out the magazine using Quark Xpress. The design was best described at simple and straightforward, mostly consisting of type on one side and image on the other.

And then . . . ?

Later, I moved on to *Yahoo! Internet Life* magazine. It was a magazine where the content was driven by what was new and happening on the Web. The identity of the magazine mimicked the vernacular of the Web by using icons such as windows, arrows, buttons, and lozenges. The typography fluidly moved across the page, images were often placed within window-like boxes, and the headers sat atop the page like navigation. The Internet-derived content influenced everything from the typography to the illustration, which was often created by illustrators who worked with 3D modeling.

You are now the design director for Jazz at Lincoln Center. Would you think of yourself as a digital designer or a graphic designer?

I am a graphic designer. I use fundamentals of graphic design to help me with all of the various components of my job. For instance, I use basic typography and hierarchy to organize information for print, as well as the Web. I use scale, proportion, and composition to extend the Jazz at Lincoln Center identity throughout all communications. I use grid systems and color theory to design the offices, theater, and other three-dimensional spaces. I use design and art history to understand how to work with photography and illustration for advertising and promotional materials.

How much of what you do at Jazz at Lincoln Center is in digital media?

When developing the Web site, I will often lay out information in a program like Illustrator or Photoshop. Our Web designer/programmer will then take the layouts and start to find ways to make it come to life online. I then work with him to decide what should be animated and what should be static. We work

together to decide what is most important and what is secondary and tertiary.

The main priority of our Web site is to promote our performances and education programs. However, it is also the easiest and most accessible way to communicate to a global audience. Therefore, there is a tremendous amount of content that has to be organized in a user-friendly way. We have limited Flash just to our home page; we offer podcasts, music samples, Jazz at Lincoln Center Orchestra interview videos, online education videos and a lot more.

So digital media is a primary component?

At Jazz at Lincoln Center we use digital media all of the time. We use digital photography, digital printing, digital screens to promote our events at the box office, digital hi-def screens with animated content in the theaters. We use digital applications from Photoshop, In-Design, Illustrator, as well as other customized programs for creating animations for our Ertegun Jazz Hall of Fame. We send promotions digitally through e-mail, and create invitations for events with e-vites. We have even created a MySpace page for promoting the jazz club to college students.

▲

John Scofield and Brad Mehldau

Art Direction: Bobby C. Martin Jr.

Design: Bobby C. Martin Jr.

Do you foresee more of the promotion and other work migrating more into the digital realm?

There are a lot of ideas floating around. There are a lot of things that we could do from an online blog or magazine. We do a lot of promotion for events digitally because most of the time we work on tight budgets and tight deadlines. E-mail has become a very important and easy way to get the word out quickly and inexpensively. We often do e-mail acquisition campaigns to gain access to potential concert goers. (We offer a chance to win tickets to an upcoming concert if they fill out information, including their e-mail address.)

Does designing for screen differ in standards from your print work?

The standard doesn't differ; I still want the design work to be as excellent as possible. I spend a lot of time on large campaign-related projects that include brochures, mailers, posters, and newspaper and magazine advertising. In print work I have to plan differently than digital work because I have to allow time for proofing, printing, folding, gluing, and mailing.

Designing for the Web differs from print mostly because of the restrictions. The type usually has to be larger and the canvas is usually smaller. The digital work that I get most excited about is animation, whether created in Flash or After Effects, the moving type and image has so much potential to be compelling.

Do you feel there are two aesthetic standards for print and multimedia?

They are slightly different experiences. I enjoy picking Pantone

colors and playing with the printing process. I was intimidated by that same process when I was right out of college; however, now I collaborate closely with printers, which helps me differentiate our work from competitors'.

I also use certain production techniques such as embossing, letterpress, metallic and Day-Glo inks, silkscreening, and various paper stocks that help create a variety of moods and expressions that I can't duplicate digitally. This bag of tricks heightens the experience of the viewer, enticing them to buy tickets, go to an event, or become a member.

In contrast, digitally I can utilize sound, animation, and other time-based techniques that can dramatically enhance an experience. These techniques can leave a positive impression that can extend past the actual user experience. It's like when I have a good song stuck in my head, I'm singing it all day long.

For the Ertegun Jazz Hall of Fame, I worked with Scott Stowell and his team at Open to develop multimedia videos for each inductee. These videos capture the legacy and the personality of the jazz musicians and their music. I find this a fascinating way to pay tribute to these artists, because it brings

their experience to life in a way that makes them relevant today.

Is there an increasing need in your art department for designers with digital skills? And are they more in the production or conception areas?

My department mostly consists of designers with good typography, organizational skills, and lots of passion. I encourage my team to develop good concepts for their projects because it builds a foundation and a starting point that allows them to be creative. Digital skills definitely help, because it's important to know how to take a campaign idea and extend it over the various touch points that the audience will encounter.

What do you look for when hiring a designer?

When hiring a designer I first try to see how passionate they are about design. Although a lot of design is often raw talent, I'd rather have a hard worker than a perfect designer. Its very important to me that I am able to collaborate with my team, so I look for people who play well with others and have a constructive working environment that we can all learn from and grow within. Of course, I look at skills, both conceptual and production, but it's not what's most important to me. ■

From Prankster to Digitalist

An interview with Patric King, cofounder of Pretty, Chicago

▲
www.radaronline.com

Client: U.S. News

Date: 2004

Designer: Patric King

Technology design: Su

©House of Pretty

At what point in your professional life did you devote yourself to the Web—or the digital world?

I've been deeply involved with the Web since 1992 or so, when I first discovered Gopher and WAIS at the University of Tennessee's library. Professionally, I started designing Thirst's online accounts exclusively in 1997, then left that agency for an online agency company in 2000. Su has, quite literally, been online for half his life, since the 1980s.

That said, we never meant to leave the world of tactile objects behind. The Web chose us. It seems that our natural interests are a few years ahead of mainstream communication, so we end up being more technologically advanced than other design studios, and therefore find it easier to adapt to new media.

In the early stage of your digital typography, there was a decided avant garde or edge-pushing thrust to your work. Do you feel that now that the digital environment has matured, you've matured, too?

I hate to say it, but I feel like my early work from the nineties was me spouting off in public and not really caring how it affected anyone. I was interested in being a prankster; being a microcelebrity; and being a morally outspoken designer. What I wasn't doing, in retrospect, was listening to the world.

And now?

I grew up a lot, and quickly, as the world itself changed after 9/11. That event was the first time I realized that Americans were perceived anywhere to be ideologically wrong, and that realization—that my world was not the center of the world—forced me to change.

I still feel that my work is very much engaged with being morally outspoken and still tricksterish. But the visual vocabulary I'm using now is a lot more accessible than it was in the early nineties. Also, a lot of other folks are using ideas of designer-as-author, which were popularized then, but not used as much. It's more accepted now. So I think it's a little of the world changing along with me, too.

You work on a lot of blogs. What is the most important design concern in this medium?

It's a lot like book design or magazine design to me. The Weblog authors who come to us are the ones who are setting off to publish with a capital P—it's not a hobby. One Weblog company we work for pulls in several thousand dollars each month in ad revenue, and they're regarded as a valid voice in their culture. Their work has to look and operate very well; otherwise, they look like amateurs.

My biggest concern in creating a Weblog's formatting is to make sure that I create a consistent and full set of possible appearances so that the author has a complete visual vocabulary at their disposal, and all displayed by common CSS tags. A blog is literally a book-in-the-making, so the design must be ready for any scenario an author throws at it.

Do you feel that Web work is diametrically different from print, or is there a common ground?
I feel that the Web is a lot more disciplined than print. In print, you are so disconnected from the systems producing your design that the work can be the product of lazy thinking more easily than that produced online.

A lot of print design is done in a bubble, because there is no interaction between designer, broadcast venue, or audience. The Web removes that bubble—if you've made a shoddy file, it might render incorrectly or not at all. If your design doesn't work for the audience, they say so, and it's suddenly a decision whether or not to honor their opinions and

perceptions. That conversation never happens in print or filmed media.

What can you do now digitally that expresses your vision that you couldn't do, say, two years ago?
I find myself spending a lot less time creating finished objects these days. I spend a lot more time creating styled building blocks, which allows our clientele to communicate well and with versatility. It wasn't as easy to do that a little while ago, because the everyday user didn't understand creating their own content as well as they do now.

How much of your concern is technics versus aesthetics?

▲ WiredDisney

Client: *Wired* Magazine   **Date:** 2003   **Designer:** Patric King   ©House of Pretty

It's fifty/fifty. Construction and technical prowess are equally as important as aesthetics. If something can't be done, I will redesign so that it can be done. The harshest part of the Web is that not only is your design up for criticism—especially in the Web's echo chamber—but so is your construction. If you're working in print, the only one who knows your production sucks is your prepress person. Online, everyone can see mistakes. And they tell you.

How would you define good design in this digital environment? And has this definition changed over time?

My personal definition of good design is design that works well, looks good, and delivers surprise and delight (when I'm in control of those ideals). In earlier years, my goal was simply to create the most visually beautiful thing I could, regardless of functionality or reaction.

What don't you know now that you must know in the near future to keep up with the field?

I'm now exploring ways to bring detailed typography into our work so that the work is visually as dense and refined as it would be on a tactile surface. Web browsers are still not elegant enough for everyday use, so typography and reading is still primitive. I want to find ways to make content management systems work in Flash's richer visual environment, which I know is possible; we've done it before. But it's rarely done or asked for, so we haven't researched it very much yet.

Are there always going to be limitations in how you design in this environment?

I doubt it. A lot of my concerns—better typography, more fluid reading spaces, multicolumn reading spaces—are actively being addressed for future browsers that work in real-world settings. I am actually very eager for the day that I can stop worrying whether something will work, and that Su and I can simply design.

Do you work with others, or is Pretty a self-contained organism?

We work with others very rarely. We usually commission others for their talent in image-craft or types of interactivity with which we don't do so well. We use a couple of frequent collaborators for our illustration and Flash work. Su and I both hate working in Flash—I'm just slow at it; he's unfamiliar with the interface—and we find ourselves needing a lot of handmade art in media we're not great with. I can draw like a fiend, and Su's an amazing typo-

▲
www.defamer.com

Client: Gawker Media

Date: 2005

Designer: Patric King

Technology Design: Gawker Technology

©House of Pretty

graphic composer, but neither of us is powerful with, say, watercolor or steelpoint pen.

What do you look for when hiring someone for Pretty?

We look for folks who can do something we can't, and in a tone of voice we wouldn't think of; someone who exhibits a fierce curiosity and technical excellence living up to our standards. Someone who understands that the work they create is not for them, but for someone else. ▪

The Language of Types

An interview with Emily King, curator and critic, London

Not since Gutenberg has there been such a revolution in type. Even phototype was not as radically significant as the digital. How would you describe what's occurred over the past decade and a half?

With all previous typesetting systems, the type functioned as a machine part. Type design was part of an industrial process, and type designers were the employees of manufacturing companies. The emergence of device-independent digital typesetting blew this relationship apart. From the late 1980s on, anyone in possession of a computer and some relatively cheap software could become a type designer. And not only could they create fonts, they could also distribute them internationally. What had once been a close-knit, some say monklike, profession became a free-for-all. I would describe the events of the last fifteen years as the deprofessionalization of type design.

What is the fundamental difference between digital typeface design and previous forms? Have more designers (and even nondesigners) been invited into a once-exclusive club?

The fundamental difference between digital type and previous forms is that its design is not linked to the manufacture of the typesetting system. When type becomes software, it can be transferred freely from one machine to another, and from one context to another. Of course, this is a liberation, but it has created a number of copyright problems. It is a rare type designer who feels that they have been paid for their work in full.

The type designers' club—that is, people who attend A Typ I conferences and the like—remains fairly exclusive. To belong at that level takes a level of commitment and skill that very few have the ability and the will to achieve. There are, however, vast numbers of widely used typefaces designed by people who have nothing to do with that scene. It is not so much that the club has invited new members; it is more that the club has become only one part of a much broader typographic universe.

In the new digital world, is it essential to understand the language of type (and type design) to be an effective participant?

It is as hard to design an effective text face as ever it was. There was a flourish of new fonts when type design software became widely available in the late 1980s and early 1990s, but since then things have calmed down; there has been something of a consolidation. There has been a general recognition that, okay, you might not need to be an employee of Monotype to design a typeface, but, all the same, you have to learn the history and acquire the understanding. That said, there are still vast numbers of easy-come-easy-go disposable display faces that are certainly effective in their own arena. Of course, these have always been around, but they are consumed more rapidly and in greater volume than ever before.

As a critic and historian, you understand the shifts in design from one era to the next. With the ability for nondesigners to use type, how has this altered design practice?

The best-used type designs in the world are now largely in the hands of amateurs—for example, Verdana—for the simple reason that amateur type users outnumber professionals by a huge margin. That said, the vast majority of nonprofessionals only use a very small proportion of the available typefaces—I bet about ten designs account for 90 percent of amateur use, and all of these will be bundled with software.

In general, professional and amateur typography are completely different spheres, although of course it is now easier for a dedicated and talented amateur to move into the professional sphere, which is obviously a good thing. To answer your question, the nondesigners' use of type has had a big impact on the typefaces that are designed with the nondesigner in mind.

On a more general note, type designers are more open to various sources of influence, particularly from popular culture, than ever before. The increase in popular interest in type that has arisen from the rise in nonprofessional design has been met with a corresponding interest in popular culture among professional designers.

You also chronicle the nexus of art and design. How have the digital technologies made designers out of artists?

Like everyone else, artists now have access to design software, and like everyone else, they want to use it. Unlike everyone else, however, they often think they are better designers than most professionals. Some of them are and some of them aren't. Of course, the artist as designer is a phenomenon that predates digital technology. Ed Ruscha, Joseph Kosuth, and Lawrence Weiner are all fabulous designers. Maybe there are more of them around now that the tools are more widely available.

On another tack, it is certainly the case that more and more designers are treating design as a found object, as a ready-made that they can turn into art by putting into a gallery, usually ignoring the fact that it was designed by someone else in the first place.

Of course, there are a set of digital artists, artists who work with software and so must understand how to use and to make it. But artists have always used tools and techniques; I don't think that artists become designers through using the same materials. On a different level, there are lots of people who choose to call themselves artists these days, and maybe they're not wrong. It is a very unfixed term. The issues at stake are cultural and economic, not technological.

Finally, as a curator, particularly interested in the new venues for digital media, how can art and design created in the ether get preserved for posterity?

I think collecting should carry on as normal. That is, curators should pick examples of work that they think are worth collecting and that fit with their institution's remit, and conservators should work out how to preserve them for the benefit of future generations. Of course, there are decisions to be made as to whether a piece of software should be shown on its original platform, but I suspect that these are best made in a piece-meal, case-by-case fashion. ■

Digital Education

Khoi Vhin (see pages 113–116) was an illustration major, Chris Capuozzo (see pages 122–125) studied comics, Mike Essl (see pages 130–134) studied type and lettering, and Elliott Earls (see pages 321–323) studied art and design. Although many of the digital designers who are at the top of the heap today did not study digital design in school, that doesn't mean that they wouldn't rather hire digital-design graduates—it just means the option wasn't available at the time. The important thing is that they all received some formal training.

Valuable lessons can be learned from any type of study, but the increasing specialization of course offerings means you may be competing for jobs with people who have training in the area. If you want to be a game designer, for example, but aren't planning on getting a formal education in game design, you should at least be prepared to explain why you made that decision, and how your other skills and experience compensate.

Presumably, you are reading this far along into this book because, more than being versed in computer technology, you want to generate integral pieces of design work that have your imprimatur. In other words, you want to design the look and feel of, if not also create content for, anything from a Web site to broadcast to a magazine or book. You want to make animation, produce typography, or invent a means of communication that will impact on audiences large and small. You want to be a designer, not a programmer, IT manager, or production coordinator.

Therefore, you want to study in an environment that enables you to both invigorate your creative side and exercise your technical prowess. This can be done through various means—undergraduate and graduate schools being only part of a viable portfolio. The following are some options that can be mixed and matched—in short, designed to meet your needs. Or you can enroll in a dedicated program to ensure your continuity of studies.

Whatever you choose, getting a formal education is important. Because it's relatively easy to make a living as a digital designer picking up projects here and there, you may be tempted to put off school or skip it altogether. There are advantages in gaining professional experience, but sooner or later you will find that you hit a wall. Reputable companies will always prefer to hire a designer who has graduated from a recognized school. In many cases, a formal education is a requirement for moving up the ranks. In New York City in 2006, the average entry-level designer was paid $33,000. Compare that to the $81,000 average of a creative director and you can see that education pays off in the long run.

The Education Matrix

We cannot categorically say whether this option comes first or last on your educational path—or at all. When or if choosing continuing education, there are benefits on both ends of life's spectrum.

For those who are already working at a job, continuing education classes and workshops (offered by art and design schools or any number of businesses, i.e., Adobe Systems, or organizations like AIGA that serve or support the industry) are doubtless the best bet to accomplish one of two things: improve design skills or learn key programs, sometimes both.

The concentrated time (usually a fifteen-week semester, but programs are also offered as intensive week units and weekends) is best for those who require immersion with a defined goal, such as embracing a typographic language, on one side, or become totally fluent in Photoshop, on the other.

Granted, it is more likely you will become fluent in Photoshop in fifteen weeks than emerge as a great typographer in the same amount of time. Both require practice, but the former is mostly about following technical guidelines, while the latter is learning to integrate the tenets of type with your talent for composition (where instinct or taste is necessary).

Yet if you are working as, say, a production assistant with ambitions to graduate into the creative realm—and you cannot afford the time or money to matriculate as a full-time undergraduate or graduate student, or you don't care whether you earn a degree—then identify the best beginning, intermediate, or advanced typography and design classes at a reputable art school or college/university art department. Reputable is important. There are some bad typographers who teach potentially good students. Schools with undergrad or grad programs often offer CE courses, sometimes with regular faculty, and other times with adjuncts who are also exemplary professional designers. When it comes to design classes, make certain your teacher has the experience necessary to impart not just skills, but also acute insight into their respective fields.

Other potential CE students are those who are skilled, even veteran designers. Everyone needs to stay current with the latest technologies, and CE provides classes designed to ratchet up your portfolio of competencies. Sometimes these ostensibly technical programs are offered at art schools and colleges. Basic programs such as Photoshop, Illustrator, and Flash are offered, and more advanced imaging software classes are increasingly popular—and essential. Additionally, technical schools that have affinities to communication arts will provide effective courses as well. In addition to technical classes, even veteran designers want to improve their craft. Don't ever assume you have completed your education, particularly since new areas of design are opening at a quick pace.

The key for everyone entering a continuing education program is to read the course descriptions, compare classes, and ask the right questions, not only of the faculty or administrators, but of yourself: What is it that I want to learn? What is it that I *need* to learn?

Undergraduate Study

This is the most critical course of study, so let's start at the beginning: As a graduating high school student, you rarely know what comes next. Most college freshmen actually major in not knowing their major—this is not a failing, but a common occurrence. Yet some are blessed with a clear focus insofar as the urge to engage in the communication arts in some form. For a few of these, the form is defined as digital design.

Young people know communication arts or VizCom because in high school they played around with Photoshop or iMovie, or maybe even Final Cut Pro. More high school classes and clubs offer these tools. They made videos and podcasts, and produced Web sites; some even invented games, and many uploaded them onto MySpace or YouTube only to find within days that hundreds or maybe thousands of people praised them for their amateur work. Perhaps more than ever this is the pathway into the world of digital design. But whatever is the overwhelming passion at the time of graduation, it is important to have a well-rounded education. It is extremely important to have a liberal arts foundation if nothing else to open doors to the vast variety of content that can be explored in the digital world.

That said, many high school grads go straight into art school or art programs in colleges and universities. While some of the latter programs require a liberal arts foundation before entering the major, other *conservatory* approaches allow students to immediately begin their specialty. Both approaches make sense to different individuals depending on you. Getting a lay of the land in a foundation or premajor program is useful in determining a viable future course. However, immersion in a major provides more time to become confident.

Now comes the tricky part: Most design programs offer the traditional typographic, concept, theory, and portfolio studio classes, along with technical instruction. Although it is usually presumed that incoming students are somewhat computer savvy, basic and advanced software classes are given either as full-semester surveys or intensive workshops. The computer is the primary tool (although it's great to use your hands, too).

Still, most design programs emphasize their specific design specialties over technological pursuit. And this is a good thing for those who want to design. But design is a broad term and field. It is possible to learn, say, Web design in a computer arts or digital communications program. It is probable that motion production, if not also motion design, will also be taught in emerging hybrid programs.

Currently there is a lot of overlap between digital photography, digital art, and other nongraphic design programs. There is also a lot of nomenclature and content fudging. A digital imaging class in one program may include typography, while in another it is only about making pictures on the screen. Scrutinize these programs and their respective classes; make certain all the subject areas that you want and need to learn are available to you. If they are not, find out where in the curriculum electives are offered to supplement your needs.

For the student who is transferring or returning to an undergraduate program from other nondesign majors or jobs, the previous suggestions are equally useful. Presumably,

Digital Photography and the New Design

In the 1930s, photography was the most progressive craze to hit graphic design and illustration. Integrating type and photo in Europe was called "TypoFoto," and throughout the world—from the United States to Japan—photomurals and photomontage were symbols of the machine age. Many of the world's leading designers were also photographers, and some even earned larger public and professional reputations from their photography.

Throughout the second half of the twentieth century, photography was the "modern" means of communicating. Although hand-drawn and painted illustrations were not dead, in certain quarters they were archaic. Today, digital photography and digital photographic programs have returned the photograph to a progressive and integral place in the field of design.

Even if you are not interested in becoming a digital photographer (a field unto itself), it is important to be somewhat skilled in digital photography. For those who want to expand their options by learning photography, continuing education and graduate classes are possible. Building competencies through technical and creative classes are useful, especially when working in video, but also in any area where the photographic image will be used as part of a digital composition.

For the professional seeking a means to broaden experiences, there are certain digital programs (e.g., at the School of Visual Arts in New York) that focus on the technical and creative needs of professional photographers, photographic educators, and visual arts professionals who are looking to advance their skills in digital image capture, asset management, and high-quality output.

As the SVA catalog notes, "Upon successful completion of the program, students will be thoroughly versed in digital imaging tools, terms and techniques; including critical networking issues, workflow strategies, color management applications and current business practices; making our graduates highly employable and prepared for the rigors of contemporary digital image-making."

those who have been out in the world or studying other worlds will be better equipped as a well-rounded designer. It can only help that other experiences underpin the design career.

Graduate Study

There is an increasing belief (and the media support this) that graduate study is a necessity rather than a luxury. The argument is that three or four years of undergraduate studies are really just an extension of high school studies. Particularly in design, for the necessary knowledge base this time frame is barely enough to prepare for the workforce. Today, students are encouraged to supplement their school learning with internships, even jobs. Some counselors even urge students to add an extra year onto their already expensive college careers.

Many students who might have taken continuing education classes to supplement their learning after graduation are now considering two- and three-year graduate schools in the hope that intensive work toward fulfillment of a graduate degree will help them in various ways. They will not only acquire more skill and knowledge, but they will be able to network with others—students and faculty—who will help them on their career paths, and get a terminal degree that in some instances will give a professional edge. In fact, it can only help—in a big way.

Still, it is useful for the undergrad to get some experience before returning to school. Although some grad schools allow students to work (and will even spread their degree study period over time, rather than forcing them to complete in two or three years), the best use of graduate school is immersion. Therefore, graduate students should enter school knowing exactly what they want and need from the considerable investment. Working for studios, firms, production companies, and so on, as assistants, art directors, producers, and even designers is the best way to identify deficiencies. Of course, the work environment will also provide experiences never received in school, but this will doubtless highlight what further needs to be learned.

Although many students with undergraduate degrees will immediately investigate grad school—and this must not be discouraged—the best use of this time is to truly have a rational goal. Ask yourself: What kind of digital designer do I want to be? Then carefully select the program—whether digital communications or traditional graphic design or multimedia art—that fits best into that pedagogic matrix.

Real-world Experience

Work experience, it begs repeating, is as important as, if not more so than, formal education. The two are an unbeatable combination, assuming the schools and jobs are giving you what you want. When in school, get those internships in the places where the work you what to do is being done. Amazing things come from internships. Try to spread them out. Although not easy, think of internships as an extension of coursework—apply for different kinds of work in different types of venues.

Once you've completed the internship route, apply for jobs that will put you in close proximity to the fields you want to practice. This may sound obvious, but in looking for work, especially with student loans, rents, food, and other expenses hanging on your shoulders, some people lose sight of what they really want. If you want to be a digital designer in any of the disciplines described in this book, seek out and get the job. Learn, learn, learn. Then decide whether further education in this field—or another related or unrelated one—will be the next step.

One thing is certain: In digital design nothing stays constant for too long. Education, whichever way you acquire it, is the edge. ■

Digital Media for Designers 101

For those who want to study motion and interactive design, the following description design teacher Melina Rodgrio is typical of the classes you will want to take.

This class introduces motion and interactive design. Students will be empowered with the software skills to produce assignments in these vital forms of visual communication. Conceptual understanding of animation and interactivity will be developed through a vocabulary of terms. Style preferences will be explored by viewing published work.

Students will gain an understanding of the concept of time and how it impacts design. Motion graphics from the 1920s to the present will be viewed. This selection will include the work of early animators such as Len Lye through the modern-day motion graphics of David Carson. Flipbooks will be made in order to understand frame-by-frame animation. The flipbooks will be converted to digital animation to better comprehend what the computer can do for us.

The complexity of motion graphics and its various elements requires collaboration. Together, students will create a combined animation. They will also be expected to teach new technical skills to the rest of the class.

By discussing the difference between motion graphics for Web, film, and television, students will comprehend the capabilities of various software. The class will view the early film titles by Saul Bass. Students will continue presenting their chosen inspirations. This section of the class will conclude with the assignment of making type come to life in a short title sequence.

Our studies of digital media will include an exploration of interactive skills. We will discuss how our favorite Web sites communicate to the user. Students will focus on aesthetics by creating 2D prototypes of their interactive design before converting their work digitally. Working in Web design, students will practice making users' actions, organizing information, and creating consequences.

All class projects will be expected to be executed with a consciousness for technology, aesthetic, and communication.

– Melina Rodrigo

Developing the Digital Designer

An interview with Anthony Dunne, chair of the design interactions department,
Royal College of Art, London

You call the department design interactions rather than interaction design. What's the difference?

Interaction design has begun to solidify as a discipline and, in my view, has become quite narrow—it is increasingly associated with a particular set of technologies. When you talk to people about interaction design, they tend to think of a computer screen. But I think that interaction design offers unique opportunities—such as involving people in the process of creating complex experiences—that you can separate from screens, computers, and electronics. I wanted to take this idea of interaction and start to explore how it might connect to other types of technology and other areas of design. By changing the name around, we emphasize the approach rather than the technology.

What's the advantage to emphasizing an approach or perspective over a set of technologies?

We don't know what the important technology will be in the future. We want our students to be able to contribute regardless of the technology—otherwise, in twenty years, they may be pigeonholed as that digital guy, when something like biotechnology is where the interesting work is being done.

In your book *Design Noir*, you discuss examples of what you call "placebo" projects. An example is the "Compass Table," which has twenty-five compasses embedded in it that twitch and spin when objects like mobile phones or laptop computers are placed on it. The table doesn't actually do anything, but serves as more of a discussion starter. Can you

talk more about the placebo approach?

With classic design the idea is generally to solve the problem or cure the ailment. If you're getting wet, you make a shelter. Placebo projects we see more as a way of negotiating a relationship to something. It's not solving a problem. Like you say, you're setting up a situation that facilitates a discussion. The more poetic the space—such as a discussion in a home about invisible fields—the more interesting the stories.

The idea of a placebo is important because it stops students from thinking in terms of "Here's a problem; now I'm going to solve it" and more in terms of, "Here's a complicated human condition. I'm going to design something that allows them to negotiate this aspect of their relationship with the world." We want students to think about

Interaction design has begun to solidify as a discipline and, in my view, has become quite narrow—it is increasingly associated with a particular set of technologies.

people in a complex way that isn't neat or containable.

What makes this perspective or approach specifically design, rather than, say, art?

Although we draw inspiration from conceptual art and from other fields, if we get plonked down as artists, for example, then the dialogue stops. Then we're just crazy artists doing whatever artists do. But when you say your work is design, people have different expectations. They expect that there's some connection to everyday life—even if it is speculative. And that expectation has the power to make design a powerful critical medium. Rather than making things consumable and easy to digest and incorporate, our interest is more about pulling back and pausing and trying to create a space of reflection. We're interested in implications, as well as applications.

For students who don't have a design background, do you teach courses in design basics?

What we do is try to get them to develop the very most basic awareness of design principles. If they're doing something on-screen, they need to think about type size or type or position or color. But we make it clear that there's no point in two years in trying to become a designer in that sense of graphics or product designer in two years. The course is postgraduate, and most people have already studied what they're coming here to do, so the course is about pushing them and also making resources available.

For example, if they want to study biotech, then we'll hook them up with a scientist. The first year is very structured, and there are workshops on electronics and such. We also do field trips—this year we went to Turkey—and work with companies on specific projects. There's also a lot of collaboration with students from

different programs: industrial design and engineering, but also business schools and science programs. Then the second year is very open, and people work on their thesis, which generally reflects what they want to do when they graduate.

How many students do you admit, and what are their interests?

Well, we admit fifteen to sixteen students a year, and it tends to be a very international group. We also try to keep a balance between people who are primarily interested in thinking and people whose primary interest is in making.

How do you know if this course is right for you?

If you're interested in the role of technology in everyday life and are dissatisfied with the design roles available, you can come here and try to discover a new way of being a designer. ■

Controlling and Manipulating Space

An interview with Louise Sandhaus, faculty, graphic design program,
California Institute of the Arts (CalArts)

Was transitioning from print and exhibition design to the digital a logical course, or did it require a new mind-set?

First, to clarify, I transitioned from print to digital to exhibition design. For me, it was a perfectly logical transition that began in the mid-eighties when I was working in Boston for a small publisher. Word of a renegade initiative at MIT called the Visual Language Workshop (now the Aesthetics and Computation Program in the MIT Media Lab) headed by the institution's well-known graphic designer, Muriel Cooper, was the buzz.

Inspired by the potential, my forward-thinking employer, Lenny, decided to attempt layout and production of our next book on the computer. Realize that was still a year or two away from PageMaker (the first desktop publishing software), and the PC (IBM) was still barely a twinkle in the consumer's eye. Lenny figured out how we could digitally typeset the book by interfacing our Compu-graphics typesetting machine with the DOS-based computer. Working blind, (since we couldn't see anything resembling a page on a screen), we fussed around writing macros until the pages output to our expectations. It was astonishing to see whole, composed pages with everything in place (even if that still had to be pasted on a board for the printer). Between that experience and watching Muriel's initiative explode, it registered for me that the real innovative design thinking wasn't about the computer as a tool to make the design and production process easier; it was about making representations that you couldn't before—new possibilities for visual language.

But, to answer your question specifically, after my life in print I could see the handwriting of change on the wall for myself and for the field of graphic design, so I went to grad school in order to engage more deeply with this transformation. After graduation, I was hired to design the interface for custom software being developed by a large corporation. Luckily, I was working with a really interesting corporate liaison, who understood that I couldn't design the interface without designing the software. For the software to function—to be able to allow users to perform certain tasks—the form, content, and function had be created simultaneously.

How did you segue into exhibition design?

My renegade spirit later turned this way of working—designing form, content, and function at once with a "user" in mind—on to museum experiences. I was fortunate enough to be given that opportunity. However, the point is that ultimately, the thinking isn't any different in print, screen-based media, or exhibition. There's a context, there's an audience, there's making something meaningful, and there's making something engaging. It's the same criteria—it just ramps up in complexity from print to digital to exhibition because there are more elements to control and utilize in making something both meaningful and compelling!

What did you have to learn about digital space that you never conceived in two dimensions?

You have to utilize and control all those additional elements having to do with making a meaningful and compelling experience.

How best do you apply the digital tools you now use?
Hire someone who really has both real talent and real skill to use, and then collaborate in thinking and making.

In work with and teaching digital design, what are the three most important characteristics that you apply and pass on?
1. Become empathetic. You need to have a real feeling for the person who will use what you are creating (same goes for readers when doing print).
2. Consider how databases containing different kinds of information can be employed to make what you're designing more interesting, meaningful, and useful.
3. Be creative in conceiving approaches to the established conventions. Organizing/structuring, writing, interface design, visual design, and programming are all highly creative realms for designers.

Some people in the digital realm become more like technicians than they would in the print world. Is this always true?

No and yes. It's just like in the print world of the seventies and eighties in which I began my career. I remember all the skilled technicians and craftspeople we worked with before digital: The photo retoucher, the typesetter, the letterer, and the production artists—all those expert technicians that were integral to our work.

It's all the same and yet different. Depends on how you define same and how you define different. But I suspect it's the expectations that have changed, because the distinction between someone who can operate the tools technically and those who are creative and can make something unique and smart isn't always distinguished. I'm not sure that the distinctions are all that clear. In the market, there are those people who need design services in different ways— those who have ideas and need someone with the skills to execute them, and those who need experts at coming up with ideas and then making them.

Is more technology required to be a digital designer?
Again, it depends on how you define the differences and how you define technology. If you define technology as stuff that has to be plugged in to work, then I suppose there's more technology.

What is your most challenging work to date, and was it more challenging because of the digital overlay?
A 50,000-square-foot exhibition (about the size of several small museums) when I'd never even designed a single teeny tiny exhibition. On the more simplistic hand, the digital technology allowed us to readily mock up how the design would look and work in the space through photo collaging and 3D software. But the biggest difference is that in a print media the organizational space in which you build hierarchies and relationships of information is less complex. When you move from the book to Web or software design, you have an additional sense of space and relationships in which things can move, transform, and build sets of relationships.

In a multidimensional space such as a museum exhibition, you have a conceptual space and you have a physical space. Visitors need to be oriented in both simultaneously. The complexity of relationships that build meaningful experiences is multiplied exponentially. So, you have to think about relationships in more complex ways.

You've heard about the end of print, but as an educator, is it more important today to teach digital methods—motion, for instance—than static type and page design?

It depends. First, print is a simple 2D space by comparison with the digital spaces. Print is where the basic principles of design are learned. You learn to manipulate and control space to make it meaningful. Once students can get a handle on flatland, then they have the foundational skills required to engage in the more complex spaces of interactivity and motion.

But it also depends on context. In L.A. it would be absurd to focus exclusively on print, since motion-based work is much more significant. But in general, an educated graphic designer today isn't fully literate in contemporary visual communications unless they can do print, Web, and motion—even though they may choose to specialize in only one of these areas—and herein lies the huge challenge for graphic design education.

What special abilities or talents do you look for in a digital designer?

They can apply different mind-sets to different realms: the content, the form, and/or the function. In my more mature age I've learned to recognize that the talents of others come in all sorts of interesting and useful creative packages. For example, I was really impressed at a recent visit to the motion graphics design office, Brand New School, where they were cultivating staff with personal interests who brought something to the table of BNS's projects, rather than preconceiving the job and retrofitting someone who would mold themselves to suit that job. I'd like to give at least a wink and nod to the digital generation who formed BNS for this kind of creative, multidimensional thinking about the workspace. Maybe that multidimensional real-world thinking is the truly interesting and valuable mind-set change of the digital revolution. ■

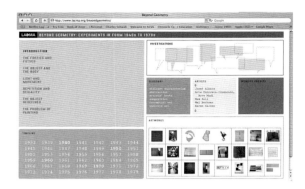

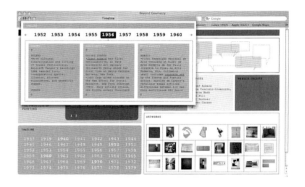

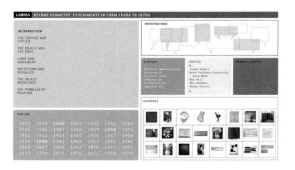

▲

Beyond Geometry

Date: 2004

Designers: Tim Durfee and Louise Sandhaus with Joel Fox

Client: Los Angeles County Museum of Art

Humanities Over All

An interview with Elliott Earls, chairperson, graphic design, Cranbrook Academy of Art, Bloomfield Hills, Michigan

Why do you design (indeed create content) in so many media?
I felt very strongly that design culture was extremely conservative, hidebound, unimaginative, against idealism, and crassly commercial. I think I realized that design was

▲
Storm Triggered Cloud King To Sex

Date: 1997
Designer: Elliott Earls
Illustrator: Elliott Earls
Client: Elliott Earls, The Apollo Program
Programs: Free Hand
© Eliott Earls

extremely powerful, if only it could be harnessed and put to use in a much more meaningful way. This is what I've attempted for most of my career. Digital media—multimedia—is the cornerstone of this effort.

Would you still call yourself a graphic designer? Or are you a digital entrepreneur? Or do you have another label you'd like to share?
The short answer is yes, but not exclusively. I've always felt that the term graphic designer was extremely problematic. Do we exclusively design graphics? No. The older, low brow archaic term commercial artist seems to be a much more appropriate term.

Obviously within academia and within the professional design field there has been a wholesale rejection of this term. Somehow graphic design is supposed to be better. For me, this naming conundrum is symptomatic of a larger (design) cultural malady. It's my opinion that graphic design culture as a whole has very low expectations and is against a kind of idealism. Graphic design culture could learn a thing

or two from the humanities, from the arts.

My personal goal has always been to try to erase the completely artificial distinction between fine art and commercial art. If we look at Jeff Koons or Damien Hirst as an example, it's impossible to contend with their work without realizing that a significant element in the work is commerce and the commodification of the work of art.

Fine artists are not somehow above the commercial realm. Damien Hirst is considered one of the wealthiest men in Great Britain. Gagosian Gallery is a moneymaking machine.

Do I identify with graphic design culture? Absolutely. Once again, I identify with our hidden history. I identify with the graphic design history that connects back to Kurt Schwitters, El Lissitzky, and the Cabaret Voltaire. I reject a kind nonideological commercialism where the designer is the bound and gagged handmaiden of industry. I believe in a kind of self-reliance and heroic authorial position that is engendered by working with media. I consider all media fair game. I primarily see myself as a creator and manipulator of media.

Your print and Web work are very complex with type and image. Is there anything you couldn't do without the aid of the digital tools?

I think you're right; my work has been very complex. I think it has been enabled by digital tools. However, the impetus comes from the profound human need to create. As romantic as this may seem, I'm absolutely driven by a powerful interpersonal need to give form to ideas and to—for lack of a better word—express myself. I reflect on my life prior to entering art school at the age of eighteen. I've given careful consideration to how my life was different. I now realize that there is a kind of inner peace and stability that I have gained through making, through being able to express myself through typography, graphics, music, and performance.

Rick Poynor wrote something to the effect that my work seems draw on a kind of anger. I use my work as a way of interrogating issues of race, class, gender, and religion. I realize now that foundation studies in undergraduate school provided me with a set of skills that have allowed me to negotiate a much more meaningful life. I bring this up because as much as I love digital media, I'm certain that I could find any number of other ways to manifest ideas within material.

How would you describe your relationship to the digital world? Are you a citizen or just passing through?

I love technology. I think what's interesting is that almost all of the hyperbole about technology being empowering is actually true. Digital media has enabled me to work with music, video, typography, graphics, programming, theater, and objects.

Expression is key in your work—and a lot of personal expression at that. How do you avoid the clichés of the media (i.e., Photoshop or Illustrator) that might fix your work in a certain time and place?

If one is committed to an authentic intellectual and emotional inquiry through design, clichés fall away like so much dead skin. Clichés within any art form, be it design or sculpture, are the result of a thin inquiry. This kind of thinness can happen for many reasons. Most often it happens because designers and artists value money or fame more than they value good work. It's my opinion that when one chases fame rather than powerful work, it's easy to look for shortcuts. I am also very aware of what tool I'm using. I think of digital tools as having the same properties as physical tools. As an example, it would seem that sculptors who work with chainsaws are given to carving bears. Seriously, as a sculptor, if I set out in a subtractive process to create a dynamic form, I will have a very hard time not producing a bear. It takes real intellectual work to establish a form of awareness that allows you to deny the tool in the process of making. Often, the mark of the tool becomes clichéd because it is so easy. It's like all of this Adobe Illustrator—based design-illustration-art that is floating around. We see this aesthetic permeate everything from Volkswagen commercials to annual reports to superflat painting—not because it's good but because it's easy.

Do you feel that it is possible for designers to create these days without reliance on the digital—either for art or craft, concept, or production?

Absolutely! I love technology. However, I love the humanities more! I love music and art and literature more than I love any one of the many tools available to create music, art, or literature. It seemed to me he was saying he loved his typewriter, not the novel he was writing. Digital media has allowed me to work within the disciplines of storytelling. My latest project is an experimental feature-length digital film titled *The Saranay Motel*. Digital media has allowed me to explore electronic forms of music. It has allowed me to design typefaces. For this, I am eternally grateful. However, if they threw me in jail and took away my paint, I'd paint with spit upon the wall.

What piece of your own work—typography, video, sound—do you believe owes the most to your digital competencies?

The digital film *Catfish* that was released by Emigre in 2001 is an experimental film that traces my

work from the studio to the stage. In a way, it begins to touch on a comprehensive view of my work. Within this film, motion graphics comingle with live-action footage. Fictional narrative mixes with reportage. The viewer gets to experience one of my

performance pieces with all of the electronics and video projections. My typeface design is woven into the actual film plane. The graphics that are onstage were produced both with the hand and digitally. The two interactive CD-ROMS that

I have produced, "Eye Sling Shot Lions" and "Throwing Apples at the Sun," lie at the heart of the performance piece that is documented in the film. So of the work that has been publicly released, this is the most comprehensive and most enabled by digital technologies.

And do you feel totally competent in the digital environment?

Totally competent is pretty encompassing. I can say that I feel pretty good about my abilities. My skills have been hard won, so (at this moment) I feel reasonably confident in my response. I should say that I'm a self-taught programmer, and I do struggle a bit with some aspects of programming. I'm self-taught in electronics, so I struggle a lot with circuit design. However, when it comes to the digital manipulation of sound and image, I feel I have a very high degree of facility. When I look back at my previous body of work I feel good about the level of craft.

Is the digital the final frontier for design?

No. The humanities are the final frontier for design. ∎

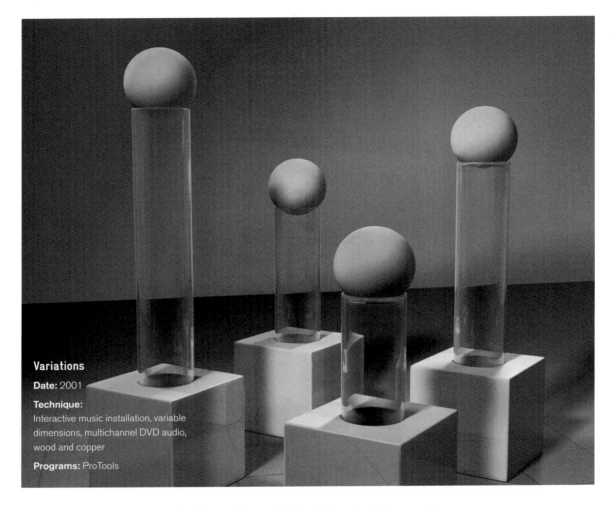

Variations

Date: 2001

Technique:
Interactive music installation, variable
dimensions, multichannel DVD audio,
wood and copper

Programs: ProTools

Digital Art Meets Digital Design

An interview with Bruce Wands, chair of MFA Computer Art, School of Visual Arts, New York City

How did you get involved in
digital art to begin with? Were
you a traditional artist?

My first exposure to digital art was
as a graduate student at Syracuse
University in 1975. I took a course
called Experimental Studios, and
made digital drawings by programming the university's mainframe
computer. We used punch cards
and it was all very primitive, but I immediately saw the potential. My creative interests at the time included
music, photography, and video.
Computer graphics offered me
new conceptual territory to explore,
and that's when I got excited about
making art with new technology.

How would you distinguish digital design from digital art? Is there an intersection?

Yes, they do blend. To me, digital art is the process of creating work for exhibition in galleries and museums, or the Internet. Digital design covers a more public realm, from advertising, to print, to industrial design, to all types of media. The line is becoming blurred, however, as contemporary art is now taking a more active role in our everyday lives. The iPod is a great example. Podcasts can range from video art and music to commercial television. Andy Warhol's images of commercial products are another example of why the border between art and design often lies in the mind of the beholder.

In your MFA program you teach animation as well as the Web. What do you want students to come away with?

The main focus of the MFA Computer Art program is to develop a strong personal creative vision and individual style that is expressed through digital media. While this may sound odd, ultimately it is not about the software. It is what you do and say with it. In addition to our studio classes, students study digital and contemporary art history and criticism. Their thesis projects include research and writing as the foundation for their creative work. Critique is also an important part of the program. Although our students do come out of the program with a very high degree of digital literacy, it is their creative work that defines their future careers.

Do you require MFA students to come into your program with advanced knowledge? What are their requirements?

When we look at our applicants, their creative portfolio and statement of intent are the two most important factors. We like to see a diverse portfolio, rather than only one type of work. Photography, drawing, and sculpture often tell us more than examples of their commercial work. We also look at DVDs and Web sites. Most students have had some professional experience as digital artists, whether it be as a Web designer, animator, or photographer. The more they know, the better they will be able to take advantage of the program once they get here. The lab is state-of-the-art, as well as experimental. Students are encouraged to push the limits of the technology to achieve their creative goals.

You've pretty much pioneered this field of education. How has it fundamentally changed over the past decade or so?

▲

Mirage

Designer: Jaeyoon Park

Date: 2006

Technique:
3D Animation, 720x405 px

To some extent, technology is slowly becoming transparent, and people are communicating more frequently through text messaging, cell phones, PDAs, and the Internet.

When I started with digital art in the mid-1970s, there were no Macintosh or PC computers. We could only create an image through programming. In the past ten years, technology has made tremendous leaps forward, as has the software that we use every day. The Internet has revolutionized global culture, communication, and business. Ten years ago, knowing the right software really well and being creative started your career off. Today, knowing the software inside and out is expected, and creativity is much more important.

Decades ago, much digital art was very impressionistic. Do you feel that students are less expression-oriented and more practice- and function-oriented today?

Because they are growing up in a very technological world, students do have a lot of fun with it. Using computers for creative ends is what they really need to learn. To some extent, technology is slowly becoming transparent, and people are communicating more frequently through text messaging, cell phones, PDAs, and the Internet. Young people today are multitaskers, and see technology as part of their daily lives. They have never known a world without computers.

What would you say is the most ambitious digital project you've seen from a student, and why?

That's a difficult one, and it depends on how you define ambitious. Most of our students want to do way more than there is time for. One of my favorite thesis projects is a 3D animation by Youngwoong Jang called Mirage. It is the story of a biomechanical being with a glass bowl for a chest, which needs water to live. It is beautifully done in a futuristic style that is totally believable and photorealistic. When you watch it with a group of people, it is so engrossing that there is dead silence in the room. It has a wonderful story and is visually stunning. Since he graduated last May, it has been in over thirty film festivals.

Carlos Saldanha is another example of an exceptional alumnus. He graduated in the early 1990s, was hired by Blue Sky Studios, and recently directed the feature film *Ice Age: The Meltdown* and codirected *Robots*. He also received an Academy Award nomination in 2004.

Can you tell me what the future holds for computer art education—at least in your domain?

The future of computer art education lies in the "art" part of that description. Our students are coming into the program more digitally literate each year. Our future tasks will be to develop their sense of responsibility as artists, to develop their creative and intellectual potential, and to provide them with a solid grounding in traditional and digital art history. Computer art education not only needs to stay abreast of current technological developments, but also needs to anticipate them. Invention and creativity go hand in hand. It is the role of the digital artist to help us see that and to use technology in a creative way. ■

Educational Resources

Colleges with Computer Art and Graphic (Digital) Design Programs

NOTE: *no progs* indicates that the college does not offer any of the above specialized programs: only general graphic design or fine art.

Academy of Art University
www.academyart.edu
Animation and Visual Effects: BFA/MFA
Computer Arts: New Media: BFA/MFA
Motion Pictures and Television: BFA/MFA
Digital Arts and Communication: BFA/MFA

University of Advanced Computer Technology
www.uat.edu
Multimedia Program BA Includes:
- Digital Animation
- Digital Art and Design
- Digital Video
- Game Design
Game Design: MA

Art Institute (various locations)
www.artinstitutes.edu
Art and Design Technology, with a concentration in Graphic Design
Art and Design Technology, with a concentration in Graphic Design: AS
Digital Design
Media Arts
Various degrees types offered, online courses available

International Academy of Design and Technology Tampa
www.academy.edu
Recording Arts: AS/BFA
Interactive Media: AS/BFA
Computer Animation: AS/BFA
Digital Photography: AS
Digital Movie Production: AS

The Art Institute of Boston at Lesley University
www.aiboston.edu
Graphic Design:
(includes courses in interactive design, digital photography)
BFA
Certificates

University of the Arts
www.uarts.edu
Graphic Design: BFA
(includes interactive courses)
Multimedia: BFA
Film/Animation: BFA
Film/Digital Video: BFA

Art Center College of Design
www.artcenter.edu
Graphic Design: BFA
(includes digital media courses)
Entertainment Design: BFA
Film: BFA
Photography and Imaging: BFA
Broadcast Cinema: MFA
Media Design: MFA

University of Baltimore
www.ubalt.edu
Simulation and Digital Entertainment:
- Undergraduate transfer students
Information Design Certificate:
- Graduate certificate
New Media Publishing Graduate Certificate

Boston University School for the Arts
www.bu.edu/cfa
Graphic Design: BFA/MFA
(including Web design courses)

Brigham Young University
www.cfac.byu.edu
College of Fine Arts and Communications
Animation BFA

California College of the Arts
www.cca.edu
Animation: BFA
Media Arts: BFA
Photography: BFA (including digital)
Design: MFA (various coursework, including interactive media)

California Institute of the Arts
www.calarts.edu
School of Art
Character Animation: BFA
Integrated Media Program in Art: MFA
Graphic Design: BFA and MFA
(includes coursework in motion graphics and interactive design)
Photography and Media: BFA/MFA

California Poly State University
www.artdesign.libart.calpoly.edu/major_graphicDesign.php
Photography and Digital Imagery Concentration: BFA
College of Design, Architecture, Art and Planning

University of Cincinnati
www.daap.uc.edu/design/
Digital Design: BFA (motion, 3D)
Master of Design: MFA
(for people with backgrounds in digital design)

The College of Arts and Architecture at Penn State School of Visual Arts
www.sova.psu.edu
New Media: BFA

The Cooper Union for the Advancement of Science and Art
www.cooper.edu
BFA: Coursework includes film, 3D, animation (generalist curriculum)

**The Corcoran School of Art
and Design**
www.corcoran.edu
Digital Media Design: BFA, AFA

Digital Media Arts College
www.dmac-edu.org
Computer Animation: BFA
Special Effects Animation: MFA

Expression College for Digital Arts
www.expression.edu
Motion Graphic Design: BA
Animation and Visual Effects: BA
Game Art and Design: BA
Sound Arts: BA

University of Florida
www.digitalmedia.arts.ufl.edu
School of Art and Art History
Digital Media: BFA, MFA

**International Academy of Design
and Technology**
www.academy.edu
Interactive Media
Digital Movie Production
Recording Arts
AA and BA degrees

Kent State University School of Art:
www.dept.kent.edu/art

**Maryland Institute College of Art
(MICA)**
www.mica.edu
Interactive Media: BFA
Experimental Animation: BFA
Video: BFA
Digital Arts: BFA/MFA
Photography (including digital courses): BFA

Massachusetts College of Arts
www.massart.edu
Media and Performing Arts:
Photography: BFA (incl. digital photography)
Media and Performing Arts: BFA Film/Video
Media and Performing Arts: Studio for Inter-
related Media: BFA (incl. digital photography
and Web design for photographers)

Communication Design: BFA Animation
Dynamic Media Institute: MFA

University of Massachusetts Amherst
www.umass.edu/art
Studio Art Program
(disciplines include digital media:
still imagery and time based): BFA/MFA

**Minneapolis College of Arts
and Design (MCAD)**
www.mcad.edu
Interactive Media: BFA/MFA
Animation: BFA/MFA
Filmmaking: BFA

University of Minnesota: no progs
www.umn.edu

**Montana State University College
of Arts and Architecture: no progs
(graphic design only)**
www.montana.edu/wwwdt

**The New England Institute of Art and
Communications**
www.aine.artinstitute.edu
Audio and Media Technology: BS
Digital Filmmaking and Video Production: BS
Interactive Media Design: BS
Media Arts and Animation: BS

**North Carolina A & T State University
School of Technology: no progs**
www.ncat.edu

Otis College of Art and Design
www.otis.edu
Digital Media: BFA
Interactive Product Design: BFA

Parsons School of Design
www.parsons.edu
Design and Technology: BFA, MFA

Pacific Northwest College of Art
www.pnca.edu
Intermedia: BFA

Pratt Institute
www.pratt.edu
Digital Arts: BFA, MFA
Media Arts: BFA
Digital Design and Interactive Media: AA
(two-year)

Rhode Island School of Design (RISD)
www.risd.edu
Film/Animation/Video: BFA
Digital Media: MFA
Computer Animation: certificate program
Web Design: certificate program

Ringling School of Art and Design
www.rsad.edu
Computer Animation: BFA
Game Art and Design: BFA
Graphic and Interactive Communication: BFA
School of Design College of Imagining Arts
and Science

Rochester Institute of Design (RIT)
www.rit.edu
Film/Video/Animation: BFA
New Media Design and Imaging: BFA
Computer Graphics Design: MFA
Imaging Arts/Computer Animation: MFA
Interactive Multimedia Development:
Certificate program

Ryerson University
www.imagearts.ryerson.ca
Graphic Communications University
Image Arts: BFA
New Media: BFA
Media Production: MA

Savannah College of Art and Design
www.scad.edu
Animation
Broadcast Design and Motion Graphics
Interactive Design and Game Development
Offer BFA, MFA, online education, and
certificates

**State University of New York at Buffalo
(SUNY)**
www.art.buffalo.edu
Communication Design: BFA, BA

School of Visual Arts (SVA)
www.sva.edu
Animation: BFA
Film and Video: BFA
Computer Art: BFA, MFA
Digital Photography: MPS

Syracuse University College of Visual and Performing Arts
www.vpa.syr.edu
Interaction Design: BFA

Temple University Tyler School of Art
www.temple.edu/tyler
Graphic and Interactive Design: BFA, MFA

Virginia Commonwealth University School of the Arts
www.vcu.edu
Photography and Film: BFA/MFA
Film (Cinema): BA

GRADUATE-ONLY PROGRAMS:
Cranbrook Academy of Art
www.cranbrookart.edu
3D Design: MFA

IIT Institute of Design
www.id.iit.edu
Communication Design: MDes

New York University Tisch School of the Arts
www.itp.nyu.edu
Interactive Telecommunications Program: MPS

Yale University School of Art
www.yale.edu/art
Graphic Design (includes filmmaking/video/ interdisciplinary courses): MFA

TWO-YEAR-ONLY PROGRAMS:
Briarcliffe College
www.bcpat.com
Multimedia and Web Design: AAS
Animation: AAS

Brooks College
www.brookscollege.edu
Animation: AS
Multimedia: AS

College of Eastern Utah: no progs
http://www.ceu.edu/

Community College of Denver: no progs
www.ccd.edu/art

Delaware College of Art and Design
www.dcad.edu
Animation: AFA

Palomar College: no progs
www.palomar.edu

Portfolio Center
www.portfoliocenter.com
Media Architecture: Certificate program

Spencerian College
www.spencerian.edu/lexington
Computer Graphic Design: AAS

Humber (in Canada)
www.humber.ca
Game Programming
3D Modeling and Visual Effects Programming
Web Design
Multimedia 3D Computer Animation
Online Only Schools:

Sessions School of Design
www.sessions.edu
Foundation and Advanced Certificates in:
Web design
Multimedia
Digital arts

OTHER PROGRAMS:
Brooks College, Long Beach
www.brookscollege.com
Multimedia: AS

Platt College San Diego Graphic Design School
www.platt.edu
Media Arts: BS
Multimedia Design: AAS
Multimedia/3D Animation: certificate program
Web Design: certificate program

Full Sail
www.fullsail.com
Computer Animation: BS
Digital Arts and Design: BS
Entertainment Design: BS
Game Development: BS
Recording Arts: BS

NONACADEMIC TRAINING:
Adobe DVDs
www.adobe.com
Total Training Videos for Broadcast and web design software

APPLE PRO TRAINING
www.apple.com/software/pro/training/
Certificate Courses in:
Motion Graphics
DVD Authoring
Special Effects and Compositing
Audio Creation

Lynda.com
www.lynda.com
online training library of videos (subscriptions service)
DVDs on software training

Desktop Images:
Visual Training for the Digital Arts
www.desktopimages.com
DVDs for:
Motion Graphics
Visual Effects
Gaming
Character Modeling and Animation

Bibliography

GENERAL DESIGN BOOKS

Albrect, Donald, Ellen Lupton, and Steven Holt
Design Culture Now: National Design Triennial
New York: Princeton Architectural Press, 2000

Bierut, Michael, and others, editor
Looking Closer: Critical Writings on Graphic Design
New York: Allworth, 1994

Blackwell, Lewis, editor
The End of Print: The Graphic Design of David Carson
San Francisco: Chronicle, 1996

Bringhurst, Robert
The Elements of Typographic Style
Vancouver: Hartley & Marks, 2004

Elam, Kimberly
Grid Systems: Principles of Organizing Type
New York: Princeton Architectural Press, 2004

Helfland, Jessica
Screen: Essays on Graphic Design,
New Media, and Visual Culture
New York: Princeton Architectural Press, 2004

Heller, Steven
Design Literacy (2nd edition)
New York: Allworth, 2004

Heller, Steven
The Education of a Typographer
New York: Allworth, 2004

Heller, Steven
Handwritten: Expressive Lettering in the Digital Age
New York/London: Thames and Hudson, 2004

Heller, Steven
Paul Rand
London: Phaidon Press LTD, 1999

Heller, Steven
Teaching Graphic Design: Course Offerings and Class
Projects from the Leading Graduate and Undergraduate
Programs New York: Allworth, 2003

Heller, Steven, and Seymour Chwast
Graphic Style: From Victorian to Digital
New York: Harry N. Abrams, 2001

Heller, Steven, and Teresa Fernandes
Becoming a Graphic Designer
New York: Wiley & Sons, 2005

Heller, Steven, and Julie Lasky
Borrowed Design: Use and Abuse of Historical Form
New York: Van Nostrand Reinhold, 1993

Heller, Steven, and Louise Fili
*Stylepedia: A Guide to Graphic Design
Mannerisms, Quirks, and Conceits*
San Francisco: Chronicle, 2006

Heller, Steven, and Louise Fili
*Typology: Type Design from the
Victorian Era to the Digital Age*
San Francisco: Chronicle, 1999

Heller, Steven, and Anne Fink
Faces on the Edge: Type in the Digital Age
New York: Van Nostrand Reinhold, 1997

Heller, Steven, and Mirko Ilic
*The Anatomy of Design: Uncovering the Influences
and Inspirations in Modern Graphic Design*
Rockport, MA: Rockport, 2007

Hollis, Richard
Graphic Design: A Concise History (2nd edition) New
York/London: (World of Art) Thames and Hudson, 2001

Lipton, Ronnie
The Practical Guide to Information Design
New York: John Wiley & Sons, Inc.

Lupton, Ellen
*Mixing Messages: Graphic Design in Contemporary
Culture* New York: Cooper-Hewitt National Design
Museum, Smithsonian Institution and Princeton Archi-
tectural Press, 1996

Lupton, Ellen
*Thinking with Type: A Critical Guide for Designers,
Writers, Editors and Students*
New York: Princeton Architectural Press, 2004

Lupton, Ellen, and Abbot Miller
Design, Writing Research: Writing on Graphic Design
London: Phaidon Press Limited, 1999

Maeda, John
Maeda @ Maeda
New York: Rizzoli, 2000

Mau, Bruce
Life Style
New York: Phaidon Press, 2000

McAlhone, Beryl, and others
A Smile in the Mind: Witty Thinking in Graphic Design
London: Phaidon Press, Ltd., 1998

Meggs, Philip B., and Alston Purvis
A History of Graphic Design (4th edition)
New York: John Wiley & Sons, 2006

Poynor, Rick
No More Rules: Graphic Design and Postmodernism
New Haven, CT: Yale University Press, 2003

Sagmeister, Stefan, and Peter Hall
Made You Look
New York: Booth-Clibborn, 2001

Samara, Timothy
*Making and Breaking the Grid:
A Graphic Design Layout Workshop*
Rockport, MA: Rockport, 2005

Shaugnhnessy, Adrian
*How to Be a Graphic Designer
Without Losing Your Soul*
New York: Princeton Architectural Press, 2005

Thorgerson, Storm, and Aubrey Powell
100 Best Album Covers
London, New York, Sydney: DK, 1999

Twemlow, Alice
What Is Graphic Design For?
London: Rotovision, 2006

DIGITAL
Drate, Spencer, David Robbins, Judith Salavetz,
and Kyle Cooper
Motion by Design (includes DVD)
London: Lawrence King, 2006

Ellison, Andy
*The Complete Guide to Digital Type: Creative Use of
Typography in the Digital Arts*
London: Collins, 2004

Goux, Melanie, and James Houff
*On Screen In Time: Transitions in Motion
Graphic Design for TV and New Media*
London: Rotovision, 2003

Greene, David
*Motion Graphics
(How Did They Do That?)*
Rockport, MA: Rockport, 2003

Harrington, Richard, Glen Stevens, and Chris Vadnais
*Broadcast Graphics on the Spot:
Timesaving Techniques Using Photoshop and
After Effects for Broadcast and Post Production*
Berkeley: CMP, 2005

Heller, Steven, and Gail Anderson
*The Designer's Guide to Astounding
Photoshop Effects*
New York: HOW, 2004

Krazner, Jon
*Motion Graphic Design and Fine Art Animation:
Principles and Practice*
Massachusetts: Focal Press, 2004

Maeda, John
Creative Code
London/New York: Thames & Hudson, 2004

Meyer, Chris, and Trish Meyer
*Creating Motion Graphics with After Effects,
vol 1: The Essentials*
San Francisco: CMP Books, 2004

Meyer, Chris, and Trish Meyer
*Creating Motion Graphics with After Effects,
vol 2: Advanced Techniques*
San Francisco: CMP Books, 2005

Miotke, Jim
The Betterphoto Guide to Digital Photography
New York: Amphoto Books, 2005

Moggridge, Bill
Designing Interactions
Cambridge: MIT, 2007

Rysinger, Lisa
Exploring Digital Video
New York: Thomson Delmar Learning, 2005

Safer, Dan
Designing for Interaction:
Creating Smart Applications and Clever Devices
Atlanta: Peach Pit Press, 2006

Salen, Katie, and Eric Zimmerman
Rules of Play: Game Design Fundamentals
Cambridge: MIT Press, 2003

Solana, Gemma, and Antonio Boneu
The Art of the Title Sequence:
Film Graphics in Motion
London: Collins, 2007

Tidwell, Jenifer
Designing Interfaces
San Francisco: O'Reilly, 2004

Wands, Bruce
Art of the Digital Age
London/New York: Thames & Hudson, 2006

Weinberger, David
Small Pieces Loosely Joined:
A Unified Theory of the Web
Perseus Books Group, 2003

Williams, Richard
The Animator's Survival Kit:
A Manual of Methods, Principles, and Formulas
for Classical, Computer, Games, Stop Motion,
and Internet Animators
Faber & Faber, 2001

Woolman, Matt
Motion Design: Moving Graphics for Television,
Music Video, Cinema, and Digital Interfaces
London: Rotovision, 2004

Woolman, Matt
Type in Motion 2
New York/London: Thames & Hudson, 2005

Woolman, Matt, and Jeffrey Bellantoni
Type in Motion: Innovations in Digital Graphics
New York/London: Thames & Hudson, 2001

Zeigler, Kathleen, and Nick Greco
MotionGraphics: Film & TV
New York: Watson-Guptill, 2002

Index of Interviews